I FEEL LOVE

I FEEL LOVE

DONNA SUMMER, GIORGIO MORODER, AND HOW THEY REINVENTED MUSIC

DAVE THOMPSON

Guilford, Connecticut

An imprint of Globe Pequot, the trade division of
The Rowman & Littlefield Publishing Group, Inc.
4501 Forbes Blvd., Ste. 200
Lanham, MD 20706
www.rowman.com

Distributed by NATIONAL BOOK NETWORK

Library of Congress Cataloging-in-Publication Data available

ISBN 978-1-4930-4980-6 (paperback)
ISBN 978-1-4930-4981-3 (e-book)

∞™ The paper used in this publication meets the minimum requirements of American National Standard for Information Sciences—Permanence of Paper for Printed Library Materials, ANSI/NISO Z39.48-1992

To Ivan Kral . . . forever dancing, barefoot or otherwise

CONTENTS

INTRODUCTION

> Merv Griffin: Tell me, Donna, is it true that every recording star needs an image?
>
> Donna Summer: Well, Merv, even a tomato has an image.
>
> *Merv Griffin Show, 1982*

This book is the story of a moment in time, of how half a dozen unique and unrelated elements, each poised and purposeful in its own stark chronology, suddenly crossed one another at precisely the same moment . . . and what happened when they touched.

The stark adventuring of electronic music, the lush orchestrations of a dirty French pop song. The nihilistic purging of punk rock, the party-before-the-bomb-drops hedonism of disco. The rise of the twelve-inch single and the fall of high street synthesizer prices. Six disparate sounds, scenes, and scenarios coming together to alter the entire course of predicted music history. To herald the dawning of a future age.

There are no heroes to this story, beyond those who snatch that mantle for themselves. Nor are there villains. There are landmarks, to be sure, and the ghost of a map, clearly marked in some spots, fogged by forest in others. Some of the story is vouchsafed by history, some is mired in conjecture and chance. If there was a grand design, it was forged in neither laboratory nor studio, and was most likely doomed to failure regardless.

"Six disparate sounds, scenes, and scenarios" . . . not even coincidence would try to be that bold. And as for "the dawning of a future age," we only had the prophets' words for that, and who believes in prophecy anymore? They just happened to get it right, that's all. Every single one of them.

It's not easy to change rock'n'roll. Yes, styles do come and go, and—to slightly paraphrase writer Nik Cohn—this year's anarchist will certainly be next year's boring old fart. But to actually stand in a studio, beneath the red light, and physically voice the words that will reinvent everything, that's hard.

Elvis did it, with "Heartbreak Hotel." More than sixty years on, one can still uncover accounts of musicians and fans alike turning to stare at the radio, their mouth open in a stunned, silent *what?* as the Pelvis paraded down lonely street.

The Byrds may have done it with "Mr. Tambourine Man," less seismic in overall impact, but significant all the same, bequeathing folk rock unto a grateful world; the Sugarhill Gang certainly did it, as "Rapper's Delight," turned R&B upside down. Some say Nirvana's "Smells like Teen Spirit" did it, but the jury might still be out on that one.

There are other contenders for similar status, but it's strange. Their claims rely more upon the circumstances under which they were heard, than the music that people were hearing. No single record defines the point at which the Beatles became a mania. Rather, it was their appearance on *The Ed Sullivan Show* in 1964 that transformed a mop-topped Anglo cult into the dominant force in sixties rock. The songs they performed that night were largely irrelevant.

David Bowie fans of a certain vintage speak still in hallowed tones of the first time they heard his breakthrough single "Starman." But again it was television—Bowie's dazzling appearance on British television's *Top of the Pops* in the summer of 1972—that beamed tomorrow into today, not a simple song about a spaceman.

The Sex Pistols birthed punk rock, and "Anarchy in the UK" was their still-resonant debut 45. But the watershed moment was not the release of the record. It was an expletive-laden appearance on local London teatime television, and the tabloid media fallout that followed.

Music, by its very definition, is an aural experience. More often than not, however, it is the accompanying visuals that make the most profound impression. This was particularly true in the early to mid-1980s, when many of the records that became major hits barely even qualified as songs, let alone music. They were simply the soundtracks to people's favorite videos.

Donna Summer's "I Feel Love," like "Heartbreak Hotel," like "Rapper's Delight," *did* change things.

Musically, it seemed to come out of nowhere. Sonically, it was like nothing on earth. And culturally, it tossed aside all predictions for what the next few years in music might sound like, and reshaped them in its own pulsating, pounding, peripatetic image.

Its commercial success only amplified its creative achievement. Far too much influential music is made under the cover of obscurity, heard by mere handfuls of people at the time of its release, and already years old before it is discovered by anything resembling the mainstream—one only needs think of the lifetime of ignominy endured by the Stooges and the Velvet Underground. Nobody denies either band's importance today. At the time, however, it was a very different story.

"I Feel Love" was recognized instantaneously. It topped charts the world over, including the United Kingdom, Australia, France, Italy, and Holland, and it reached the Top 10 almost everywhere else.

Its success, however, is, and always will be, secondary to its impact. To the ideas it uncaged in countless musical minds around the world; to the sense of excitement and liberation that it forged in the souls of all who heard it. To the sheer weight of adventure and artistry that it was responsible for unleashing.

It is routinely featured toward the top of manifold "greatest song" Top 100s; it is included in the Library of Congress's National Recording Registry (one of just a handful of non-US recordings featured therein); and the *Financial Times*—scarcely the first place one looks for musical commentary, it is true, but nothing to be sniffed at regardless—described "I Feel Love" as, indeed, "one of the most influential records ever made."

On the streets of New York and London, the rising punk hordes were spellbound by the record. It pumped from the sound system at Max's Kansas City in New York; it thudded from the disc jockey booth at the Vortex in London.

The thrill of "I Feel Love" would become a key component in Blondie's set list, and evolve into their own "Heart of Glass"—which the band then utterly subverted by covering "I Feel Love" as well.

The discipline of "I Feel Love" would be reflected in the strivings of a horde of bedroom synthesizer acolytes, to create a sound that reduced even Summer's icy symphony to minimalist poetry, a duet for disassociated voice and cold waves of sound.

And the questing innovation of "I Feel Love" would tattoo itself onto the consciousness of a generation.

Musicians who might never have considered listening to the music of Donna Summer, or the productions of Giorgio Moroder, suddenly found themselves compelled to pay attention. Not only to the record, not only to the performance. In the words of Brian Eno, himself regarded as the patron saint of the electronic music of the day, they found themselves face to face with "the sound of the future."

"I Feel Love," Eno is said to have told David Bowie, is "going to change the sound of club music for the next fifteen years." Which, Bowie later concluded, "was more or less right."

Except, fifteen years was an underestimate. "I Feel Love" is almost three times that age, and people are *still* discovering it, whether through one more spin for the original record, from cover versions that stretch from Bronski Beat and Marc

Almond, to the Blue Man Group and Sam Smith, or from performances of *Summer: The Donna Summer Musical.*

Not everybody likes the song. History is subjective, and music history especially so. A record that one person regards as the most scintillating sound that has ever been made will routinely be dismissed by another as trash, and vice versa. It has always been that way, just as that condemnation has not always been dependent upon a record's own merits.

Its influence across the musical spectrum notwithstanding, for some listeners "I Feel Love" has never escaped its generally accepted branding as a "disco" record, with all of the attendant baggage and opprobrium which that entails. Four decades on from its peak period of usage, "disco sucks" remains one of the best remembered slogans of the seventies: "I Feel Love" was disco. Therefore, it sucked. End of conversation.

It was a pernicious debate, and a lingering one as well. The "disco sucks" movement, created on a slow night by DJ Steve Dahl, arguably hit its peak with the Disco Demolition Night at Chicago's Comiskey Park on July 12, 1979, where the crowds applauded as a crate of disco records was blown up. The event was only ever intended as a promotional device for the local White Sox baseball side, but it touched a nationwide nerve regardless.

In New York the following year, Jimi Lalumia and the Psychotic Frogs scored a local hit with "Death to Disco"; touring the United States, later in 1979, Ian Hunter rewrote the chorus of his song "Cleveland Rocks" as "Disco sucks," and rooms full of fans sang lustily along.

As late as 1981, opening for the Rolling Stones in Los Angeles, the still largely unknown Prince was forced offstage after just three numbers by an audience that was hurling abuse, trash, and antidisco catcalls at him—and this from a crowd that, later in the night, would be applauding "Miss You," the Stones' own contribution to the disco inferno. A few years later, they were probably also singing along to "1999" and "Little Red Corvette," and lining up for tickets to Prince's own headline shows. But that's not the point. Disco had apparently stopped sucking by then.

Donna Summer herself remains as controversial a figure as the music she championed. In 1983, the born-again Christian found herself lambasted for remarks she allegedly made to a fan, describing AIDS (then a newly emergent and barely understood disease) as God's punishment for homosexuality.

She didn't say it. Decades of denials by Summer, years of forensic research by fans and journalists, and ultimately, a $50 million libel payout, all of these things heap scorn upon the story. Yet still it persists, haunting the fringes of popular culture, ready to be raised whenever Summer's name is mentioned in certain company, and pathetically poised to poison any dialogue regarding her contributions to popular music.

Which, in truth, would never eclipse "I Feel Love," but that is neither here nor there. In 2020, a budget-busting thirty-three CD box set of (almost) her entire works, aptly titled *Encore*, was topping Amazon UK's best-sellers chart a full two months before it was released.

Besides, even music's most unassailable geniuses can count on the fingers of one hand the number of genuinely unique accomplishments in their repertoire, but most artists don't even manage one.

Summer's own recollections insisted that she was simply the singer of the song, and had nothing whatsoever to do with its subsequent impact. Of course, that isn't true—if it were, then every subsequent cover (some more than others, it is true) would not try so hard to replicate her soaring, swooping, keening vocal line.

But her words do acknowledge that the music, the arrangement, the performance, and the production were indeed the work of just one man, Italian-born, Germany-based studio maestro Giorgio Moroder. And he would, and could, follow it up. The most important question there is, did he even need to?

• • •

Although the phrase itself is of relatively recent coinage, the notion of "alternative facts," like "fake news," is now an integral staple within both our language and culture; a viewpoint that, no matter how absurd it might appear to the orderly mind, is treated with both validity and even acceptance by today's media.

The concept, however, is far, far, older than a 2017 Kellyanne Conway sound bite. Whether intended as disinformation or misinformation (there *is* a difference), a slip of the tongue or a genuine belief, the idea that there is often a gulf between what we are "told" and what we should "hear" is as old as language, or at least, conversation.

We find "alternate facts" in the most ancient writings; in the histories penned by the Greeks and Romans; in the teachings of the philosophers; in the theories of academics; in the promises of politicians; in the pledges of propagandists.

It is not always done to deceive—or, at least, not *only* done for that purpose. Sometimes, the evidence of one's own eyes, or ears, screams so loudly against what others term reality that one simply cannot take any other viewpoint seriously.

Neither is it the "big issues" alone that are subject to this. A misheard song lyric is as much an alternative fact as any grand pronouncement from our political leaders. (Does Rod Stewart really admonish Maggie May with the caution "my love, you didn't need two Cokes"? Does Bob Dylan's Lily, of Rosemary and the Jack of Hearts fame, really take "a cabbage into town"?)

Likewise, anybody with a genuine intellectual death wish needs only spend a few evenings browsing sundry Internet musical forums to encounter any number of equally thoughtful projections.

The pros and cons of disco—the dreaded D, the D-word, the D-bomb—are definitely a popular topic for debate within such realms, even if it is the negative ("it sucks") viewpoint that is guaranteed the most traction. For that reason, one is advised to treat this book with a certain amount of caution, and again to remember that history is not, and never should be, regarded as a mere procession of straightforward facts.

It is the enduring conflict of cause and effect; the awareness that nothing . . . not even flashes of absolute brilliance . . . can be forged in a vacuum, no matter how obscure its constituent elements might be. Just because you've not heard of something, that doesn't mean it doesn't exist. And that's the problem with alternative facts. Sometimes, they're the correct ones.

There are going to be a lot of alternative facts in this book. A lot of unpalatable observations and untenable quotations. Not every disco record was a musical hate crime. Electronic music is not going to be celebrated in the fashion that others believe it ought to be. Punk rock will be lionized more for what it made possible than for what it actually was.

The point is to tell the story of this one single song from every direction.

To pinpoint not only the ideas and emotions that went into its creation, but also those that comprised the world into which it was released, there to become the focal point from which an entire new wave of talent and creativity would radiate. And yes, the pun was intended, for at least some of the music that emerged on the other side was tagged "new wave" by the media. But by no means all of it.

Much of this book is set, as expected, against the turbulent, fractured backdrop of midseventies club and dance floor life. But contrarily, the story opens with the ultimate slow dance floor filler, Serge Gainsbourg and Jane Birkin's "Je t'aime . . . moi non plus," and the tsunami of suggestiveness that oozed out in its wake.

From there, it journeys into the worlds of an American nightclub singer, touring the US Air Force bases of West Germany; an Italian-born producer scoring pop hits out of his studio in Munich; and their own contribution to that still fractured debate, the even slower dance floor filler "Love to Love You Baby."

The story shifts with the song, from the studios where Moroder and a wealth of other synthesized mavericks created their icicle symphonies, each placing their own mark upon the slow rise to prominence of electronic music, to the hedonistic Wild West of the American disco scene, where Summer's US record label, Casablanca, became a synonym for excess, corruption, and coke-fueled madness. And thence to the scorching earth of the punk explosion, where nihilism and anarchy met steaming teenaged hormones in a frenzy of outsider art attacks, only for "I Feel Love" to stop the clock and reset it in its own image.

From the discordant dramatics of New York's no wave scene, to the masturbatory basement laboratories in which a generation of would-be musicians were toying with homemade oscillators and electronica, searching for the sound that would synthesize their dreams of pop stardom with their love of their own new noises. From cold wave to synthipop, house, rave, industrial, all have at least a root firmly implanted in the sound of Munich, circa 1977.

Yet still "I Feel Love" transcended them all. A single, some say simple, song that did not simply cross musical boundaries. It erased them; and, from what observers already termed an unlikely marriage of musical extremes, there would stream the most unexpected offspring.

In the rock mainstream of the day, artists as far apart as David Bowie, Joy Division, and Bob Geldof's Boomtown Rats were swift to incorporate "I Feel Love's" vision into their music. David Sylvian's art-punk (!) outfit Japan headed for Munich to record with Giorgio Moroder; as they marched toward 1979's watershed *Quiet Life* album, new wave Ultravox! traveled to Cologne to record with Kraftwerk's early mentor, Conny Plank. Their first album had already proclaimed "I Want to Be a Machine"; now German studio technology was going to show them how to achieve that ambition.

But at least most of those bands had synthesizers. What about Sparks, who *didn't* have synthesizers, but wanted to discover what would happen if they did? Yes, disco sucked. It sucked everybody in.

Jane Birkin and Serge Gainsbourg, 1971. (Photofest)

Great swaths of what, in the early 1980s, would be seen as the first wave of MTV-generated hit artists shared the same Road to Damascus moment as their more veteran peers, and "I Feel Love"'s imprimatur can be found throughout their output. The singing half of synthesized pop duo Soft Cell, Marc Almond, even scored a major hit when he teamed with fellow electronic acolytes Bronski Beat to cover "I Feel Love" in 1984, and time had not erased the song's inventiveness.

Both Moroder and Summer would go on to further monster successes, side by side and, later, separately. Moroder's post–"I Feel Love" career includes work alongside some of the biggest names in seventies and eighties rock history, including Bowie, Blondie, Janet Jackson, Kylie Minogue, and more; Summer, until her death in 2012, remained among the few true legends of the so-called disco generation.

But still "I Feel Love" worked its magic. In the mid-1990s, in the heart of the then-burgeoning industrial music scene, Thomas Thorn of Electric Hellfire Club declared, "We'd all grown up with [the Who's] 'Baba O'Reilly' and understood that rock music could be written and played around a sequencer.

"But it was 'I Feel Love' that showed us that sequence could not only carry the song, it could *be* the song. You could feel it. Pulsing. Pounding. For some of us, that first foray into programming sound, whether it was holding down three keys on a secondhand synth while the arpeggiator churned or actually looping the first sequence you ever wrote, was magical."

Don Gordon of fabled Canadian noise terrorists Numb insisted, "'I Feel Love' was *the* jumping-off point for electronic music." Athan Maroulis, whose band Spahn Ranch would spearhead the 1990s dance revolution that the media tagged "noir," continued, "I was driving in the car recently, and 'I Feel Love' came on the radio. I was, like, 'wow, Moroder really had it down.'"

Today, too, "I Feel Love" remains a touchstone for all who loved it.

Tim Bowness, one half (with Steve Wilson) of modern prog leviathan No-Man, recalls, "When [we] first starting working [together], we discovered that three of our shared earliest influences . . . were the film music of John Barry, Pink Floyd's 'Shine On [You Crazy Diamond]'/'Echoes' long-form pieces and the Donna Summer albums produced and cowritten with Giorgio Moroder.

"We both loved the ambition of the numerous side-long epics, and pulsating synths of 'I Feel Love.'" A love which was revealed in all its glory across No-Man's 2019 *Love You to Bits* LP. Even the album's promotional video featured a mirror ball!

Modern remixes, too, draw fresh ears to the original record. But, arguably, no single record or artist plays as great a role in perpetuating the influence of "I Feel Love" as the original "oldie" itself. Because even that is a key to the song's importance; the fact that it can *never* be described as an "oldie."

It still sounds like the future.

1

SEVEN MINUTES TO MIDNIGHT

People were *so* easy to offend back then.

In early 1969, sensitive ears across western Europe were outraged when the latest single by French songwriter and performer Serge Gainsbourg, nominally a duet with his girlfriend, English actress Jane Birkin, turned out to be nothing less than a heavily orchestrated recording of the pair. . . .

. . . well, it sounded like they were fucking. Yes, that's *exactly* what it sounded like.

Gainsbourg already had a reputation, in his homeland at least, as something of a provocateur; had, in fact, attempted to record "Je t'aime . . . moi non plus" ("I love you . . . neither do I") once before, with actress Brigitte Bardot. The fruits of their labors, however, went unheard. The moment Bardot's husband got wind of how she'd spent her time with Gainsbourg, he demanded the recording be scrapped. Bardot, too, had second thoughts about her role in the affair. Gainsbourg acceded to their wishes.

Birkin was less squeamish. "I got a bit carried away with the heavy breathing," she told writer Celia Walden. "So much so, in fact, that I was told to calm down, which meant that at one point I stopped breathing altogether. If you listen to the record now, you can still hear that little gap."

You could apparently hear a lot more than that. According to the media of the day, few people doubted that the couple were genuinely making love, and neither Gainsbourg nor Birkin seemed inclined to contradict them.

Indeed, in those days when anything even remotely resembling actual sex was still banned from television, radio, print, and film (many television couples still slept in single beds), the record was already selling heavily on the strength of that belief when another rumor emerged. Pope Paul VI had personally excommunicated the record company man responsible for releasing the record in the first place. Sales jumped even higher.

Radio, naturally, was incensed by the song, by both its content and its success. Indeed, the bigger "Je t'aime . . . moi non plus" became, the more frustrated the disc jockeys grew. The performance could never be broadcast; in fact, many stations enacted full broadcast bans. It didn't matter how many listeners called in requesting to hear the song. It remained unplayed. It remained unplay*able*.

The bans did not make a difference. In Italy, Spain, Portugal, and Sweden, four of the European nations to outlaw the song, word of mouth alone was sufficient to propel "Je t'aime . . . moi non plus" up the chart.

In the United States, where there was no central authority for such authoritarian crackdowns, radio didn't so much ban "Je t'aime . . . moi non plus" as bow down to the general belief that it was obscene, and shunt it quietly off to one side. It still reached number 58 on the *Billboard* listings.

Even in France, where Gainsbourg's mischievous proclivities were already an open secret, and the song's—actually, rather sweet and sensitive—lyric was a lot less explicit than it sounded to non-French-speakers, it was agreed that stations should not play the record before eleven p.m.

In the United Kingdom, the record was not simply banned. Gainsbourg's record label of the time, Fontana, actually withdrew "Je t'aime . . . moi non plus" from sale . . . but only after it had soared to number 2 on the chart on the strength of the outcry alone.

Of course another label promptly stepped in to pick up the slack and "Je t'aime . . . moi non plus" became both the first foreign-language record ever to top the national chart, and the first to do so under the confines of a broadcast ban. (It would be fifteen years more before Frankie Goes to Hollywood's "Relax" duplicated the latter feat.)

Elsewhere, too, "Je t'aime . . . moi non plus" worked its magic. In Jamaica, it failed to chart, but it entered the national consciousness regardless. A decade later, Gainsbourg hired a clutch of crack Jamaican session men, ace rhythm section Sly and Robbie among them, to accompany him on his latest album, *Aux Armes et caetera*.

It was an uneasy partnership from the start, and matters only worsened when Gainsbourg asked his bandmates whether they knew any French music. Once the musicians had finished laughing, Sly acknowledged that they liked one song, an old instrumental with a woman groaning over the strings.

It was "Je t'aime . . . moi non plus."

The sessions relaxed after that, and Sly and Robbie not only cut a second album with Gainsbourg, they also toured France with him.

Genuinely seductive, genuinely sexy, and framed by a genuinely lovely melody, "Je t'aime . . . moi non plus" has been compared to everything from art house erotica to backstreet pornography. Certainly it was a unique record by the standards of the time. But it was not to remain unparalleled for long.

Canadian composer Mort Garson had already recorded a couple of electronic albums, dedicated to the signs of the zodiac (see chapter 2) and highlights from *Hair*, when he turned his attention to musical lovemaking in 1971. *Music for Sensuous Lovers*, released under the singular pseudonym of Z, was effectively twenty-six minutes of background electronic textures, over which a woman moaned, groaned, giggled, and gasped.

Recorded in response to the similarly mysterious J's best-selling book *The Sensuous Woman*, it really isn't particularly erotic . . . in fact, it's rather boring. It's certainly not a patch on "Je t'aime . . . moi non plus," and it had nothing on the more or less contemporaneous "Jungle Fever," either.

Los Chakachas, one of Belgium's longest-running bands, a Latin ensemble formed in the late 1950s, had accumulated a clutch of local and occasional international hits long before recording "Jungle Fever" in 1971.

That, however, would become the performance for which they would become best remembered, a frenzied, seething Latin beat, a percussive swamp inhabited by menacing horns and lurking guitars, over which . . . with a title like that, surely the young lady at the microphone was in the throes of some dreadful tropical illness, moaning and groaning with such conviction that you could almost hear the sweat forming on her fevered brow.

Nice try, but it didn't work. Any more than Jamaican singer Max Romeo succeeded in convincing people that his hit "Wet Dream" was about trying to sleep in a bed beneath a leaky roof, and his repeated insistence of "lie down girl, let me push it up" was simply him asking his girlfriend to get out of the way so he could prop up the sagging ceiling.

Clearly, European radio's overseers agreed, the only sickness involved in "Jungle Fever" was lodged in the mind of the people who thought a woman . . . *another* woman . . . in the throes of a wild and unconstrained orgasm was suitable material for a pop record. "Jungle Fever" was banned and it galloped into the Top 30 across a lot of the continent.

In the United States, on the other hand, it again wasn't banned, and it doesn't appear to have roused too many hackles, either. Not if its eventual chart peak of number 8, and a Recording Industry Association of America (RIAA) gold disc, are anything to go by.

Perhaps surprisingly, given the generally, slavishly, imitative nature of great swaths of the music industry, the success of "Jungle Fever" (*Billboard* later proclaimed it the fifty-first most successful single of 1972) did not provoke a rash of similar sounding recordings.

It lived on the dance floors for a while, of course, and, possibly apocryphally, made sufficient impact on the West Coast porno scene that it was a shoo-in for the soundtrack of the movie *Boogie Nights* in 1997.

As incipient musical genres go, however, orchestrated orgasms felt like a non-starter, even in an age when every parental boudoir was alleged to possess a well-thumbed copy of *The Joy of Sex*, one of *the* runaway best sellers of the early 1970s. Even when *Cosmopolitan* rounded up "12 songs that feature sex noises" in 2017, neither "Je t'aime . . . moi non plus" nor "Jungle Fever" made it onto the list.

Not in person, anyway.

In 1973, the singularly named Sylvia released "Pillow Talk," an exaltedly sensual ballad that only grew steamier as it approached its fade. And the following year, British producer Mike Hurst conceived a positively steaming reinvention of the Troggs' sixties chest-beater, "Wild Thing."

A lascivious bass line throbbed obtrusively through the ether, a scythed guitar hacked one of rock's most memorable riffs, a synthesizer line sounded like gelatin dripping from vertiginous heights, and over it all, a young lady in a seemingly serious state of sexual arousal moaned, "wild thing, I think you . . . move me?"

Oh, "Pillow Talk" had nothing on singer Helen Court, and Helen Court, it swiftly transpired, often had nothing on. A former *Penthouse* Pet, and therefore well versed in the vicarious manipulation of juvenile male hormones, Ms. Court turned in what remains one of the most pointedly sexual vocal performances ever to transfix an American radio audience. No wonder her band was called Fancy.

Producer Mike Hurst explained. "One night back in [summer] 1973, I thought the time was right to do a new, rocked up version of . . . 'Wild Thing.'" He recruited guitarist Ray Fenwick to the cause, and it was Fenwick who "immediately went for the idea of using a female vocal . . . it made it sound more raunchy, especially when we found Helen . . . to sing, or perhaps I should say breathe, the words."

Moroder and the mustache he confessed to hating. (Photofest)

Needlessly, perhaps, Hurst reiterates the track's best-remembered qualities: "It was a dirty, low-down track, with all the heavy breathing and suggestive orgasmic guitar and bass work."

Indeed.

Hopes to have their creation storm the UK charts were dismissed when Hurst could not find a single label in the land willing to unleash such a smorgasbord of squelchiness upon the innocent ears of the public. The American Big Tree label, however, was somewhat less squeamish, and in June 1974, "Wild Thing" thrust a tentative toe into the *Billboard* Top 100.

It eventually peaked at number 14 in America, and won Fancy an utterly unexpected gold disc. But its antics were only just beginning. In short order, "Wild Thing" crossed the Pacific to charm the Australian Top 20; it charted across most of continental Europe, and it became one of the biggest hits of the year in Holland and Belgium.

It even, in the end, impacted in Britain in an odd sort of way, when the Goodies comedy trio released their own take on "Wild Thing," while drawing Fancy's original sexiness out to its ultimate conclusion. "Come on, hold me tight," breathed vocalist Bill Oddie. And then . . . "uuurrgggh, not *that* tight."

If the United Kingdom missed out on "Wild Thing," there was some consolation to be drawn from a reissue of "Je t'aime . . . moi non plus," and it was around that same time that an ex-patriate American nightclub singer named Donna Summer told her Germany-based producers, Giorgio Moroder and Pete Bellotte, that she'd had a stab at writing her own, similarly veined, song.

She only had a lyric, she explained, although she thought it might double as the title, "I'd Love to Love You Baby." She had a ghost of a melody. Some thoughts for an arrangement. Her main concern was that it should be sexy. As sexy as "Je t'aime . . . moi non plus."

The end result, in the hands of her associates, would become the oldest (forty-plus years) and longest (close to seventeen minutes) song on the *Cosmopolitan* list.

It features, depending upon which account you read, either twenty-two or twenty-three separate orgasms; it made a star of Donna Summer; and it did so with not much more airplay than you'd expect from a description like that.

Twenty-three orgasms in seventeen minutes. That's some going. Especially when you listen to the record and realize she experienced most of them in the first nine minutes!

• • •

Boston born, on New Year's Eve 1948, LaDonna Adrian Gaines joined her first band, the Crow, in her late teens. Most heavily influenced by the then-soaring jazz-rockers Blood, Sweat & Tears, the Crow played around Boston for a while, and eventually made it to New York City. That was where RCA spotted the band and commenced making overtures. All along, however, it was clear that the record company's interest really lay in their tall, cool, beautiful vocalist alone.

Gaines took the bait. The band was beginning to crumble, and a record deal was not going to solve that. Barely had she started recording demos, however, than Gaines was offered a role in the upcoming German production of the musical *Hair*—a six-month contract that turned into an eight-year stay.

An immediate success in *Hair*, Gaines moved onto stints in both *Godspell* and *The Black Experience.* She also married the man from whom she would take (and which a typo on her first single would accidentally amend) her eventual stage name, Austrian actor Helmuth Sommer. and she gave birth to her first child, daughter Mimi.

In her autobiography *Ordinary Girl—The Journey*, Donna Summer talks far more about her personal life (which seemed to stagger from turmoil to tumult with unbecoming grace) than her early career, suggesting that she basically just got on with things. By night, she would play her role in the theater; by day, she'd do what needed to be done.

She does note, with what was surely a smile, that there weren't many black women in Germany at the time; so few, in fact, that sometimes she found it hard to even walk down the street without photographers coming up to her, "wanting to snap their first picture of a black woman in an Afro."

The people around her, for the most part, were people she met through the stage, and although Germany itself was undergoing a vast period of social change at the time, it appears to have barely touched her.

Why would it? When Summer went out dancing with friends, she generally chose those places where the American military congregated, on and off base. When she listened to the radio, it would be the American Armed Forces Network that she automatically tuned to. Few people living and working in a foreign land would do anything different.

She had no interest in the politics that saw German society creased by a fiercely militant civil rights movement, one that spilled over not only across the arts, but into violent resistance, too. Summer was largely based in Munich, but she was probably not even aware that the Amon Düül art commune not only included members of the rock band Amon Düül II, but also several founding members of the Red Army Faction (a.k.a. the Baader-Meinhof Gang), whose campaign of bombings,

Donna Summer—loving to love you. (Photofest)

kidnappings, and assassinations would dominate the country's news for much of the 1970s.

And when Summer did make her way into the local music scene, in 1973, it was not into the arms of the musicians and producers who, for the past five years, had been scheming the sonic landscapes that the (non-German) media was quick to label Krautrock . . . the likes of Can, Cluster, Tangerine Dream, and, indeed, Amon Düül II . . . but one who had remained resolutely outside of it. ("Writers for British music magazines were quite inventive when referring to our music!" chuckled Popol Vuh's Florian Fricke.)

Like Summer, Giovanni Giorgio Moroder was "foreign," born in Italy in 1940. Trained as an architect before dropping out after a year, he had lived in Germany for close to a decade, entering the local music scene in Aachen, before relocating to West Berlin.

Armed with a mustache that he later confessed to hating ("but I couldn't get rid of it"), he launched himself as the singularly named Giorgio in the mid-1960s, and released a string of pop singles, among them 1969's million-selling "Looky Looky."

A self-produced slice of utterly irresistible bubblegum nonsense, "Looky Looky" had great swaths of neighboring Switzerland dancing and grinning idiotically all summer long; imagine the Beach Boys running into the 1910 Fruitgum Company, and then jamming around the old "Papa Ooh Mow Mow" vocal refrain.

As writer Chris Azzopardi mused almost half a century later, "Could anyone have predicted that Giorgio Moroder would change the future of music? Probably. But in 1969, the only evidence of his ingenuity was 'Looky Looky.'"

Outside of Switzerland, where it was a Top 3 smash, "Looky Looky" was not a huge hit. Belgian buyers pushed it into the lower reaches of the Top 20; Germany, about ten places below that.

But it was ubiquitous, and even today, it sounds fantastic. At the time, it was utterly revolutionary, a mash of so many sounds and ideas that any other artist would probably have spread them over half a dozen singles. Giorgio just crammed them into one, and then traveled even further afield across his first LP, *That's Bubblegum—That's Giorgio*.

The long-player largely comprised covers, from "Yummy Yummy Yummy" and "Gimme Gimme Good Lovin'" from the Kasenetz-Katz songwriting empire, to a brace of Creedence Clearwater Revival rockers, "Bad Moon Rising" and "Proud Mary." He even tackled a couple of numbers from *Hair*—"Let the Sun Shine In" and "Aquarius"—little dreaming that fate would soon be engineering an even closer link between the musical and himself.

By 1971, Moroder had relocated his base of operations to Munich. He set up his own Musicland studio in the basement of the newly completed Arabella-Hochhaus building, a twenty-three-story apartment/hotel complex close to the airport, built in part to accommodate visitors to the 1972 Munich Olympics.

There, he promptly set about scheming his next major hit, producing and co-writing veteran singer Michael Holm's "Nachts scheint die Sonne" ("In the Night Shines the Sun")—or, as it rapidly became better known, "Son of My Father."

Again, it was deathly contagious, an ear worm for the ages. Even if you loathed it (and many people do), it was impossible to get "Nachts scheint die Sonne" out of your head, a trap that was laid in the song's opening moments as a burbling Moog synthesizer picked out a riff and then stuck resolutely to it. Everything else, even the soaring chorus and the nursery rhyme rhythm, was simply icing on the cake.

Holm's original version was released in Germany alone. However, with a new English lyric by Pete Bellotte, another member of the Musicland team, Moroder then rerecorded it under his own name for release elsewhere, and this became a middle-size hit—in fact, it charted higher in the United States, where it reached number 46, than it did in Germany (number 47).

Elsewhere, however, a hitherto all-but unknown British band called Chicory Tip recorded what we will politely describe as a *very* faithful cover version, and all hell broke loose.

Nothing could stand in its way. In Britain, where glam rock was just beginning to establish itself around the twin bridgeheads of Slade and Marc Bolan's T. Rex, Chicory Tip dressed themselves glammier than either, and pushed T. Rex's "Telegram Sam" off the number 1 slot. "Son of My Father" topped charts in Spain, Argentina, Belgium, and South Africa; it was Top 10 in Ireland, Norway, and Holland; and it outsold the song's own cowriter to go Top 20 in Germany.

Chicory Tip themselves never flew so high again. A second Moroder number, "Good Grief Christina," gave them a brief glimpse inside the UK Top 20 the following spring, but that was it for them.

Neither were Moroder and Pete Bellotte especially inclined to repeat the experiment. Moroder had only ever used the synth out of curiosity, having first heard the instrument on Walter (now Wendy) Carlos's *Switched-On Bach* album. As he told interviewer Torsten Schmidt, "It sounded absolutely intriguing to me, to have one instrument which would play an oboe, a violin, and a piano. So I tried to find out who has one, because I wanted to hear it."

He learned that the classical composer Eberhard Schoener had recently taken delivery of only the second Moog ever to come off the production line. It was a huge piece of kit, and it did its job on a few recordings. But Moroder quickly decided it was far more trouble than it was worth.

Quoted in Tim Lawrence's disco history *Love Saves the Day*, Moroder was dismissive of the instrument's potential. "I used it as a source for gimmicky sounds in the early seventies, but then gave it up because the audience response wasn't really there, and I was always a commercial composer-producer."

Moroder undersells his achievement. It is difficult today to comprehend just how revolutionary "Son of My Father"'s Moog line was. Today, with streaming and online video services having rendered the entirety of music history a flat, context-free playing field on which one can call up any record one wants to hear without any understanding of why people may have wanted to play it in the past, "Son of My

Chicory Tip cover Moroder's "Good Grief Christina." (Author Collection)

Father"—any version—is just one more old pop song with a novelty synth line burbling through it. Nothing to see here, move along please.

We will (or could) be repeating this argument later in this book. But in order for a record to be appreciated both for what it is, and what its original listeners *thought* it was, it has to be heard in the context of the time in which it was released. Otherwise, it's just one more can of baked beans on the supermarket shelf, and all of them have their sell-by date covered up. It doesn't even matter how much you like baked beans.

In January 1972, when "Son of My Father" first hit radios around the world, the vast majority of listeners—schoolchildren preparing for another day in class, housewives getting ready for another day of domesticity, factory employees sitting down for another shift of mindless repetition—had *never* heard anything like it.

Yes, they may have encountered the Moog on a handful of earlier electronic albums (see chapter 2). They, too, might have admired it across *Switched-On Bach.* They might even have wondered how the sound effects were made on the clutch of mostly sci-fi movies that had been using electronics since the 1950s. Beyond that, however, the instrument was simply a bubble and squeak effect in the background, a wash of sound that might have painted fresh colors, but was scarcely something that the majority of listeners took any particular note of. They certainly didn't know what it was.

To them, Emerson, Lake & Palmer, to name one of the instrument's most dedicated rock exponents, sounded more like a firm of solicitors than a musical concern. *Switched-On Bach* did break through in commercial terms but, for many people, it remained that weird thing which the neighbors played when they invited folk round to see their latest fondue set. And, as for Beaver and Krause, that was probably some newfangled obscenity that the hippies got up to.

"Son of My Father," on the other hand . . . you could sing along to it, and sundry English football crowds *still* unleash choruses of the song when they're in the mood. It was danceable. It was bouncy, it was boppy, it made you feel happy. And you could always raise a laugh by pretending to know the lyrics, and then admitting that the second line of the chorus might still have been in the original German, for all the sense that anyone could make of it.

In fact, for those people who would grow to hate the synthesizer's subsequent dominance of the pop scene, and abhor the production-line plasticity of its sound, that second line was remarkably prescient.

"Moulded, I was folded, I was preform-packed."

2

AN ELECTRIC HISTORY OF UNPOPULAR MUSIC

It's not a hard-and-fast rule, but beyond the realms of scholarship and musicianship, there were just two primary entrances into the world of electronic music—either the sheer novelty of it, or its use in television and film.

In the first instance, the easiest point of entry was simply to stumble across it by accident. Veteran American producer and rocker Todd Rundgren spoke for many when he recalled how, back in high school in the late 1950s/early 1960s Philadelphia, "I started buying electronic records out of the cut-out bins at the record stall in the shopping mall, because they were sixty-nine cents and ninety-nine cents, and they had really psychedelic covers.

"I was like, 'what is this?' I was really interested in it, and there'd be all these weird bloops and bleeps and cut-up tapes, and I found it made sense to me. It all still sounded like music to me."

Or, in the second instance, it would come to you. John Foxx, founder and leader of the British band Ultravox! across their first three albums, and still one of the electronic scene's leading visionaries, remembered, "The first electronic music I was conscious of hearing was the soundtrack of *Forbidden Planet.* I saw it when it was first released in the mid- to late 1950s—I was seven or eight years old. After that movie, electronics were forever connected with sci-fi and futuristic otherworldliness."

Weird bloops and bleeps, futuristic otherworldliness. That just about sums it up. Although, of course, there is a long and distinguished history to the genre, one that reaches back almost to the discovery of electricity, and certainly to the end of the nineteenth century, as the first . . . they called themselves futurists . . . commenced experimenting with, literally, generated sounds.

Names like Ferruccio Busoni, inventions like the Telharmonium, these are the dinosaurs of electronica, precious pioneers who not only isolated the manifold possibilities of the field, but who predicted its future, too.

Busoni's *Sketch of a New Esthetic of Music* is widely regarded among the ur-documents of electronica; Francesco Balilla Pratella and Luigi Russolo's manifesto *The Arts of Noise* would, close to a century later, (almost) name one of the 1980s most popular and successful electronic bands, Trevor Horn's The *Art* of Noise.

For perhaps obvious reasons, through the first half of the twentieth century, electronica was the preserve of the avant-garde. Charles Ives, Edgard Varèse, John Cage, Pierre Schaeffer, Karlheinz Stockhausen . . . how easy it is to skip through the names, registering their familiarity but never truly appreciating precisely what they did.

How it was their fascination with the field that paved the way for almost all that we today take for granted; how, without their explorations, manipulations, and creations, we would still be banging rocks against electric guitars and asking if *that* sounded like a Martian war machine.

But we *do* skip them over because, for the vast majority of people, even those who profess to love music as much as life itself, the vast majority of them were completely unknown. If these people made records, they were released on tiny specialist labels to the delight of tiny specialist audiences. If they gave performances, they took place far from the venues that the average music lover might attend. If you picked up the sheet music, it looked like a wiring diagram.

Occasionally, a name would break the surface. John Cage never worked exclusively within electronic parameters; indeed, his best-known work, 1952's "4.33," is completely silent. But his *Imaginary Work for Prepared Piano*, in 1939, is a set text for anybody exploring the history of the music. Likewise Stockhausen, whose *Electronic Studies* of 1953 and 1954 might now be viewed as massively influential pieces of work but were, in fact, his first ever published attempts at making electronic music.

Even Robert Moog, the inventor of the synthesizer that bears his name, is widely known and celebrated *because* he had the forethought to name his creation after himself. (Or, more accurately, after the company he founded in 1953, Moog Music.) If he had named it something else . . . for its capabilities or its shape or whatever . . . doubtless he would be as bereft of mainstream recognition as any of his predecessors.

All of which is not to say that the general public was completely unaware of electronic music. They may not have been versed in its development, or the intricacies involved in creating certain sounds. But certainly by the mid-1950s, as science fiction movies came to the fore in the drive-ins and cinemas of America, anything that sounded like nothing on earth was probably produced with some kind of electronic contraption.

Karlheinz Stockhausen. (Photo by Rob Croes/Anefo/Wikimedia Commons)

Forbidden Planet—the 1956 movie that introduced John Foxx to electronics—is generally regarded as the first major movie to deploy such techniques. Utilizing sounds created by the husband-and-wife team of Bebe and Louis Baron, whose base in Greenwich Village is widely regarded as the first electronic recording studio in America (it opened in 1949), *Forbidden Planet* completely obliterated the divide between music and sound effects.

Four years later, Alfred Hitchcock's *The Birds* followed in its footsteps. Hallmarked by what is widely regarded among the greatest movie soundtracks ever recorded, it is equally notable for having no conventional score whatsoever. Rather, Hitchcock recruited German composer Oskar Sala and the American Remi Gassmann to handle the soundtrack's "electronic sound production and composition," as the movie credits put it, utilizing a device that Hitchcock himself first heard on the radio while visiting Berlin in the 1930s. The sound of the rampaging birds that is the movie's most dramatic sonic takeaway was created on an electroacoustic Mixtur-Trautonium.

It was sci-fi, too, that influenced what is now regarded among the most important electronic albums of the early rock'n'roll era, when the search for ever more revolutionary studio techniques birthed the magnificent sonic landscapes of record producer Joe Meek.

Often described as the British Phil Spector (although neither would have appreciated the comparison), Meek was responsible, as producer, for over 250 records, and the engineer of probably as many again. Up there with any of his studio counterparts, and that includes both Spector and Beatles producer George Martin, Meek revolutionized the infant rock'n'roll industry. The difference is, whereas those others are now firmly ensconced within the annals of the establishment, Meek remains, sixty-plus years after his death, an outsider, an unpredictable wildcat who was as prone to intolerable excess as he was unparalleled genius.

Even Meek's most indulgent biographers acknowledge that there are great swaths of his catalog which they find utterly unlistenable; even his greatest fans will swear they could happily die tomorrow if it meant they would never hear some personal nightmare recording again.

What these otherwise reasonable viewpoints overlook, however, is the very thing that made Meek so important, the sheer unpredictability that was the nature of his game. For it was not the wavering of genius, nor the arrogance of ego, which prompted Meek to make some truly dreadful records. Rather, it was the same relentless drive and fervent imagination that also allowed him to make some great ones. It was just that sometimes, the experiment failed. In every single instance, it was not the end result which mattered. It was the loving labor that went into the creation. "We love Joe Meek's take on everything," says electro band Astralasia's Marc Swordfish. "Very inspirational."

Not for Meek the comfortable, well-equipped surroundings within which Martin, Spector, and Co. did their job. Meek worked from home, an apartment above a leather goods store on a busy north London high street, within a sprawling warren of junk-piled cupboards that he referred to as "the bathroom."

Wires trailed wildly across every surface, and a visitor who managed to remain undetected while Meek worked his magic was as likely to see a musician striking an ashtray with a signet ring, as strumming guitar or playing the drums. If Meek couldn't create the sound he wanted by conventional means, he would start looking for the unconventional. Sometimes he took a shortcut and didn't even look at the conventional means.

He was a lifelong tinkerer. Even as a child, Meek delighted in nothing so much as taking apart and reassembling (often as something else) old radios, cameras, and gramophones. One of his most treasured childhood Christmas presents was a *Practical Wireless* book. He was just nine years old at the time.

By the age of fourteen, he was running what would today be called a mobile discotheque with a wind-up gramophone and amplifier. He built a television set, regardless of the fact that his part of the country did not even receive television signals, and in 1947, he breezed into the Royal Air Force as a radar mechanic.

His focus, however, was always on music. He built a disc cutter, and started recording local dance bands; he landed a job as sound engineer at the BBC; and, by the late 1950s, he was engineer at one of the most prestigious recording studios in London, IBC. (He later moved on to the similarly grand Lansdowne Studios.) And he kept on tinkering.

It was in 1959, that Meek began planning an album composed entirely of electronic sounds. He titled it *I Hear a New World* and, following one argument too many with his superiors at the studio, he could now see a new world, too.

Meek began recording the album at Lansdowne, but soon moved his base of operations to the home studio he was now equipping precisely to his own specifications. His favorite tool was the Clavioline, another ancestor of the modern synthesizer, with which he intended creating his science fiction suite. But in truth, he saw boundless musical potential in virtually anything he could lay his hands on, from a comb and paper, to a fork banging on the furniture; from knives and rulers vibrating on a table, to blowing bubbles in a glass with a drinking straw.

He recorded the sound of the toilet flushing, then played it backward. He threw things down the stairs, and taped the crashing. He rattled things, shook them, hit them; anything to provoke an unusual effect. One of his favorite tricks was to short out an electrical circuit, and capture the resultant "phhhzzz." Today, his activities would be referred to as "sampling." Back then, it was simply madness.

I Hear a New World would employ many of these effects, and more.

The project was insanely ambitious. It was recorded in stereo, a trick that even the major studios had yet to satisfactorily master (or market); it featured sounds unlike anything anyone had ever heard before; and songs that sounded quite unlike any ever recorded.

The only problem lay in actually getting the thing released. Having set up a production deal with the tiny Triumph label, Meek was confident in having an outlet for his productions—he was already making records with heartthrob actor John Leyton, bodybuilder Ricky Wayne, four-year-old Smiley, and more.

But, while Triumph did produce very limited (ninety-nine copies) promotional extended-play discs (EPs) featuring four selections from *I Hear a New World*, the album itself would remain unheard throughout the remainder of Meek's life (he committed suicide in 1967), and for more than twenty years thereafter.

The 1991 CD reissue of Joe Meek's *I Hear a New World*. (Author Collection)

It was finally made available in 1991, at which point it ought to have been little more than a niche release, of interest only to Meek collectors alone. Instead, it became one of the most talked about albums of the year, eminently tuneful, but utterly "out there," too—a demonstration album for every piece of electronica Meek could lay his hands on, pushed to limits that even modern manipulators would be hard-pressed to emulate.

Meek's own belief in the project is evidenced by the number of ideas and effects that he would retain for transplant into other projects—his 1962 global smash "Telstar," recorded by the Tornados, is unquestionably the child of *I Hear a New*

World, and listened to in the context of other electronic music from the late 1950s and early 1960s, it is clear that Meek was not only well aware of what was happening elsewhere, but was intent on bettering it, too. Indeed, his liner notes for the original EP suggest he could have gone even further out.

"At first I was going to make a record with music that was completely out of this world, but realized it would have very little entertainment value"—the curse of so many other electronic pioneers, of course. "So, I kept the construction of the music down to earth and wrote tunes that I hope you will grow to like."

In terms of mainstreaming electronic music, Meek's only serious contemporary, let alone competitor, was the staff of the BBC Radiophonic Workshop, a tiny operation in the bowels of Broadcasting House.

"The Beeb" had a long history of recording unusual sounds . . . its archive of wildlife calls and the noise of nature dates back to the 1930s, and that tradition would continue; would, in fact, provide some of the first tools that the BBC Radiophonic Workshop had at its disposal.

Founded in 1958, under the aegis of electronics musician Daphne Oram and sound engineer Desmond Briscoe, the Workshop was the department charged with creating the sounds that television and radio shows demanded, but which regular musical recordings could not deliver. Everything from the rumble of a stomach for an episode of the long-running comedy series *The Goon Show*, to the sands of the Sahara for a serious documentary.

It was exacting work. Perfectionists one and all, pottering around the studio in the white lab coats that the BBC demanded they don, the men and women of the Workshop were never satisfied until their sonic creations were indistinguishable from the real thing, even if nobody had any idea what the "real thing" was. But they knew what they *thought* (for example) a meteorite crashing into the hide of an alien monster would sound like, and that is what the Workshop would deliver.

The job was not well recompensed, at least in terms of credits. Famously, the theme music to the long-running science fiction television program *Doctor Who* may have been composed by Ron Grainer, but it was realized by Delia Derbyshire, a twenty-six-year-old former trainee assistant studio manager, who had only recently won a transfer to the Workshop.

Doctor Who was just one more job of work, then, although it was one of which Derbyshire would be inordinately and justly proud. The theme that she delivered was not a simple performance, after all. Every single note in the short piece of music was painstakingly crafted from one or other of a variety of sources, the hum of a test-tone oscillator, a single plucked string, a burst of white noise. Each would be recorded and then sliced or spliced, sped up or slowed down, played backward or forward, any which way-ward.

If a piece of tape could be tortured, it would be. Oscillators were manhandled into creating a melody; whooshes and hisses would be carved from white noise. And it was all done on tape. There were no computers on which to compose, no samplers to store a universe of noises, no programs with which to "see" the sounds. Every single note was created manually; every piece of tape was marked with china marker, then spliced with razor blades and sticky tape.

The end result, the piece of recorded music that would open and close adventures of *Doctor Who* every week for years to come, so impressed composer Grainer that he offered Derbyshire a cocomposition credit, ensuring she would receive royalties from the piece for as long as the show continued.

The BBC, however, refused to allow her to accept it, and Derbyshire never achieved any official recognition for her contribution to what remains one of the BBC's flagship properties, still in production almost sixty years on, and still using a variation on Grainer and Derbyshire's original vision. It also, throughout at least the first ten or so years of that span, probably influenced more future musicians than any other piece of electronic music in history.

At its peak, in the mid-1970s, *Doctor Who* was drawing in between ten and twelve million viewers a week in the United Kingdom alone—one reason that, when Kraftwerk (see chapter 6) scored the surprise hit "Autobahn" in 1975, a lot of people simply referred to it as "*Doctor Who* music." That theme was their only reference point to the sounds that the German quartet was making.

Similarly, the work that Derbyshire would go on to create, countless pieces for the BBC, and several works of her own, remains both darkly challenging and eminently listenable even today. One project in which she was involved, 1969's *An Electric Storm* (credited to White Noise—Derbyshire, fellow Workshop veteran Brian Hodgson, and David Vorhaus) even received a release on the progressive-pop themed Island Records.

Of course, *Doctor Who* was scarcely the first, or only, example of electronics being corralled for a television theme. In the United Kingdom, after all, that had always been part of the BBC Radiophonic Workshop's job, to make readily recognizable sounds for a wealth of programming. A host of US shows, too, looked in electronic directions, particularly once the aforementioned Robert Moog launched his eponymous synthesizer onto the market in the mid-1960s.

In "rock'n'roll" terms, the Moog received its first public airing when electronic pioneers Paul Beaver and Bernie Krause staged a demonstration of its capabilities at the Monterey Pop Festival in 1967. Already, however, the Beaver half of the equation had teamed up with Canadian composer Mort Garson to create the first ever all-Moog LP, *The Zodiac: Cosmic Sounds*, reinterpreting all twelve astrological symbols as wild, weird, musical extravaganzas, and preluding a subsequent (1969) Garson project in which he devoted twelve entire albums to each of the signs in turn.

From thereon, Beaver became *the* go-to man for almost anybody wanting to incorporate the Moog into their music. Over the next few months, Emil Richards's *New Sound Element—Stones*, the Electric Flag's *The Trip*, Hal Blaine's *Psychedelic Percussion*, the Doors' *Strange Days*, the Monkees' *Pisces Aquarius Capricorn & Jones Ltd*, and the Byrds' *Notorious Byrd Brothers* albums all featured Beaver and his box of electronic tricks in some capacity or another.

He was not alone in spreading the gospel, either. Over at Motown, engineer Lawrence Horne was equally fascinated by the instrument's possibilities, and as he worked on the latest single by Diana Ross and the Supremes, he saw the perfect opportunity to showcase them.

Lyricist Eddie Holland recalled, "Lawrence had got hold of a synthesizer, at a time when they were still very, very new on the market, and he was playing with it, making all these strange noises, and he wanted to add them to 'Reflections.' Brian [Holland, Eddie's brother and cowriter] didn't like it at all. He said it sounded artificial, but I listened to it on the demo and I liked it. Yes, it was different, but it also sounded really new, really fresh.

"I'm not usually a big fan of 'technology' in the studio, because so many people use it in the wrong way. They hear a new drum effect, for instance, on somebody else's record, and decide to do it themselves, not because it works with the song but because it makes them sound 'up to date.' And synthesizers would go that way. But not yet."

Indeed. Because it is that "not yet" that is the key ingredient here. Synthesizers would eventually become *the* go-to instrument for any and every artist looking for unusual sounds and effects on their records.

The newborn progressive rock crowd would acquire them, and set about transforming every melody they could into a writhing snake-pit of beeps, burps, whooshes, and wheeeeees. Others would be more refined, but still the synth was on its way to becoming both a creatively crucial and musically superfluous addition to many modern bands' equipment van.

But there were frontrunners who remained leaps and bounds ahead of these bandwagon jumpers.

A New York City outfit called United States of America released what is now regarded as a highly influential, self-titled LP in 1969, but which at the time simply caused people's jaws to drop. A rock'n'roll band without guitars. They deployed synthesizers instead.

The United States of America was poised closer to performance art than pop; to willful experimentation than chart-bound chutzpah; even today, it tends to be mentioned only when discussing the latter-day bands that most obviously fell in love with it—the late lamented Broadcast for one.

Little about it, after all, conformed to anything one might term "radio-friendly," and yet it's difficult to listen through without one's head filling up with ear worms, even as titles like "The American Metaphysical Circus," "I Won't Leave My Wooden Wife for You, Sugar," and "Love Song for the Dead Che" serve up reminders that the musicians came to the group from backgrounds in political radicalism, ethnomusicology, and the avant-garde extremes of Fluxus.

All of which, and more, found resonant echoes within, to create as shimmering a monument to late-sixties New York City experimental rock sensibilities as, a decade later, the debut albums by Patti Smith, Television, and Richard Hell personified what those currents would eventually become.

Equally forceful was the work of Frenchman Jean-Jacques Perrey and German-born Gershon Kingsley.

This distinctly boffinlike pair came together in 1964, following careers that had already taken them through associations with such giants of the avant-garde as John Cage and Robert Moog (Kingsley), George Jenny and Pierre Schaeffer (Perrey); indeed, it was Perrey's work with Jenny, the inventor of the proto-synth Ondioline, that brought him to the attention of French chanteuse Edith Piaf. She, in turn, introduced him to New York entrepreneur Carroll Bratman and, in 1962, Perrey had his first ever American LP release, *Musique Electronique du Cosmos* (*Electronic Music from Outer Space*).

Kingsley, meanwhile, was working as an arranger at Vanguard Records, overseeing the esoteric European folk recordings that the label was then releasing. Intrigued by Perrey's bizarre electronics, Kingsley arranged a meeting and, in 1966, the pair recorded their first album together, *The In Sound from Way Out.*

John Cage. (Photo by Rob Bogaerts/Anefo/Wikimedia Commons)

Based around a series of tape loops that Perrey constructed in his own Manhattan studio, *The In Sound* seems incredibly naive by today's electronic standards. The genre, at that time, was still more fascinated with unusual (read: "novelty") effects than musical expression and, while *The In Sound* at least dignifies its primitiveness with the veneer of science fiction weirdness (song titles include "The Little Man from Mars," "Barnyard in Orbit," and "Computer in Love"), prolonged listening nevertheless reveals the limitations of the instrumentation. Remove the duck call and baby yowl from the soundscapes and one is left with some very thin gruel indeed.

Regardless of all that, the album attracted sufficient attention to merit a follow-up and, in 1967, Perrey-Kingsley reconvened for *Kaleidoscopic Vibrations: Spotlight on the Moog*, a collection of popular hits fed through the Moog synthesizer.

A squelchy "Strangers in the Night," a ricocheting "Spanish Flea," and a "Baroque Hoedown" (the musical theme for Disney's Main Street Electrical Parade for much of the next thirty years), are the standouts here and, had the duo remained together, they might well have derailed the entire future course of classical rock.

Instead, they parted (amicably) to pursue solo careers as writers and performers. Over the next few years, Perrey cut two further albums for Vanguard, and gained further learned plaudits. Kingsley, on the other hand, scored a massive international hit as the composer of Hot Butter's 1972 electronic novelty smash "Popcorn."

Surely ranked among the most infuriatingly catchy pieces of music ever created, "Popcorn" was only the second all-Moog hit ever to grace the American chart; the first, three years previous, was Dick Hyman and his Electric Eclectics' "The Minotaur."

Others followed Hyman's lead (Gil Trythall's "Yakkety Moog," from 1970, was an especially joyous successor), but could never replicate his success, and even "The Minotaur" is scarcely remembered today. Hot Butter, contrarily, still feels inescapable. Particularly if you are making popcorn.

Hot Butter themselves were a side project for Stan Free, one of Kingsley's colleagues in the First Moog Quartet, the first electronic act ever to appear at Carnegie Hall. Free alone played the synthesizer; his bandmates—Dave Mullaney, John Abbott, Danny Jordan, and the brothers Bill and Steve Jerome—plied "conventional" instrumentation. But the only sound that anybody heard was the popping of the popcorn and the incessant toytown melody that percolated above it, and two million worldwide record buyers declared it irresistible.

It was never anything more than a novelty hit, though, and that'd be where things remained. To the average UK and US consumer, synthesizers remained either a funny noise box or a mood machine. When David Bowie took to opening his 1972–1973 live shows with Wendy Carlos's synthesized rendition of Beethoven's Ninth Symphony (from 1971's *A Clockwork Orange* soundtrack), it was simply one more piece of futuristic weirdness to add to all the others he propagated.

When the Los Angeles witch Louise Huebner was searching for a suitably outré backdrop to her *Seduction Through Witchcraft* collection of spells and magic, she turned to *Forbidden Planet* masterminds Bebe and Louis Baron. The effect, Huebner's darkly erotic text, a voice deep-laden with mystery and promise, and the Barons' unhinged, and even terrifying musical accompaniment, remains a long way from many people's idea of mainstream music.

But the two forces, experiment and acceptance, were growing closer all the time.

3

KEYCHAINS AND ICE STORMS

"Son of My Father" was the first number 1 in any country to feature a Moog in a leading role, and not much happened over the next few years to disturb its supremacy in that respect.

True, popular legends claim the Osmonds deployed a synth with much gusto across their worldwide breakthrough "Crazy Horses," later that same year, 1972, but Jay Osmond insisted "it was something [we found] on Donny's organ," and so it was.

Many artists disdained the synthesizer's influence upon music making. A sleeve notation on Queen's self-titled first album in 1973 proudly proclaimed, "Nobody played synthesizer"; while French keyboard player Philippe Besombes looked back upon his early use of electronics, and admitted, "Synths weren't the soul of my music, just a help when I needed electronic sound." The album *Besombes—Rizet—Pôle* (1975) was dedicated to the idea that "we are using synthesizers because some music shop provided [them to] us, but we don't really like them!"

Elsewhere, however, the synthesizer's acolytes were proud. Keith Emerson, one-third (with Greg Lake and Carl Palmer) of the synthesizer's most accomplished and successful prog rock exponents, recalled, "the Moog gave me so much freedom, and the more I understood about its capabilities, the more I was able to express on record."

Todd Rundgren purchased his first synthesizer in 1969, as he transitioned from a member of the rock band the Nazz to a solo career. "It was one of the first synths that wasn't made by Moog or ARP, the Putney [VCS3] synth, which was made in England by EMS."

He saw it, he recalled, in the window of the legendary New York music store Manny's, on Forty-Eighth Street.

"I said, 'I have to have that.' It was the only one they had, and a couple of weeks later, I got a call and it's Dave Gilmour from Pink Floyd. He wanted one, but when he went to Manny's, they said, 'Sorry, the only one we had, we sold to Todd

Rundgren.' So he called me and came over to my house so he could muck around with it a little bit. So, I accidentally introduced Pink Floyd to synths. . . ."

In the years that followed, and the decades, too, Rundgren would become of the synthesizer's most pronounced operators, genuinely transitioning it into his sound from within the confines of the Secret Sound studio that he and keyboard player Moogy Klingman set up on New York City's Thirty-Eighth Street.

His efforts were not always appreciated. Among the harshest reviews for his 1974 album *Todd* was Robert Christgau's withering *Creem* magazine précis, complaining of the "mess of electronic studio junk" that obscured the album's "useful bits." But the following year's *Initiation* only followed *Todd*'s direction, and rubbed its distractors' noses in the dirt with the triumphant "Born to Synthesize"—which he chose to perform a cappella.

On the other side of the Atlantic, John Foxx, too, had taken the electronic bull by the horns at the earliest opportunity.

"The first electronic instrument I remember actually operating was in the 1960s—a wee device made from a transistor radio by a friend in Chorley, Tony Bassett. He was the local genius—made things using those circuit diagrams in science and electronics magazines.

"This one was a sort of theremin. It had no keyboard and operated by proximity—the nearer your hand got to the aerial, the louder it squawked. Tony couldn't decide if it was a burglar alarm or a musical instrument. I was deeply impressed by the raw noises it made."

His listening habits developed alongside this fascination. Electronic television themes and classical adaptations. "[Wendy] Carlos and *A Clockwork Orange* [1971]. The Velvet Underground using cacophony as a device, mostly from [John] Cale's music and I liked this idea of noise as art, and music as organized noise—that's exactly what synths actually do. I subscribed right away.

"I also liked the whole psychedelic thing—[the Beatles'] 'Tomorrow Never Knows' and all that. But its awful tendency to sweetness and infantilism needed tempering with more savage elements—the early Who and the Velvets and [Andy] Warhol supplied that. That's where I come from."

Naturally, then, when he transitioned from listening to music to making his own, "I wanted to include synthesizers because I was interested in a certain kind of embrace of transcendent mayhem and joy. They could supply that."

Now a student at London's Royal College of Music, Foxx found himself with access to a Mini Moog—the instrument's eponymous designer's earliest attempt to slim his hitherto bulky and expensive synthesizer down to something more manageable, both in size and cost.

"I began to play with that. I also bought a reel-to-reel recorder I could bounce tracks down with, so I could make multilayered pieces, not very good quality, but good enough to develop a few early ideas I could sing along to. [Although] I couldn't record the vocals until an art-school friend, Darrall Thompson, bought a four-track and we were able to make some proper demos." When he started auditioning musicians for what became his first band, Tiger Lily, it was those demos that Foxx played to the musicians who passed through.

• • •

In 1972, American entrepreneur Harvey Matusow organized what is widely regarded as the first ever worldwide gathering of the electronic clans, beneath the umbrella of the even vaster International Carnival of Experimental Sound . . . the ICES festival.

Staged at London's Roundhouse, a barely converted former railway building that had also served decades as a gun warehouse, ICES was a hugely ambitious month-long celebration of the avant-garde in all its guises, both musical and artistic—highlights included a BBC Proms performance of John Cage's *HPSCHD*, a performance by the so-called "naked cellist," Charlotte Moorman, and an appearance by Japanese percussionist Storm'u Yamashta.

There was also a showing by perhaps the premier British electronic act of the time, Gentle Fire. Formed in London in 1968, veterans of the Drury Lane Arts Lab, Gentle Fire were armed with a repertoire that balanced their own compositions with Cage, Kagel, and Stockhausen; it was Gentle Fire that gave the first ever UK performances of the latter's *Mikrophonie II* and *Kuzwellen*, while they were also involved in the recording of his *Sternklang*.

Led by English musicologist (and Stockhausen's assistant) Hugh Davies, Gentle Fire's blend of found sounds, synthesizers, and what author Ian Helliwell calls "amplified junk" was among the select handful of acts to physically welcome a new day at the legendary 1971 Glastonbury Festival, the premiere of the electronic Group Composition IV ringing out as dawn broke over the festival's so-distinctive silver pyramid stage. Later in 1972, they would also be appearing at the Munich Olympics.

ICES, however, would find Gentle Fire playing to an audience of their peers, as it became clear that they were not alone in their electronic explorations. A universe of untrammeled exploration was out there, and ICES brought it all together. Tristram Cary, whose course in electronic music at the Royal College of Music, London, shed light on the aspirations of a host of future electronic pioneers, was in attendance; so was his assistant, Lawrence Casserley.

There were appearances from Americans Stephen Allen Whealton, JB Floyd's Electric Stereopticon, and Amra/Arma, made up from the editorial staff of the pioneering *The Source: Music of the Avant-Garde* magazine. From Holland, STEAM, Michael Waisvisz, and Jaap Schoonhoven; from Japan, Takeshisa Kosugi and the Taj Mahal Travellers . . . it was truly a worldwide celebration, not only of electronica, but of experimental music in general.

David Rosenboom demonstrated his revolutionary biofeedback equipment ("'gee whiz' in those days," recalled JB Floyd); "I had brought with me four portable, battery-driven EEG monitors that could produce clicking sounds in response to things like alpha wave detection, and maybe other features. I believe I invited people to try this experience informally while we were all hanging around in the Roundhouse.

"I recall that quite a few people were interested in all this, and several took it very seriously. . . ."

A combination of poor promotion and haphazard organization ensured, sadly, that ICES would remain woefully underattended for almost its entire run. But for those people who did attend (most of them performers, awaiting their turn on the stage), it was an invaluable experience, as Amra/Arma's Stanley Lunetta explained.

"A lot of people there saw what other people were doing, and how they were doing it, and they would not have seen it had they not been there at the festival. We knew what most people were going to do . . . But, because a lot of the people were adventurous, you *had* to see their performance. You could read about it and say 'yeah, that's interesting,' but if you *saw* it, you had more than that."

Now a mainstay of the performance group Sound, Light and Space, Lawrence Casserley continued, "My overall impression of ICES was the sheer range and variety of what happened there—some extraordinary strangenesses, some deep banality, some over-egged pomposity—but mostly a great generosity between people who were all doing very different things, but all (or mostly all) stretching the bounds of the possible, and understanding that even those whose work you didn't much like were also doing that."

Oddly, there was one significant contributor to the electronic field that was not represented at the International Carnival—significant because West Germany was perhaps the one nation where electronic experimentation was already more or less a mainstream pursuit. (The two countries, the democratic West and the communist East, would not become one until 1990.)

Various theories abound as to why West Germany would become such an early trailblazer, many of them settling down to the belief that, with their homeland's musical heritage irredeemably tarnished by associations with the Nazi party, and its sole successor the imports brought in by the occupying Americans and British, young German musicians of the 1960s had no choice but to start again from scratch. Or, as the French playwright and poet Guillaume Apollinaire put it, before his death in 1918, "*à la fin tu es lac de ce monde ancien*"—"when it comes to it, you've had enough of that ancient world."

In terms of establishing a historical hierarchy, it's an appealing notion. Unfortunately, it overlooks one key figure in Germany's musical development whose work and reputation were tarnished by neither war nor peace, Karlheinz Stockhausen.

Both Irmin Schmidt and Holger Czukay, founder members of the band Can, studied under Stockhausen, and Czukay later remarked, "We didn't listen to what was going on on the radio, because that was just a tiny corner of what was happening. For us, people like Stockhausen and [French composer Pierre] Boulez were far more contemporary than people like James Brown and the Grateful Dead, because they were making modern music, whereas the rock-and-roll people were just remaking the music they grew up listening to."

In fact, Can are rarely spoken of among the era's key electronic acts, and that perhaps is the point. "Other people were still listening to Stockhausen. We had already heard him."

Popol Vuh were another pacesetter, the brainchild of the classically trained German musician, Florian Fricke. Popol Vuh's first album, *Affenstunde* (*Ape Hour*), signaled what Fricke described as "the beginning of a type of electronic music that contributed to the zeitgeist of the period. Unlike [the electronic music] that preceded it, this new type could more or less be played live before an audience. It was also generally classified as a sort of pop music."

This is an interesting point, and one that Fricke could only assume corresponded with the then prevalent desire "for new listening experiences, new sensations. Although I'm not able to go into details on that, I think these facts didn't only apply to Popol Vuh, but were also significant for the other groups [operating at this time]."

He continued, "We were acquainted with some of [those bands]. At that time, we had a vivid exchange of ideas with Amon Düül II, because they lived and worked in the Munich area, as we did, and of course we came to know Giorgio Moroder, although we had less in common with him."

Fricke also came in contact with another band working in this field, the one that would ultimately cast electronic music into its brightest spotlight yet.

Kraftwerk were the brainchild of Ralf Hütter and Florian Schneider, classically trained musicians from Düsseldorf, in what was then West Germany.

They met at the Academy of Arts in nearby Remscheid around 1968, but Düsseldorf remained their home base, both physically and creatively. Stockhausen's electronic studio was just twenty miles away in Cologne; they were close, too, to the French studio where Pierre Boulez constructed many of his greatest works.

Electronic music, it seemed, was a part of their local heritage. Stockhausen regularly performed in the area, while local radio also hosted several shows dedicated to electronic music. With all of that at their disposal, the pair's future interests should have surprised nobody. As Hütter later told *Keyboard* magazine, "We always considered ourselves the second generation of electronic explorers, after Stockhausen."

The pair formed their first group, Organisation, in 1968, a feedback and fury four-piece fed from the frenzy of experimental rock that was then the German underground.

In the studio with producer Conny Plank, himself just stepping out on the career that would establish him among the most visionary producers of the seventies and beyond, Organisation became the first German group of their generation to land an international record deal, with RCA in London.

Unfortunately, the label didn't have a clue how to market them, finally settling on a prog rock angle that could only alienate any Moody Blues or King Crimson fans who might wander into earshot. And if the album was a failure in the United Kingdom, it was an even bigger disappointment in Germany, where it was available only as an expensive import!

Organisation did not survive the shock. The album, *Tone Float*, had barely been released before Organisation sundered, and Hütter and Schneider commenced scheming a completely new outfit—the first member of which was their own recording studio, in Düsseldorf.

Concluding that the only way to approach the music they wanted to make was to do so in their own time, on their own territory, the duo opted to work first, and worry about record labels later.

But they did at least come up with a catchy name, and one that a local audience, at least, would swiftly appreciate. Düsseldorf lies deep within Germany's industrial heartland, in the shadow of myriad power plants. "Power plant" in German is *Kraftwerk*.

Augmented by the returning Conny Plank, work on what would become Kraftwerk's self-titled debut album stretched through July and August, 1970, and would reach the shops at the end of the year. Hütter and Schneider wrote and performed almost every instrument.

Only drums were provided by outside musicians and, long before Kraftwerk attained any substantial success, it was clear that there were only two "real" band members. Anyone else would simply be hired on for the duration, to come and go as their paymasters pleased, in the knowledge that neither their presence nor absence would ever truly damage the founders' vision of Kraftwerk.

One early departure, however, almost derailed the project before it had even got going. Early in 1971, Hütter himself quit.

Schneider didn't replace him. Working now with drummer Klaus Dinger and guitarist Michael Rother, Kraftwerk made their television debut as a trio, performing eleven minutes of "Truckstop Gondolero," surrounded by traffic cones, on *Beat Club*.

The performance owes little to Kraftwerk, past or present—rather, it veers very much in the direction of Neu!—the band that Dinger and Rother themselves would form following their departure from Kraftwerk during the summer of 1971. Hütter meanwhile returned and *Kraftwerk 2* followed, its relentless beats provided by the cheap drum machine that now completed the group. They would remain a duo for the eminently sensibly titled third album, *Ralf and Florian*, but that would soon be changing.

In 1973, Kraftwerk expanded their lineup again, to include guitarist Klaus Roeder from the band Spirit of Sound. Six months later, on the eve of the group's appearance on the German music show *Aspekte*, they added Roeder's former bandmate, drummer Wolfgang Flür.

"They had heard me playing in a club somewhere, and told me, 'You are not the best drummer in the world, but that is okay. That is just the thing we are looking for, a drummer who plays little and has good timing.'"

Flür agreed with their reasoning. "That was me. I was not the jazzy stylish drummer who always wanted to bore the people with his paradiddles, I played very little, just what was necessary inside a song.

The two-man Kraftwerk's sensibly titled third album. (Author Collection)

"I learned my trade from listening to the Beatles; that was my entrance to music, to copy Ringo Starr. He was my idol. So, Ralf and Florian asked me to join, and I said, 'No, it's boring. I don't like this music, I've heard you at a festival.' But later on, I thought about it and thought about it, and when they came back, I said yes."

Kraftwerk had been booked to perform three songs on *Aspekte*: two from *Ralf and Florian*, "Heimatklange," and "Tanzmusik," and one new piece, "Morgenspaziergang."

Flür continued, "They asked me to practice those three songs and join them maybe only for that one appearance. They wanted to pay me, so I said okay. But I went to the studio, and you know what happened? We played, and it wasn't very interesting for me. But there was a little tool in the studio which looked very interesting; it had little knobs on the side, some slides, and I asked Florian, 'What is this?'

"He says 'Oh, I don't know, something from an old Farfisa organ, it's very old but it plays rhythms.' I had a look at it; there was a waltz and a samba, then there was 'rhythm beat one,' 'rhythm beat two,' and that interested me.

"'What is beat one?' He plugged it into an amplifier and it went 'bum-to-tum.' 'What is beat two?' It played fill ins. So we connected it to the big speaker cabinet, then I found some switches which let you control it tone by tone, sound by sound, with my fingertips, switches like on a harmonium. Then, we plugged an effects machine in, a tape echo, and suddenly we had this really spacey sound, and we were all running around, 'This is great! How can we use that on the TV?'"

Within three days, the group had built their first electronic instrument, a bizarre contraption with what Flür describes as "sticks on wires which you could touch and make noises with, and I could play it standing up without sweating. And we got to Berlin, to the television studios, and all the cameramen with the big lenses were running up to film me playing that crazy instrument which no-one had seen before.

"It looked so unusual, a little bit scary, a little bit funny, and that was it for me. I was proud of it, it worked, and that was the reason I stayed with Kraftwerk. And once we started recording [our next album], of course, I loved it more and more because of the romantic melodies inside. That was my style, and that was already in me."

A year passed, a year during which Kraftwerk jumped onto the synthesizer bandwagon, then watched in disgust at what their fellow passengers were doing to it. The instrument, Hütter and Schneider were sure, had infinitely more potential than had been demonstrated so far.

The freaky whooshes of Hawkwind, the morose contemplations of Tangerine Dream, the pompous pounding of Keith Emerson, the quirky rhythms of "Popcorn," these elements were so predictable, so uninteresting. Kraftwerk were looking for new applications, new purposes, new pop. And they were destined to find them.

4

THERE'S A NEW SENSATION

In 1972—that is, the same year that "Son of My Father" was such a huge hit and "Popcorn" reverberated through every eardrum in the west; as ICES melted in the London summer heat and Tangerine Dream turned their entire attention to electronic music—a new British band called Roxy Music exploded out with a single ("Virginia Plain") and self-titled debut album, and introduced the world to Brian Eno.

Eno today is cited as perhaps *the* most influential artist working in electronic music since the grand old days of Cage and company. From the outset, he was many observers' choice for Roxy Music's focal (and, in terms of gossip, vocal) point, more so even than vocalist Bryan Ferry.

He looked fabulous, an alien disguised as a leopard-skinned peacock, lurid alongside the box of wires, buttons, dials, and doohickeys with which he twisted Roxy's sound into sonics unknown.

How the rumors flew about him! He was heir to a vast pharmaceutical fortune—Eno's was a well-known indigestion remedy. He was a genius, he was glam, he was (of course!) an alien, an emissary from God Himself . . . Eno is an anagram of One.

In fact, he was plain old Brian Peter George St Baptiste de la Salle Eno, an East Anglian lad who probably never dreamed that he was destined to bear the longest name in rock history. As a youth, he wanted to become a painter, but the art that he once slapped on canvas slowly gave way to the notions of sound as a painting in itself.

He already a disciple of the avant-garde by the time he arrived at the University of Winchester in 1966, both lyrically (he attended the legendary First International Poetry Incarnation at the Royal Albert Hall in 1965) and musically, through the encouraging auspices of a tutor at art college. Eno proved a rabid student.

The young man studied theoretical sound paintings; discovered the possibilities of tape recorders; involved himself in soundscapes that were as deliberately notated and planned as any conventional piece of music.

He subscribed to *The Source: Music of the Avant-Garde* magazine, and it was at Winchester that Eno staged his first "happenings"—as art events of the age were known. Singer Robyn Hitchcock, one of his contemporaries there, recalled this one for Eno biographer David Sheppard.

It took place "in a 14th century flint-walled cellar—essentially a dungeon with electricity. He had unscrewed the college 60 watt lightbulb and inserted his own blue bulb. A reel-to-reel tape recorder stood on a bare table beneath the light, playing Dylan's 'Ballad of Hollis Brown' backwards, while somebody . . . was bowing a one-string violin. A microphone ran from the tape machine into the audience."

The performance was witnessed by "about fifteen boys, chaperoned by one of the younger, hipper teachers," and when it was over, the teacher was the first to respond to Eno's "any questions?"

"Er, would you call this kind of thing music, as such?"

By late 1968, the ever-questing Eno had combined a loose aggregation of like-minded souls into a musical ensemble, Merchant Taylor's Simultaneous Cabinet, and was staging a performance of George Brecht's "Drip Event"—an event in itself that Eno later described as "one of the best things I did in my art school days."

He branched out, reaching into the loosely connected network of student unions to arrange a series of guest appearances at other universities; Eno alone with his Ferrograph reel-to-reel, performing both his own manipulated pieces, and others'—Tōru Takemitsu's *Piano Distance* among them.

It was at one of these appearances at Reading University, that he met a sympathetic soul named Andy Mackay, an oboist whose musical tastes likewise ranged from the Velvet Underground to John Cage and beyond.

The friendship that developed saw Mackay's student band, the New Arts Group, invited to perform at Winchester, and the pair, Eno and Mackay, even discussed forming a band together, to be named Brian Iron and the Crowbars. It faded from view when Mackay was offered a postgraduate teaching position in Rome, Italy, but the pair would remain in touch.

Eno next teamed up with guitarist Anthony Grafton in Maxwell Demon, a duo that intended melding explosive rock guitar with Eno's sonic textures.

Eno sang, Grafton improvised alongside him, and Eno recalled, "the first thing I did in rock was an instant success"—a pair of songs called "Ellis B. Compton Blues" and "Mr. Johnson." "We rehearsed a great deal and recorded very little," Eno told the *New Musical Express*'s Ian MacDonald in 1977.

Another band, Dandelion and the War Damage, augmented Maxwell Demon with bass (Dave Hallows), keyboards (Jim Johnson), and drums (Alf MacDonald), and even undertook a short tour of other south England colleges.

Eno picked up a guitar and a fuzzbox without caring to learn either, celebrating his disinterest with a limited-edition book published by the college's print department, *Music for Non-Musicians*. And, by summer 1969, their studies at an end, the band had relocated to London—and essentially fizzled out.

Eno found paid employment with printmaker Ian Tyson—among whose regular clients was Gavin Bryars; "Ian printed a lot of the scores that I prepared for the Experimental Music Catalogue," the composer recalled. And when Bryars moved out of his small Kilburn flat for a new home in Ladbroke Grove, Eno moved in. "[I'm] not sure exactly how I met Brian," Bryars mused. "But he told me that he used to come to the concerts that John Tilbury and I did on the South Bank in 1969 to 1971."

Eno would also become involved in the Portsmouth Sinfonia, an orchestra that Bryars launched with the sole intent of allowing nonmusicians to perform music.

The notion of an orchestra whose members needed be either nonmusicians or, if they could play something, taking on an altogether different instrument, was not Bryars's alone; Cornelius Cardew's similarly inclined Scratch Orchestra got off the ground around a year earlier, although there were few similarities in either intention or direction.

As a short article in *Source* magazine (issue 10) pointed out, the Sinfonia "had nothing to do with . . . the fringe of chaos [the Scratch Orchestra's stated destination]; its members were interested in playing the popular classics to the best of their ability, without the gloss of technical expertise, but with a true enthusiasm for the enjoyment of their real entertainment value."

Neither was it to be a one-off, after all. Enthusiasm for the Sinfonia's debut performance in Portsmouth was such that other appearances soon followed.

The orchestra's first recording, a flexi-disc massacre of that first performance's rendition of the *William Tell* Overture, left listeners as divided as Bryars doubtless hoped, but word of the venture spread, not least of all to the ears of Brian Eno.

Arming himself with a clarinet—his father's favorite instrument, in which the younger Eno had never expressed any interest whatsoever—he joined shortly before the Sinfonia appeared at *Beethoven Today*, a celebration being staged at the prestigious Queen Elizabeth Hall in London in December 1970. It was only the Sinfonia's second-ever public performance. Eighteen months later, Eno appeared again with the Sinfonia at the ICES festival, in the same week as he and Roxy Music starred on television's *Top of the Pops*. In terms of audience appreciation, there can be few more ironic contrasts.

It was a chance meeting with his old friend Andy Mackay that introduced Eno to Roxy Music, originally enrolling as their technical adviser. But he didn't do too much advising. While Roxy rehearsed, Eno would be behind the mixing desk at the back of the hall, doing strange things to the music with an array of equipment that even his band members only half-understood. Eno's gradual transition from soundboard to stage only occurred as the band's eye for image took root in the glam rock firmament of the day,

Eno remained with Roxy for two albums, before quitting during the summer of 1973. He was growing bored with rock'n'roll and, although he immediately turned around and recorded two albums that still rank among the most important left-field pop records ever (*Here Come the Warm Jets* and *Taking Tiger Mountain by Strategy*), it was clear that his eyes were elsewhere.

But where? Successive Eno albums have proven as individual and, in their uniqueness, intoxicating as any other avant-gardist's. It still seems improbable, if not impossible, that as early as 1972, he was recording what became *(No Pussyfooting)* with King Crimson's Robert Fripp, a series of indefinable burps, bleeps, and drones that nevertheless proved such compulsive listening that, the first time Eno met David Bowie, the latter claimed to be able to hum the whole thing. And then proceeded to do so.

(No Pussyfooting) was utterly opposed to anything that fans of Roxy Music (or even King Crimson) might have expected to fork out hard cash for . . . one reason why Island released it in its budget-priced line.

"It was the two of us making one sound," Eno explained to *Mojo* magazine in 1995. "[Fripp] did all the clever stuff, for sure, but the sound that he was hearing was routed through my machinery, I was changing it and he was responding to what I was doing. This was really a new idea, the notion that two people could make one sound in that way. That kind of got me into the idea of the studio, not as a place for reproducing music but as a place for changing it, or re-creating it from scratch."

As a precursor of the "ambient" genre that Eno would both create and pioneer a couple of years later, *(No Pussyfooting)*'s importance is inestimable; as an example to a

Fripp and Eno's *(No Pussyfooting)*. (Author Collection)

still-youthful generation of kids that would come of age in the postpunk age of cheap synths and ice blasts, it would become a peerless tutor.

More music followed, and continues to do so today. *Discreet Music*, *Music for Airports*, *Music for Films*, *Possible Musics* . . . Eno's albums through the 1970s and early 1980s, in particular, not only defined, but also *created* what would become known as ambient music. Rob Brown, of the electronic band Autechre, remains adamant that "there have only been five truly ambient records ever made—and two of them (*Music for Airports* and *Atmospheres*) are by Eno."

Even before he ignited that sequence, however (*Discreet Music* was first, in 1975), Eno's impact and influence was palpable. Guest appearances as far afield as Genesis and Robert Wyatt's Matching Mole confirmed his role as something more than a quirky singer-songwriter, an architect of sound whose use of loops, drones, and rhythms was as farsighted as it was otherworldly.

Eno launched his own record label, Obscure, home to intriguing albums by Gavin Bryars, John Cage, Harold Budd, and the Penguin Cafe Orchestra; collaborated with the German electronic band Harmonia; and, in the process, rewrote the rule book that had hitherto governed electronic music.

John Foxx: "It was clear that synths could make sounds never heard before, and that also fascinated me. I made a sort of loop of two tracks from *Another Green World* [Eno's third album, in 1975], 'Becalmed,' and played 'Sky Saw' full volume." When Foxx's band Tiger Lily became Ultravox! in 1976, and signed with Island Records, it was their love of that loop which inspired them to ask Eno to produce their first album.

• • •

Brian Eno, "Popcorn," *Doctor Who*, Chicory Tip, a bunch of mysterious German groups, and a man who made records in his bedroom. They may not be the scholar's choices for the principal figures in the history of electronic music. But to kids growing up on both sides of the Atlantic Ocean in the mid-1970s, they were certainly the most pronounced.

Now, all somebody needed do was find a way to synthesize their influence as deftly as the musicians themselves created those sounds.

Ike and Tina Turner came close. Released in 1973, "Nutbush City Limits" was a storming dance rocker, a compulsive beat beneath Tina's trademark shriek, across which Ike draped one of the wildest synth solos of all. It sounded fabulous, the ultimate consummation of the instrument's long-running love affair with weird and wacky noises.

But that was all it was. "Nutbush City Limits," like so many other records that roped a Moog into the music, would have existed just as effectively without one. It was an integral part of the record, but not of the song. That, to borrow from the title of Tangerine Dream's next scheduled album *Rubycon*, was the Rubicon that rock still needed to cross.

In simple pop chart terms, the Moog had retreated to its original background role, providing color and emphasis to any number of hits, but seldom stepping out into a spotlight of its own. When Keith Emerson struck out for a solo career, his first single was a honky-tonk piano piece.

Neither did Giorgio Moroder and Pete Bellotte appear overly interested in traveling again the same Moog-driven road as had guided "Son of My Father" to glory.

Yes, they remained intent on forging a singular Musicland sound, a musical signature that could not be anybody but them (at least until the world flooded to

Brian Eno—the longest given name in rock. (Island/Photofest)

emulate it, as is always the case for pioneering producers). But they were not especially dedicated to electronics per se, regarding them, and utilizing them, as simply one more weapon in the arsenal.

Moroder maintained his own stream of Giorgio singles in the wake of the hit. "London Traffic" was a sing-along driven by percussion and what sounded a bit like a flute; "Take It, Shake It, Break My Heart" was the misbegotten love child of "Here Comes the Sun" and a roomful of brass instruments; "The Future Is Past" (another number that Chicory Tip covered) was a surprisingly plodding rocker; and "Lonely Lovers Symphony" would have been a synth driven reworking of Beethoven's "Für Elise," were it not for the truckload of drums, strings, horns, and figurative kitchen sinks that Moroder dropped into earshot about ten seconds in.

It is a spectacular production, vast and overwhelming, demanding your attention and kicking the rug away from beneath you if you don't at least turn to the stereo and mouth your surprise. And yes, there is a synth solo in the middle.

But again, the electronics are not the heart of the record; are not its be-all and end-all. Few people would disagree that "Son of My Father" would have been a mere shadow of its eventual self had the riff been knocked out on a guitar or a sax. But they would also agree that "Lonely Lovers Symphony" would not have suffered one iota if there had not been an ounce of electronic technology brought to bear on it.

Moroder was already a brilliant record producer. Everybody who heard his music agreed that. But that specific Musicland sound that he sought remained out of reach. Probably not by much, it is true—consistency, after all, is at least part of the battle, and vision is another. But that final step was elusive all the same.

And then Donna Summer walked into the room.

A friend introduced them, telling her about a local producer who had put out the call for "new voices." There was no guarantee that hers would be among those he required, but she went along anyway, and when Moroder learned that she'd appeared in *Hair*, he asked her to run through a few of the numbers from that. She complied, and Moroder asked for more—show tunes, mostly—and then told her she'd passed the audition.

They got on well together, matching their humor, their drive, their outlook on life. Moroder looked at Summer and yes, he heard a phenomenal voice. But he also saw the ability to stretch it, to take chances, to throw herself into new arenas just to find out what they felt like.

They were qualities that he recognized in himself, of course, but Summer had more—a determination to actually launch her own career as a singer, as opposed to simply being one more face on a crowded theater stage. She was a natural performer; she needed to perform.

Soon, Summer was spending every day at the Arabella, and deep within Moroder's personal vaults, one hopes there is still a shelf or three of tapes, each one preserving another couple of hours of their early work together, Summer demoing the new material that Moroder and Bellotte were pouring onto paper; the ideas that they would follow through to fruition, and then either keep or discard according to their success.

Summer's 2003 autobiography sizes up the competition that Moroder had already identified, the preponderance of "blandly generic Tin Pan Alley" pop. The belief that "everyone on the charts sounded more or less the same."

Because that was something else that Moroder was aiming for in his quest for the Musicsound signature. Not just to make great records that didn't sound like anyone else's. They also had to be successful. Very successful. He didn't want critical acclaim—or rather, he did. But he didn't want critical acclaim alone. He wanted major hit records. And he wanted them on his own terms.

Not that every waking moment in the studio was spent in the quest for that particular grail. Musicland was a working studio, and Moroder was a jobbing producer-songwriter. The bread and butter needed to be cared for as much as whatever delicious topping he spread over it.

A who's who of German pop streamed through the premises, names like *Schlager* singer Miriam; Anthony (actually Anton Monn, later to become a producer in his own right); Mon Thys, an alias that allowed a young singer named Gerd Müller to not be mistaken for the world-famous German soccer player; bands like the soft orchestral Pete's Band, Rock Devil, and Sugar.

Moroder and Bellotte maintained their own seemingly endless stream of hit-hunting releases, both under the Giorgio name and a host of aliases. Spinach . . . Einzelgänger (we'll get back to that one later) . . . Inter-mission. And the pair were constantly submitting new compositions to any band they hoped might want to record them. The first session Summer ever recorded for Moroder was for some songs that he was pitching to Three Dog Night.

For Summer's own career, Moroder already knew that he wanted to pitch her in a different direction to the majority of soulful female singers . . . a different one, too, to the pair of lackluster 45s she'd already recorded elsewhere, "If You Go Walkin' Alone" in 1969 and "Sally Go Round the Roses" a couple of years later. Anybody could sing songs like that. He wanted to challenge her with material that nobody else could pull off.

He succeeded, too, with their very first single together.

He had already recorded "The Hostage" once before, with another of the session singers he sometimes employed. Ultimately unreleased, the song told the story of a woman who has just discovered that her man has been kidnapped.

It's a harrowing piece of work, opening with the ringing phone that lets her know what's happened; interrupted midway through by the kidnapped man's pleas for her to do what she is told; and buoyed by one of the most unlikely choruses of the age—"he was a hostage . . . his life was in their hands. His life depending on their demands. . . ."

The woman obeys. She follows the kidnappers' instructions; she pays the ransom. But she also involves the police, and, in the chaos of the shoot-out that concludes the drama, there is no happy ending. One of the kidnappers escapes; but "[My husband's] funeral's tomorrow." Those are her final words.

All round, it would have been an odd topic for a potential hit single at any time. In early 1973, however, it was positively suicidal. Across Germany, the Red Army Faction had already proved that even the jailing of its leaders, Andreas Baader and

Pete Bellotte (left) and Giorgio Moroder (right) working with singer Andrea.
(INTERFOTO/Personalities/Alamy Stock Photo)

Ulrike Meinhof, would not staunch its campaign of high-profile attacks on establishment figureheads; Munich itself had just undergone the trauma of the real-life hostage situation that shattered the 1972 Olympic Games. "The Hostage" was simply *too* topical to be released.

Moroder shelved the track, and might even have forgotten about it, had he not heard Donna Summer sing. In early 1974, he resurrected the song, to be rerecorded with Summer on magnificently melodramatic vocals.

It was still too soon—German radio slapped an immediate ban on it; might have done so even after hearing its title, let alone listening to the song. But elsewhere in Europe, and in Holland in particular, broadcasters were not so sensitive. Summer herself had returned to Boston for a vacation with her daughter, when she received the excited message from Munich. "You've got a hit. They want you on television."

The initial plan was for her to stay for just a few days, and then return to the United States. She ended up remaining on the continent for the next three weeks, such was the demand for more Dutch television slots. One appearance, a comedy sketch based around "The Hostage," even won a Best of Year award.

"The Hostage" went on to reach number 2 in Holland, and it marked the onset of a remarkable succession of Summer singles . . . remarkable because, again, not one of them adhered to anything remotely approaching standard hit material.

"Lady of the Night" felt like an updated sixties girl group song celebrating a streetwalker. The Dutch sent it to number 4. Less successful in chart terms, but equally powerful, "Denver Dream" was a lament for an orphan girl who runs away and leaves her little sister to face the future alone. "Virgin Mary" was the slow-burning tragedy of a homeless former beauty.

It was as if Shadow Morton and the Shangri-Las had been uprooted from midsixties New York, and dropped into the heart of the next decade's love for daytime soap opera drama; the last great glimmering of Brill Building girl group tragedy, with Summer's vocal and Moroder's production melding into one grand, grandiose, whole.

Even the B-sides were phenomenal.

The singles did not come easily, however. Summer recalled take after take after take until Moroder was satisfied; could hear them, as she remarked in her autobiography, "the way [he] heard them in his head."

It was, she continued, the ultimate education in studio craft, honing every nuance to perfection. It also encouraged her to show Moroder a song idea that she'd been batting around, although she admitted that it really wasn't much more than a title, "I'd Love to Love You, Baby," harnessed to the sensuality of "Je t'aime . . . moi non plus."

Moroder flipped. "He paused for a second and then said, excitedly, 'Donna, I like this!'" Watching him as he digested the idea and then flooded it with notions of his own, stalking the studio and conducting the unfolding symphony in his head, Summer later described him as resembling "a mad scientist from some B horror movie."

She left him to his thoughts and went home. The following morning, there was a knock on the door of her telephone-less apartment, Moroder's girlfriend Helga, telling her that Giorgio needed to see her immediately.

Summer arrived at the studio to find Moroder already waiting to start recording. All night long, he'd been working on a backing track, a tapping cymbal, a funky guitar, a pounding beat, a slowburn bass, rising strings. It was simple, it was gentle, and it was five minutes' worth of compulsive, irresistible seduction. Pete Bellotte had constructed a handful of lyrics around Summer's original title. All Moroder wanted to know now was how she wanted to sing it.

Standing sipping a cup of herbal tea, Summer admitted she didn't know. She'd not even thought about the song since she left the studio the previous day; that she would suddenly be asked to perform it was the furthest thing on her mind.

Through the morning the two worked, trying different ideas, different moods. Suddenly, an image of Marilyn Monroe popped into Summer's head, "singing the song in that light and fluffy, but highly sensual voice of hers." She knew that was how she wanted to perform.

One take is all it took. By noon, the record—or, at least, a workable demo—was complete. Now to find somebody to release it.

Holland was no problem. Groovy Records had already released Summer's first album, titled for "Lady of the Night," and were now looking for fresh material. Atlantic picked up the record in Germany, a follow-up of sorts to Fancy's moan and groan–laden cover of "Wild Thing." In the United Kingdom, the tape was leased to GTO, the newly launched label spin-off from the production company of the same name.

America was the egg that Moroder wanted to crack, however. And the American discotheque was the world he wanted to rule. "Love to Love You," he sensed, might well accomplish both.

5

IF YOU NEVER PULLED A MUSCLE, YOU NEVER DID THE HUSTLE

The story of what we insist upon calling disco music, even though most of it really wasn't, is a bizarre, convoluted fable. A lot of people have told it, it is true, and some of those tellers even lived it. More often, however, they didn't. Or they did, but they didn't like it.

We could devote this entire chapter to telling jokes about polyester suits. About *Saturday Night Fever*, forever enshrined as too many people's notion of disco's quintessence, and that moment therein where the hero, Tony Manero, freezes midmove, and jabs one arm up in the air. How many people, after watching the movie, took that gesture onto the dance floor and thought they looked cool?

The falsetto warbles, the wacka-wacka guitars, the peeping of the whistles, and the booping of the electric drums. The choruses of "woooo woooo" that may have been lifted from Michael Zager's 1978 hit "Let's All Chant," but just as likely may not. He claimed to have been inspired by a New York discotheque audience that was chorusing "ooooh ah." Either way . . . let's all laugh.

And what's with those frenetically revolving mirror balls, sending shards of light like shrapnel into the dancers in the dark? The ultraviolet strobes that transformed the whole crowd into stop-action spastic crabs, all shaking their groove things and ringing their bells?

Or the dark side of the era, the mountains of cocaine and the nightclub backroom orgies, the ever-present crack of discarded popper capsules beneath the dancers' feet. The stench of sweat, amyl nitrate and rags soaked in ethyl chloride. Studio 54. Oh, the sheer hedonism of it all. . . .

Yeah, disco sucks.

Except, for most people . . . the majority, in fact . . . it wasn't like that.

Well, not *all* the time.

Because if you forget the pet rocks and allow literature to be your guide; if you travel back to a time, as novelist Andrew Holleran so eloquently puts it, "before journalists discovered the discotheques of Manhattan . . . before they became another possession of the middle class," you will find yourself in a very different world.

Dancer from the Dance, Holleran's 1978 novel of the nascent New York discotheque scene, captures that world exquisitely; better, in fact, than any other writing on the subject, whether factual or fictional. But what he wrote of one city could be applied with equal accuracy to dance scenes anywhere; on the West Coast in America, across the ocean to the United Kingdom, north to Scandinavia, east to West Berlin, at that time an isolated pocket of Western decadence within the communist state of East Germany, and then farther east as well, to the gaggles of kids huddled in the stone-faced heart of the Soviet Union, dancing to songs taped from Western radio broadcasts.

Everywhere, the scene was the same. A rarified world where the stairs were narrow, the rooms were tiny, and the guest lists exclusive; where the records were played not by disc jockeys but *discaires.* Where the bulk of the clientele may or may not have been gay, but was always dangerously good looking; and where everyone in the room was a stranger who just happened to have fucked everybody else. Or would have, very soon.

Who were bound together, as Holleran put it, not by the drugs they took or the drinks they drank, the clothes they removed, or the sweat they sweated, or even by the sex they'd just had.

They were bound "by a common love of a certain kind of music, physical beauty and style. . . . A core of people who seemed to have no existence at all outside this room." But whose bones were turned to jelly by a certain song, and now they were out on the dance floor, "heads back, eyes nearly closed, in the ecstasy of saints receiving the stigmata."

Disco music was sex music, then, just as disco dancing was a form of foreplay, to be consummated . . . whenever. Wherever. With whoever. But rarely, despite the rumors that circulated around the choicest dances and dancers, rarely did that consummation take place on the dance floor.

Bob Casey, who installed the sound system at several of New York City's midseventies discotheques, confirmed that when he told author Tim Lawrence, "Anybody could get their dick sucked in any number of places. A busy disco would not have been anyone's first choice." Or, as dance floor remixer Patrick Cowley noted in his journal, "In a group, we walk home from the Disco, all loose from dancing, and his interest is as apparent as mine. 'My bus or yours?'"

But more than one disc jockey traded blow jobs in exchange for allowing fans to sign their name on the wall of his booth (for the disc jockey was the star of the show, never forget that), usually after they'd first gazed in wonder at the autographs scrawled there already.

"Really . . .

"*Really?*

"REALLY?????"

More than one discaire, too, grew tired of hauling his duplicate singles to the nearest used records emporium, and instead built up a private trade with a coterie of young, hungry collectors: "A boxful of twelve-inchers for a mouthful of six."

Such reportage sounds sleazy now, sordid and even distasteful. Maybe it did at the time. One thing, however, is certain. Whatever one did, and wherever one did it, it had the greatest soundtrack on earth. It is said of the sixties that if you remember them, you weren't there. It ought to be said of the seventies, or this particular pocket of them, that if you were there, then you remember the songs.

Everyone had their favorites: Zulema's "Giving Up." "Wild Safari" by Barrabás. Curtis Mayfield producing "Make Me Believe in You" for Patti Jo. Hamilton Bohannon's "South African Man." Different years, different songs, but always, the same rush of adrenaline and drive, hunger and lust, and absolutely unquenchable happiness.

Outsiders often view things through a very refracted prism—either envy for the high points that they think they could have shared in, or scorn (or worse) for everything else. The disco era, exemplified as it is by so many cultural stereotypes, is a sitting target.

To begin with, what *was* the disco era? History tends to peg it as roughly 1975–1980, although true believers would tell you that '75 was the end of the day, and all that came after was simply the corpse's zombie twitching. Certainly discotheques, the clubs from which the music took its name (and which itself was derived from the French *disque*, meaning "record" and *-thèque*, from *bibliothèque*, "library") had been around since long before that. Still it was the mid-1960s before the term really entered the English language, following the opening of New York's Le Club on New Year's Eve 1962, the Whisky a Go Go in Los Angeles two years later, and Arthur's, back in New York in 1965.

But Paris's legendary Chez Régine opened in 1956, and is still routinely described as the world's first discotheque (a New York branch opened in 1975), and Jamaica had been enjoying the sound systems—effectively mobile discotheques—since the 1940s. Nor did it take long for the newly invented portable record players of the 1950s to move into youth clubs across the United States and western Europe. Turn down the lights, turn up the music—hey presto, you've got a discotheque.

For as long as there is music that people want to dance to, they will go to discotheques and the only variable is, what they call the places they are going to.

The dance halls of Jamaica, breeding ground for almost all of that island's music, are effectively discotheques—they just don't call them that. In early 1960s America, you were more likely to go to "the hop" than a discotheque; in mid-70s Britain, you just went out dancing.

But the people still wound up at the same place. The discotheque. And what did they do when they got there? They danced. Maybe they drank, maybe they took whatever the drug du jour might be, maybe they picked up partners and went home together. But the rest of the time, they danced.

What did they wear? Whatever was fashionable, whatever looked good.

And what did they dance to? Dance music, played through some of the best sound systems in the world. Canadian songwriter Phil Rambow remembers going to New York City's Danceteria, sometime around the mid-1970s, simply because "the music sounded amazing. The sound was as good as any sound system in the big London studios like AIR or Olympic. It was off the scale sensational."

Sometimes, yes, the music being played did slip into what we might call generic disco territory—simple call and response–style danceable ditties that got bodies on the floor but not much more; records like that, it was generally agreed, had more in common with sixties bubblegum, "Simon says 'shake your groove thang,'" than anything else.

But wasn't that a part of the fun? Knowing that a good DJ mixed the good with the bad, the tough with the smooth, depending upon the mood of the crowd?

There's a terrific scene in the movie *Rockers*, a hard-baked Jamaican production set at the sleazier end of the late seventies reggae scene, and soundtracked by Bunny Wailer's title song, one of the stateliest roots records of the age. Leroy "Horsemouth" Wallace and Dirty Harry are visiting a dance hall, and in any other movie, the walls would have been pounding to some deep, dark dub cut. In *Rockers*, the entire crowd is getting down to Roundtree's "Get On Up (Get On Down)." An American disco record. And not a particularly great one, at that.

It wasn't an anomaly. Never had been. In England in the early 1970s, a reissue of rock guitar legend Jeff Beck's 1967 hit "Hi Ho Silver Lining" was as big a hit in the discos of the age as Beck's then bandmate Rod Stewart's "Do Ya Think I'm Sexy?" would prove six years later.

At the Button nightclub in Fort Lauderdale in 1975, Led Zeppelin's "Whole Lotta Love" was a regular favorite; and, across the world later that year, the same band's "Trampled Underfoot" was inescapable. A few years on at Greenwich Village's Paradise Garage, DJ Larry Levan would shift from Jamaican dub to the Clash's "Magnificent Seven"; from Rhode Island art schoolers' Talking Heads to Afro-beat progenitor Fela Kuti.

In 1976, the Ritchie Family had a massive hit with "The Best Disco in Town." But there were places that more than merited that description which probably never even played that record. "Disco music" was whatever discotheque audiences demanded, and that demand shifted from town to town, from venue to venue.

Years before the Palladium became ground zero for the New York salsa scene, a little place called El Teatro Puerto Rico, tucked away in the South Bronx, served a similar purpose. In Dalston, East London, the Four Aces was a reggae club, dark and secretive, the air thick with pot smoke, the sound system pounding out the latest imported Jamaican hits for an audience that cared little for outside pop.

But they were both as much a discotheque as Galaxy 21 in New York, the Jungle in West Berlin, Bachelor in San Juan, L'Esprit in Detroit, and Le Sept in Paris, and no less capable of launching their favorites onto the national scene than any of them.

But were they actually disco music? Or did they only become that once they escaped the (as far as mainstream white audiences were concerned) obscurity in which they once existed, and were blended in with all the other records that a less specialized DJ spun that evening?

The point is, again, every disco was different, and the music that they played was different as well. Weekly between late 1974 and the end of 1978, the American trade paper *Record World* published selected Top 10s from discotheques around the country, And even there, it was unusual for any of them to have more than a few songs in common, because each club had its own established disc jockeys who played their own choice in music.

Indeed, the DJs were as much a part of the experience as the music and the dancing. More so, in some cases, as they gathered their own devoted fan bases who would follow them from club to club, for performances that were often as energetic and exciting as any conventional "live" act.

Some DJs (and fans as well) would even tape an evening's set to copy and trade with other aficionados, creating a febrile underground market in well-constructed dance that would ultimately give birth to the mixtape culture of early hip-hop and rap.

For they did not simply stick on a record and then sit back while it played. A good disc jockey mixed the music while it was spinning, inserting sound effects, voice-overs, rhythms, slicing sequences from other songs and slipping them seamlessly into another. And a *really* good DJ . . . you didn't even realize that he was doing it, till you went out and bought the record yourself, played it, and wondered where the best bits had all gone.

The best bits. . . . Across the entire spectrum of what is now labeled "disco" music, you are more likely to find common ground between pesticides and penis pumps than lies between, say, "You Can Do Magic" (Limmie & the Family Cookin's signature 1973 hit) and "Funky Town" (Lipps Inc.'s fin de siècle floor filler from 1980).

Between the gorgeously flamboyant Disco Tex and the Sex-O-Lettes demanding "I Wanna Dance Wit' Choo," and the Jimmy Castor Bunch's bizarre "E-Man Boogie"; between Spaghetti Head's "Big Noise from Winnetka"—a tribal drum solo with more peaks than a mountain range and Rufus ripping back to old-school R&B with the frenzied "Once You Get Started."

And that's before the DJ turns down the lights for the latest slice of Philly soul to slip out of the Gamble and Huff hit factory; the glorious productions with which Eddie and Brian Holland gifted the mid-1970s Supremes and Michael Jackson; the slow funk of James Brown, the wild peaks of George Clinton.

The seventies were a decade of change and turmoil, politically, culturally, and stylistically. Not that every decade doesn't have its dramas and disasters, but hindsight insists that there was a palpable darkness overhanging the seventies, a combination (in the United States) of the grinding humiliation, and resolution, of the Vietnam War, the resignation of President Richard Nixon, the oil crisis, the gas lines, soaring food prices, the bankrupting of New York City . . . and (in the United Kingdom), skyrocketing unemployment, sky-high inflation, industrial unrest, never-ending strikes . . . and, in both countries, governments that seemed powerless to resolve any of it.

So, the kids found their own solutions.

In Britain, the headlines were hogged by glam rock, a fabulous flowering of fantasy and fun that was sheer escapism from star-studded start to glittering finish. How could you even pretend to be depressed when "The Ballroom Blitz" was pounding out of the radio . . . and sounding fantastic on the dance floor as well? Then, when glam didn't work and things continued to worsen, punk came along, a sociopolitical conflagration whose loudest voice might have been music, but whose cultural footprint has defined underground British politics ever since.

A far larger country, with a far wider demographic spectrum, the United States has never followed British youth's tribal trends—Beatlemania was probably the last time the entire country (or, at least, great swaths of it) was wholly bound up in a single musical phenomenon. Other "explosions"—psychedelia, new wave, and so on—tended to gather geographically, never to truly coalesce into a nationwide movement.

What did bring people together was dancing.

Dance music has been the default setting for the American hot 100 ever since the early to mid-1960s, when Motown first set its sights on topping *Billboard*'s pop listings with the same ease as it was already topping the R&B chart. Across the decade that followed, the doors that Motown kicked down—including, but not restricted to, institutional racism and cultural snobbery—flew open.

In 1967, three out of twenty *Billboard* chart toppers were also major R&B hits. In 1974, twelve out of thirty-seven were performed by African American acts, and whereas the earlier total was the work of just two artists, the Supremes and Aretha Franklin, 1974 saw number 1s for Al Wilson, MFSB, and the Three Degrees, Barry White, the Love Unlimited Orchestra, the Hues Corporation, George McCrae, Roberta Flack, Andy Kim, Billy Preston, Dionne Warwick, Stevie Wonder, and Carl Douglas.

Vince Aletti outlined more disco break-out hits in a fall 1973 *Rolling Stone* feature: the O'Jays' "Love Train," Eddie Kendricks's "Girl You Need a Change of Mind," the Intruders' admittedly mawkish "I'll Always Love My Mama," the Pointer Sisters' "Yes We Can," and the Temptations' "Papa Was a Rolling Stone" "were broken or made in discotheques." Almost unnecessarily, he adds, "Their acceptance aboveground was nothing compared to their popularity with the dance crowd."

Mainstream white rock artists began paying attention. Again, there had always been outliers, pioneers, if you will. But it is no coincidence that David Bowie's first major US hit was "Fame," a funk number taken from an album, *Young Americans*, that Bowie himself described as plastic soul, and which he followed up by becoming one of the first white performers ever to appear on *Soul Train*.

Todd Rundgren's sweet soulful "I Saw the Light." Robert Palmer's superslinky "Sneaking Sally through the Alley." Humble Pie teaming up with the soul vocal trio the Blackberries for the majestic *Eat It* album. The Rolling Stones' "Hot Stuff" (in fact, almost anything from 1976's *Black and Blue* album), Roxy Music's seductively funk-laden "Love Is the Drug"—another US breakthrough for what hitherto had been little more than a cult attraction. Practically anything by Hall and Oates.

Elton John released "Philadelphia Freedom" and it became the first record by a white artist ever to be played on WBLS, the leading black radio station in New York. He was even interviewed on air by DJ Frankie Crocker, the self-styled Chief Rocker whose ear for hits was so legendary that his Wikipedia entry is basically a list of the records he was responsible for turning into New York hits.

They are dance music, one and all. But disco music? Not so much.

The dancers themselves were dedicated, fierce, even. Andrew Holleran writes of one audience, "It was a serious crowd—the kind of crowd who one night burned down a discotheque in the Bronx because the music had been bad." These were not audiences to be messed with; they took their fun seriously.

In terms of the music they listened to, however, the word *disco* was nowhere in sight. Later, that would change. For now, as Holleran put it in a later magazine article, it was disco "which did not know it was disco." It was "simply a song played in a room where we gathered to dance.

"Songs you could dance to for a long time, because they concentrated energy rather than evaporated it; songs that went inside you, rather than lodging in your feet and joints. [It] was our fado, our flamenco, our blues; it spoke of things in a voice partly melancholic, partly bemused by life and wholly sexual."

If the word *disco* did surface within this ferment, it was strictly a marketing term, as a handful of the more opportunistic labels began utilizing the abbreviation in their promotional material.

But when you picked up an Atlantic Records "Disco Disc," you weren't buying "disco music," as we understand it today. You were buying music that the label believed would be popular in discotheques.

When Motown put together a couple of compilations under the banner title *Disc-O-Tech*, it wasn't because it had suddenly discovered a whole new musical genre lurking within those old Junior Walker, Jackson Five, and Shorty Long hits. It was because Motown, too, thought that the songs made sense on the modern dance floor, and one LP even blended its contents together, to create a seamless, nonstop disco-style party.

And when the UK-based Pye Records launched its "Disco Demand" imprint, it was because these were records that they assumed would be . . . yes, demanded by discotheques, and what a glorious sequence was aimed at that target: classic sixties American soul reissues by the Casualeers, Jerry Williams, Maxine Brown, and Al Wilson; lost British oldies like Wayne Gibson's "Under My Thumb"; modern homegrown performers like Wigan's Chosen Few and the amusingly named Nosmo King.

In fact, it is with "Disco Demand" that we truly see just how facile and meaningless the term *disco music* is.

Beginning in the early 1970s, the English industrial north had been nurturing a vital, vivacious dance scene known, so prosaically, as Northern Soul. Centered on such venues as Wigan's Casino and Manchester's Twisted Wheel, Northern Soul audiences were renowned for their love of obscure soul sides from the sixties, Motown outtakes and the like, with the true faithful even making trips to the United States to bulk buy forgotten 45s from out-of-business warehouses and distributors.

From the Delfonics' so soulful "La La Means I Love You" to the frenzied popping of the Peppers' "Pepper Box," a wordless squealing synth solo that percolated first from the French clubs to those across the water; from Guy Darrell's "I've Been Hurt" to the short-lived popularity of the Footsee dance, Northern Soul itself would never break into the clubs on a national scale. But a lot of the music and (in the case of the Footsee) dances that it enjoyed would.

The Tams' "Hey Girl, Don't Bother Me" and Tami Lynn's "I'm Gonna Run Away with You" were both forgotten American oldies until Northern Soul shoved them into disco rotation, but new music got a look in as well. A new release in 1977, Gene Farrow's "You Should Be Dancing" confounded many a dancer by virtue of a "stick groove" at the end of the instrumental B-side, which gave the impression of the record going on forever. (With peculiar circularity, a cover of "You Should Be Dancing" was the last single released by "Popcorn" hit-makers Hot Butter, in 1977—see chapter 2.)

That was the audience that the "Disco Demand" imprint was pursuing, and it did it well. Northern Soul adherents would rather boil in a bag than hear their nightclub meccas described as discos. But, in marketing terms, that's what they were.

We're still in 1974, 1975 here. Later, things would change. Later, formulae would emerge, just as they do in any musical setting—how many heavy metal records sound essentially the same? How many punk singles, grungy growlers, boy band sensations? It's the nature of the beast; the leaders lead, the rest of the pack just scrambles to make the same noises, in the hope that *please, can some of your magic rub off on me?*

It's kinda sad, the dearth of talent, the death of creativity. But it's inevitable.

Certain rituals were beginning to coalesce, however. Again, we remember that spending a night out dancing was as old a tradition as music—or, at least, dance clubs. And dressing up for the occasion was part and parcel of that. Some discos even had their own dress codes; others relied upon peer pressure to keep the scruffier elements out.

On June 7, 1975, *New York* magazine published what remains another of the key contemporary documents of period "disco," and once again, a reminder that we are speaking here of the bricks and mortar, not the music therein.

Englishman Nik Cohn's "Tribal Rights of the Saturday Night" is justly celebrated as the essay from which the hit movie *Saturday Night Fever* was born, but its true worth lies in its utter dissimilarity to the movie itself.

Cohn's style of writing is journalism at its best: fast, but never rushed; easy but never lazy; informative, but never schoolmasterly. At his finest—the rock'n'roll history *Pop from the Beginning* or the New York City travelers' guide *Heart of the City*—Cohn brings an almost fictional feel to the facts at hand, transforming the driest tidbit into fascinating anecdote, creating images which linger long after the page is turned. Indeed, he makes an event out of even turning the page, just to see where the latest sentence is going to go.

So it was, and so it still is, with "Tribal Rights of the Saturday Night."

Cohn is the observer, but it is the reader who is in the room, watching the blue-collar Brooklynites hop and hustle across the floor, living out a fantasy world which is as real as the paychecks which they collected that week (and which they'd probably blow that night).

• • •

It was not written as a movie. In fact, some six months earlier, Cohn had been sitting in entrepreneur Robert Stigwood's office, talking with him about possibly writing a screenplay. Stigwood admitted he'd be interested and asked Cohn to come back when he had something solid to pitch. Apparently, the first thing Stigwood did once he'd read the essay was call up Cohn and told him he was crazy. "Why didn't you bring me this to begin with?"

Stigwood was correct; "Tribal Rights of the New Saturday Night" was a strong theme for a film. It just needed someone like Stigwood, forever alert to the incidentals that other onlookers might overlook, to notice that. All the movie had to do was take (or, rather, create) one of the people that Cohn described in his essay and bring him to cinematic life—Tony Manero, an Italian American who spends his days in the paint store where he works, and his nights in a bedroom decorated with posters for *Rocky*, Al Pacino, and Farrah Fawcett-Majors.

He runs with a gang, he argues with his parents, and exactly like the kids who populated Cohn's essay, he lives for just one thing, the Saturday night discotheque. And that's the crucial distinction. It is the discotheque that defines Tony. It was only later, once the movie became a hit, that Tony came to define the discotheque.

Spahn Ranch vocalist Athan Maroulis was growing up in Brooklyn at the time, mere streets away from what became the *Saturday Night Fever* location set.

"You have to understand that Brooklyn at that time *was Saturday Night Fever*; the leather jackets, the medallions and the shirts opened to the waist and the plastic hair. That was real. Brooklyn was really taken by this whole thing. It seemed [to us] as if the whole disco thing was already big in Brooklyn. *Saturday Night Fever* was just putting it on the map."

Actor John Travolta, preparing for the role of Manero, confirmed this with his own study of the kind of people he would be representing. He told *Rolling Stone*, "I concentrated on every detail of their behavior I could . . ."; the manner in which "their whole way of dancing, moving, conversing, relating to their girls, was ritualistic. It had its set rules. . . . Tony Manero's whole male-chauvinist thing, I got from watching those guys in the disco."

The suggestion in the essay, codified by the movie, is that the average discotheque goer was wholly resistant to any kind of cultural evolution; some might argue, in fact, that the sheer popularity of the movie caused a form of de-evolution, instead.

But the music that they danced to never stopped changing.

For all its preeminence in earlier years (and the hopefulness of the aforementioned *Disc-O* compilations), the music industry at large was surprisingly slow off the mark when it came to matching the newest developments on the dance floor.

Interviewed in 1994, Marvin Gaye's brother Frankie explained, "Motown had led the Black music world for so long that when disco came along, they naturally assumed that they would be able to lead that as well."

Marvin's own "Let's Get It On" (cited by writer Michael Gomes as the first true "disco record"), Eddie Kendricks's "Keep On Truckin'" and the Jackson Five's "Dancing Machine" (all 1973), Michael Jackson's "Forever Came Today" and Stevie Wonder's wife, Syreeta's "Harmour Love" (both 1975) all presented the label with what later historians would rightly proclaim proto-disco hits; and, in those terms, Diana Ross's "Love Hangover" was a very logical progression. So much so that the post–"Love to Love You Baby" Donna Summer, when asked about the similarity between her record and Ross's, said she took the song as a compliment.

As Gaye continued, however, "the label's strengths simply didn't go in that direction. There was an element in disco, or maybe missing from it, which Motown simply couldn't come to terms with."

Not yet. Later, Yvonne Fair's storming "It Shoulda Been Me," Marvin Gaye's "Got to Give It Up," and the Commodores' slow dance epics "Easy" and "Three Times a Lady" would unleash a veritable late-in-the-day storm.

But Motown's only other major dance floor hit in these early years was Thelma Houston's "Don't Leave Me This Way" (1976) and the label had to search far beyond Hitsville for that, to the Philadelphia-based Kenny Gamble and Leon Huff house of hits. (Both Ross and Houston, incidentally, were included—alongside a couple of Donna Summer sides—on positively the greatest dance music soundtrack of the age, *Looking for Mr. Goodbar*.)

Throughout the first half of the 1970s, Gamble and Huff dominated the dance floor as thoroughly as Motown ever had in the 1960s. Characterized by the lushest strings and the sweetest voices, their Philly International label became home to the likes of the O'Jays, Harold Melvin and the Blue Notes (fronted by the ethereal perfection of Teddy Pendergrass), the Three Degrees, and more. All were at the top of their game, all set standards of technical perfection that have seldom been surpassed.

Of all Gamble and Huff's major acts, Billy Paul was perhaps the most unlikely. His roots lay in soft jazz and, had the stars only been inclined slightly differently, he might have out-Bensoned George Benson. But then "Me and Mrs. Jones" came along to become one of the hottest hits of 1972, and with the cast-iron inevitability of a determined kitten walking across the keyboard while you type, his career careened off in a whole new direction.

Although not always the direction that most people expected.

War of the Gods was his fifth album, and his first to be made from a position of stardom, but Paul was clearly not relying on Mrs. Jones for support.

The album itself is like nothing else in either Paul's canon or Gamble and Huff's empire. Taking the threads that the Temptations were picking at across their last albums of the sixties, feeding them through a battery of synthesizers and electronica, and then mashing psychedelia, funk, jazz piano, and the incredible Paul voice into the ensuing brew, the end of the world had never, ever, sounded so alluring.

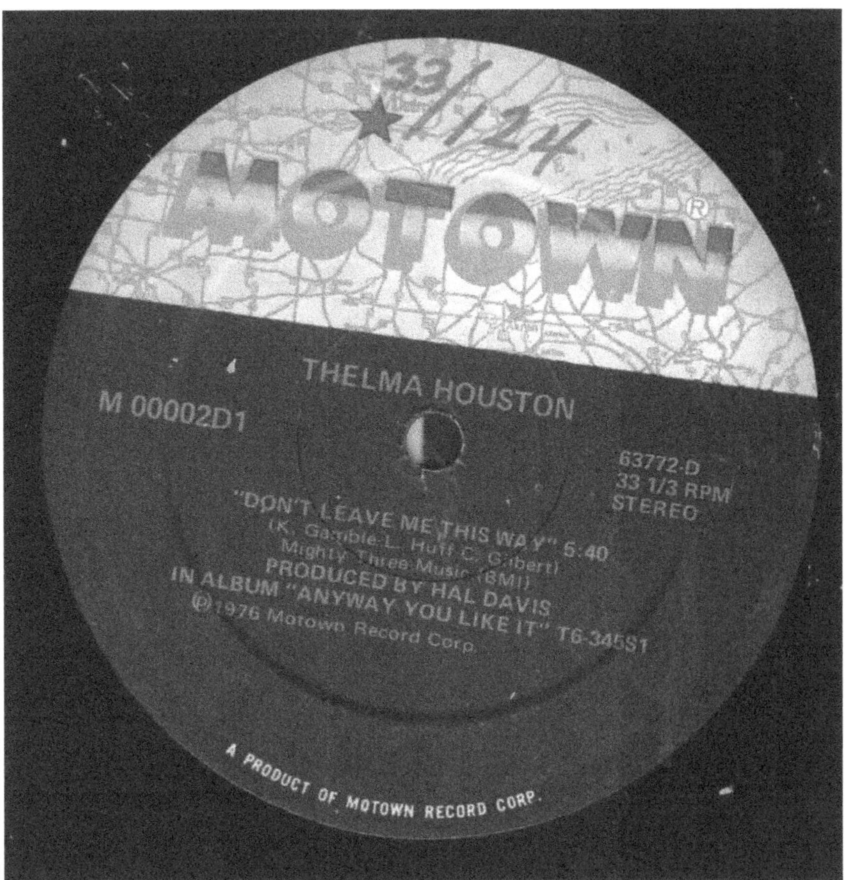

Thelma Houston's "Don't Leave Me This Way" 12-inch. (Author Collection)

Opening with the shriek of electronic alarms, buoyed throughout by Moog-ish mayhem, the album's apocalyptic title track devours ten minutes of your time, and if the rest of the record sinks back into more familiar Paul territory, that is only because it didn't need to do more. "War of the Gods" had already worn the machines out.

Ingenuity aside, Gamble and Huff's ace-in-the-hole was Philly International's in-house soul orchestra MFSB. The group not only scored a string of hits in its own right, it also established new precedents to fire the musical imagination of both Barry White and Van McCoy. By late 1972, White in particular was traveling in MFSB's wake with his own newly formed Love Unlimited Orchestra, one-third of a triple shot that also spun off hits for White himself, and the vocal trio Love Unlimited.

Again, White's biggest hits came during the first half of the decade, as the Orchestra's "Love's Theme" and Love Unlimited's "I Belong to You" joined his own "I'm Gonna Love You Just a Little Bit More," "You're the First, the Last, My Everything," and "Can't Get Enough of Your Love, Babe" at the top of both the pop and R&B charts. Then, when the hits slowed down, White's influence remained all-pervasive, every time a sultry male voice oozed soft-core sex over a lush string soundtrack.

Even he, however, would never have imagined just how far that influence could be taken, over and over and over again. Following on the heels of a man whom the press dubbed "the walrus of love," a world of aspiring hopefuls suddenly discovered that sex didn't just push the boundaries. It sold. Lots.

Moroder knew that when he first recorded "Love to Love You." Now, he just needed to find some other Americans who would agree with him.

6

"I DON'T UNDERSTAND WHAT THE PROBLEM IS . . ."

"The great genius of disco music is that it is all about the heartbeat, steady and throbbing," writes author Mike Edison. "It's easy to relate to the rhythm—you are already living it.

"Most disco songs are just slightly quicker than the average resting heartbeat of a moderately excited adult human, enough for a thrill, but without actually being threatening, like that demonic rock music.

"Listening to disco actually raised your pulse beat and gave you a cheap rush, but it didn't kill you, either, which is why disco was so popular at bar mitzvahs as well as in actual discotheques: because it was the perfect tempo for dancing, doing drugs, and fucking all night long, but Grandma could do the Hustle with little chance of falling over dead."

That second-to-last bit is where Moroder fit in; where Donna Summer fit in; and where "Love to Love You" fit in: "the perfect tempo for dancing, doing drugs, and fucking all night long."

Because, if you listened to it under the precise right circumstances—which were those that only a dance floor could provide—that was exactly what it made you want to do. Dance, do drugs, and fuck. For seventeen minutes, anyway, and maybe that's why old record players had the auto-return function. You just placed the needle on the record, and it would play forever.

In November 1974, Giorgio Moroder's representative Trudy Meisel arrived in New York City to meet with different record labels, Casablanca Records head Neil Bogart among them.

Casablanca was very much the new kid on the block in terms of American labels, founded by former Buddha Records supremo Bogart in 1973; named for the movie that starred his Hollywood namesake Humphrey; and effectively launched with the first releases by KISS—destined to become the fire-breathing, drummer-levitating, anaconda-tongued metal sensation of America's adolescent seventies.

KISS were still struggling to take off right now; still battling against a wall of critical mirth that might have derailed any less tenacious operation. Bogart was convinced that KISS would make it, though; he just needed a few hits to keep things ticking over until they did.

The music that Meisel played him sounded like it had potential. There was another of Moroder's solo projects, the experimental *Einzelgänger*, and the lumbering heavy metal debut by Schloss; and then there was "Love to Love You."

Bogart and the rest of his team were interested in all three, but then matters returned to the one issue that was still haunting Casablanca. Money. They needed a hit to be able to afford future hits, and Moroder's music wasn't coming cheaply.

Meisel departed, but Bogart schemed on; and, by morning, he had an offer in place. Instead of hard cash, would Moroder accept his own American record label, distributed by Casablanca?

The answer was yes, with one condition. Moroder already had his Oasis label up and running in Germany. He wanted to use the same name in America. And, because nobody could come up with a single reason that a label called Casablanca should not have an oasis (and most people thought it was a masterpiece of wordplay), Bogart agreed.

There was one other element in the story, though, enshrined in legend by both Summer and Moroder. According to them, Bogart wasn't especially interested in "Love to Love You" until he played the demo at a party he was throwing, just to see what people thought.

First, his guests asked to hear it again. Then, they asked to hear it once more. Then, somebody knocked into the table where the record player stood, and jogged the stylus back to the beginning of the song, effectively doubling its length. And still people couldn't get enough.

Over and over, Bogart spun the demo, and when he and his wife went to bed, she asked him to put it on again. And the only problem with that, he said, was that the record finished before he did.

A deal was struck the following day.

Whatever happened, by March 1975 the US wing of Oasis was in business with the release of the *Einselgänger* album. "Love to Love You Baby" (it was Bogart's idea to change the title a little) was scheduled to follow in August.

The Donna Summer recordings that Trudy Meisel played the Casablanca crowd were the least finessed of all her offerings; demos, and sketches, as opposed to an actual LP. Further material had been recorded for it, of course, but still it seemed weak.

"Love to Love You Baby," on the other hand, grew more powerful every time you heard it. Especially if you kept playing it, over and over again.

So, what to do about that? Bogart didn't even need to think about it.

Make the track longer. Much longer. Take the little demo and transform it into a symphony. Then plaster it across one full side of Summer's next LP. Bogart already knew that once radio (if they dared play it) and, more important, the discotheques got to hear it, they wouldn't care whether it was marketed as an album, a single, or a box of frogs. For however many minutes Moroder dedicated to "Love to Love You Baby," the dance floor would be packed with smooching lovers.

The producer settled upon just a little shy of seventeen minutes, allowing the original demo version to approach its close before laying in a whole new bass line and allowing that to propel the new material.

There was no scientific or biological reason for his choosing that particular length, at least that he has ever acknowledged. But that's how long the track was when he called Summer back into the studio, and told her to make it sound sexy. Make it sound *real* sexy.

Down went the lights. Candles were lit, cushions were arranged on the floor in the vocal booth. And Summer lay back, relaxed, and gave it everything she had. Where there were no lyrics, she breathed and moaned. When there *were* lyrics, she sighed and gasped.

She allowed her voice to crack, her emotions to overwhelm the power of speech. Out went Marilyn Monroe, in came . . . Summer never revealed exactly what she was thinking as the session went on, just that it involved her boyfriend, Pete. All she knew, as she wrote in her autobiography, was that "sometimes magic happens when you're just trying to figure out how to get the rabbit into the hat in the first place."

At the end of the session, she came out of the booth and whoever was in the studio was still standing there in silence . . . just looking. By the time Moroder was finished with preproduction, that scene would be repeated everywhere . . . in the studios where radio disc jockeys first heard it. In homes, when radio *listeners* encountered it. And on dance floors across the planet, as the disc jockey would murmur something like, "We're going to slow things down a little now . . . enjoy . . ." and then disappear off for seventeen minutes, while his audience . . . well, they did what he said. They enjoyed.

The original Dutch single release of "Love to Love You Baby," before an extra word was added to the title. (Author Collection)

In pure historical terms, you could say that Moroder had accomplished nothing that Mort Garson's Z pseudonym had not pulled off three years earlier, with *Music for Sensuous Lovers* (see chapter 1). In listening terms, however, there was no competition. Garson's lady effectively grunted for twenty-six minutes while the synthesizer twittered behind her. Summer purred in the orchestra's embrace. The two worlds were poles apart.

The media pounced. *Rolling Stone*'s Richard Cromelin encountered Summer in 1976, and the ensuing exchange was much the same as she'd had (and would continue) to endure, every time a journalist approached her.

"Everyone's asking, 'Were you alone in the studio?' Yes, I was alone in the studio.

"'Did you touch yourself?' Yes, well, actually I had my hand on my knee."

She admitted, once the record was a hit, "If I'd known seven years ago that all I had to do was groan, I would have been groaning!" And she acknowledged that, once the session was over, the last thing she wanted to hear was a playback.

"I didn't want to hear it. I heard a couple of oohs and aahs once and I—black people don't get red—I was blue! I love the music, I just wished that I hadn't sung it."

Another *Rolling Stone* writer, Mikal Gilmore, went on to describe "Love to Love You Baby" as the sound of a "servile vixen with a whispery voice, intoning and moaning over a metronomic beat that had all the intensity of a sex act between consenting androids"—an odd interpretation, but an intriguing one regardless.

The session, Summer continued in a delightfully candid *Penthouse* interview with Elliot Mitz in 1979, "was approached as an acting piece, as what I imagined it to be like for a man seeing his wife for the first time, or for a woman seeing a man for the first time. I've been in that situation.

"There wasn't anything to say. I was in ecstasy without even being touched. I was breathing heavy just from the thought that my dream was right there, in front of me. Ecstasy comes in many forms; it's not just physical. But my song conjured up physical fantasies for people. . . . People believed the story I was acting."

She talked of the letters she received from fans, and drawings as well. The fan who fantasized, across four pages, of watching a whip-wielding Summer in a scene with actors Raquel Welch and Ann Margret; of the fact that many of her male fans tended to be blond; and how baffled she was by the fact she was so beloved by the gay community.

But all of that was still to come.

Unquestioningly, Casablanca targeted the bulk of its promotion at the discotheques and, in an interview with *Record Mirror*'s Robin Katz, Moroder nodded his agreement. "The criticism of disco music is that the rhythm is monotonous. The rhythm is identical from song to song.

"Admittedly, outside a [discotheque], it becomes tedious quickly. But inside a good disco, records get strung together so you don't even realize you're going from one song to the next.

"The result on the dancer is almost hypnotic. Your body goes by itself. So, I'm not surprised when you say audiences don't hear what they dance to anymore. They may not. But the input of music and lights is just incredible."

The world of the New York discotheques heard the record for the first time at the regular Record Pool, a Prince Street gathering of some two hundred city disc jockeys, at which around forty different labels (at that time—both numbers would soon increase) would throw their latest releases, in the hope that some would stick.

Record Pool was launched in June 1975 and, according to *Record World*, one single meeting in late August saw more than ten thousand records handed out in New York alone—similar organizations would soon be springing up in other major cities. And back in Manhattan, if anyone missed out on a favorite at the pool, a visit to the all-night Colony Records store, in the Brill Building on Broadway, or the sensibly named Downstairs, in the subway arcade beneath Sixth Avenue and Forty-Second Street, would quickly put them right. Those retailers, too, knew enough to keep the disc jockeys' favorite spins in stock.

What all of these DJs, be they the pulse-beat of the smartest new niterie, or ringmaster of the grimiest dive, had in common was, they searched for the new, but they sought out the nuanced as well. They looked for records that not only met the requirements of their individual audiences, but those which also might exceed them.

In musical terms, it had already been a good year for the discotheques, all the more so since the very term disco had started slipping away from the venues alone, and being applied to the kind of music that they played.

It remained a marketing move, but such terms . . . pigeonholes, labels, call them what you will . . . also serve another purpose. Musicians themselves tend to resent having their art thrown into a catchall category. But, from a fan's point of view, asked what kind of music they like, it's a lot easier to simply say "disco" (or whatever), than to stand there listing individual artists.

Still, at this time, even attempting to affix a single, all-encompassing, label upon that music was akin to trying to take a pineapple seriously.

Still a few years short of the formulaic death knell that would eventually descend upon the dance music of the late 1970s, and the stylistic absurdities that would become its visual signature, discotheque tastes remained a wild west, a place where you were as likely to hear the swamp-soaked Cajun sexuality of Labelle's "Lady Marmalade" ("*voulez vous couchez avec moi, ce soir?*") as the daft martial artistry of Carl Douglas's "Kung Fu Fighting"; a world in which Minnie Ripperton's supremely sweet "Loving You" vied with Barry White's sultry "You're the First, the Last, My Everything."

"The whole disco scene was going on simultaneously to the punk scene," Blondie drummer Clem Burke recalled for author Kembrew McLeod of these formative years. Television played their first live show in 1974, Blondie, the Ramones and the Patti

Smith Group, too. And they gigged wherever they could get gigs. Discotheques were one of the options available. Indeed, when Max's Kansas City reopened under new management after dominating New York's underground art society since the late 1960s, owner Tommy Dean initially intended it to be a discotheque, with no live acts at all. He quickly had a change of heart, but a staff of house DJs kept the earlier option open.

The basement housing Club 82, too, was both a popular live venue and a disco, and they were not alone. Burke continued, "Blondie used to play with . . . lots of our friends in gay clubs and drag clubs, and the music that was playing was dance music. I always point out that disco music was probably more subversive than punk. That whole lifestyle—the underground clubs, the gay culture, the leather scene—all that stuff revolved around disco. [It] was definitely a left of center movement, the same way punk was."

"Love to Love You Baby," slinky and sexy and, in terms of what you normally heard on a major record label, subversive, was as left of center as any of that.

DJ Phil Gill, a mainstay of the Brooklyn club scene, was the one who brought *Love to Love You Baby* (the album was titled for its main attraction) into Record Pool—he had received a superadvance copy from Casablanca, close to two months shy of the album's release. He put it on, then sat back while everyone else in the room came rushing over, to demand to know what they were hearing.

Record World magazine's Vince Aletti reviewed the album in his September 20 column, one of two new releases that he described as "the . . . most talked-about album cuts in New York discos right now." One was "Every Beat of My Heart" by Crown Heights Affair; the other was . . . the "*extraordinary*" "Love to Love You Baby."

It was, Aletti enthused, "like nothing I've heard before," taking off "from a few flimsy 'Pillow Talk' style lyrics, delivered with breathy abandon by Summer, who does little else but moan passionately and repeat the title. She fades out . . . and the orchestra wells up, then falls back to reveal her in the throes of even deeper passion as the record builds wave by wave. . . . Deliciously excessive."

Forty years on, Aletti could still remember the first time he heard "Love to Love You Baby" in a club setting, at the Loft in New York. He was, he told *Interview* magazine's Sarah Nechamkin, "amazed that it could work the way it did—that it could be that overwhelming and sexy and danceable at 15 minutes plus."

The Loft was the perfect environment for such an experience. For a start, it wasn't actually a disco. Situated on the corner of Broadway and Bleecker Street, it had been operating since 1971, when owner David Mancuso established it as an exclusive invitation-only private party. Not a club, not a discotheque. A private party.

There was no curfew—private parties can go on as long as they like. There were no firemen banging on the doors to check occupancy rates. There were no permits required, or licenses. True, it meant Mancuso could not sell his guests alcohol, but they didn't seem to mind. They just brought their own drugs instead.

Dawn was often breaking before all the dancers departed.

Aletti: "I don't remember a song before that proceeded so much like love-making [as "Love to Love You Baby"]. Donna's voice was so thoroughly woven into the music, but it was really this overall sense of eroticism that made it work. It had the length that you could really flow with it and let it completely take you away. The length, the sensuality, the storytelling and the sense of a new sound coming up—it really did start there with Donna Summer."

Aletti's enthusiasm was contagious, his observations spot on. The following week, "Love to Love You Baby" was solidly locked in among the most requested songs as far afield as New York and Florida. Boston and Detroit, Los Angeles and Seattle. When Donna Summer visited New York, she dropped by the Record Pool to thank the disc jockeys for their part in the record's success, then played a show at a Manhattan discotheque, where she was greeted by a life-size replica of herself, made out of cake.

As the record soared on the dance floors, so it climbed the charts.

The regular seven-inch single, edited down to a quarter of its long-playing length, hit number 1 on *Billboard*'s Dance Club listings, number 2 on the national Top 100, 3 on the R&B listings, 4 in the United Kingdom; 5 in Sweden, 6 in West Germany.

Canada sent the single to number 1, and the album was reliably Top 20 across Europe and the Americas. The four weeks *Love to Love You Baby* took to rise to the top of *Record World*'s Disco File top twenty established it as that highly influential chart's fastest mover of the year; while the album ended the year at number 3 (behind Silver Convention and the Salsoul Orchestra) on the same publication's Essential Albums of 1975 listing. Significantly, the single edit did not even bother the "essential singles" Top 60.

Even more amazingly, it achieved all this with just a modicum of airplay. Like "Je t'aime . . . moi non plus," like "Jungle Fever," and maybe more so than either, the sound of a woman having *that* many orgasms in *that* short a time just didn't seem like the sort of thing any responsible broadcaster should be forcing down people's throat with their cornflakes.

The bans amused Summer. The fuss had made people "curious enough to go out now listening for the record. But I truly don't understand what the problem is."

She talked of how she had spent time in London earlier in her career, "[and] I remember things like the dirty strip clubs in Soho. Why don't these people turn their attention to that kind of thing because that's a million times more damaging than my record. After all, what is wrong with making love? It isn't as vicious and negative as some small-minded people obviously think it is . . . and unless you have experienced making love, how can you talk about it on the strength of what other people say?"

If radio tended to avoid the record during the day, however, night-time was a completely different matter. "You know what I used to tell people in the beginning?" Neil Bogart was quoted as asking in period ads for the record. And then he'd deliver his answer. "Take Donna home and make love to her—the album, that is. It'll become part of your family.'"

Over at WBLS, Frankie Crocker took to playing the record every night after midnight, a move that inspired Casablanca to sponsor midnight airings for the full-length album track elsewhere, under the banner "seventeen minutes of love with Donna Summer."

Neither did Summer balk at her newfound role as the sex queen of the seventies. When New York's Infinity discotheque debuted in a former envelope factory at 653 Broadway that fall, Summer was among the merry throng who danced beneath the six-foot pink neon penis that was a highlight of the opening-night decor. She gave interviews to the adult-oriented *Penthouse* and *Oui* magazines, and she openly discussed sex with any journalist who cared to ask about it.

Journalists were not the only people affected by the song. One night at the Crypt in west London's Earl's Court, "Love to Love You Baby" incited such a rush for the dance floor that one onlooker turned to another and quipped, "The only record that turns all the straight boys queer. At least for a quarter of an hour" And then he joined the rush as well.

It all helped. When *Billboard* magazine staged its second Disco Forum at the Americana Hotel, Casablanca was named disco label of the year. By the end of the seventies, with the likes of Parliament, the Village People, Paul Jabara, Love & Kisses, Cameo, Santa Esmeralda, and more also on the roster, it was most people's idea of the disco label of the decade.

For all of that, Casablanca was not necessarily a happy family. "Each [artist] hated the other," Giorgio Moroder told journalist Torsten Schmidt. "KISS said, . . . 'How can you have that disco girl?' And then the disco girl, Donna, was like, 'How can you have the . . . Village People?' . . . it was a little bit of a conflict. Thank God we never met together."

But that didn't matter. All but overnight, all that Neil Bogart had prophesied for his record label; all that Giorgio Moroder had been planning for his "sound," and everything that Donna Summer had ever hoped might happen to her had slipped into place.

And all she had to do was groan.

7

AND WE'LL HAVE FAHR'N FAHR'N FAHR'N

"Love to Love You Baby" was not the only album side–size German Goliath to bestride the US singles charts during 1975.

Krautrock, like disco music, was going gangbusters. By 1975, the heavily synth-laden Tangerine Dream were old hands at climbing the UK album charts, and had headlined some of the country's most prestigious venues, the Royal Albert Hall among them.

Amon Düül II had just signed with Atlantic Records in the United States; Nektar (a British band, but one that was formed and based in Germany) had scored two successive American Top 40 hits, and were preparing to relocate to New Jersey. And Giorgio Moroder's harshly electronic, robotic-pop *Einzelgänger* project had launched his own Oasis label in that same country, and received encouraging reviews all over.

The brightest light, however, was being shone on Kraftwerk. Or it would be, once their latest studio sojourn was complete.

"Having a real guitarist and a real drummer was a little unusual within our setup," Wolfgang Flür reflected. "Other bands did that, but we were maybe more electronic, or less rock, than they were, so we were unusual at the time."

"We are German," bandmate Ralf Hütter remarked in the *New Musical Express* several years later, "and there is a fatalistic German quality of going all the way. There is never a question of maybe using a little computer here and plugging it into the synthesizer there and keeping the rest of the group as it was before. We close the door . . . and don't open it. We try to do it all the way, imposing the process as a discipline on ourselves, really taking all the way and then going out of the room to see where that takes us. I think that is very Germanic."

Flür: "What we played then was not the classical style of conventional pop songs, we developed that later; much much later. For a long period, what we played was music that made the audience really go into it with their feelings and their imagination."

The new album was titled *Autobahn*, after its side-long title track, and it is tragic that history has not recorded whose idea it was to edit the original, twenty-two-minute piece down to a snappy three minutes; nor does it recall the looks on the faces of the sales reps who were handed advance copies of it, and told to do their job.

But few records have ever seemed so unlikely, so unsuited, so *unsingle-like* as "Autobahn." And few have turned all those presumptions so thoroughly on their head, and become the complete and utter opposite. Top 30 in America, Top 20 in the United Kingdom, "Autobahn" (and in its wake, its parent album) became the surprise hit of the year, of the decade-so-far. And that despite (or possibly because of) a surprisingly popular misinterpretation of the record's lyric convincing listeners that the group were singing "fun fun fun on the autobahn," to conjure visions of grinning Teutonic Beach Boys.

Not everybody took that comparison seriously, although few would deny its validity. John Foxx: "I think 'Autobahn' came over as a sort of one-off novelty record in the public mind, being a tongue in cheek conversion of 'Barbara Ann' by the Beach Boys into motorway music with traffic noises. Of course, it was far, far more significant than that, but that's how it was generally perceived."

But Flür was unequivocal. "No! Someone else told me that they thought the way we speak in German, *Fahr'n*, which means 'driving,' sounds like the English word *fun*. 'Fahr'n Fahr'n Fahr'n,' 'fun fun fun.' That is wrong. But it works. Driving is fun. We had no speed limit on the autobahn, we could race through the highways, through the alps, so yes, 'Fahr'n Fahr'n Fahr'n, fun fun fun,' but it wasn't anything to do with the Beach Boys!

"We used to drive a lot. We used to listen to the sound of driving, the wind, passing cars and lorries, the rain, every moment the sounds around you are changing, and the idea was to rebuild those sounds on the synthesizer."

As a major international hit single, "Autobahn" completely rewrote the rock rulebook. There was simply nothing to relate it to. Nothing except—it really did sound like a road trip. Trucks raced by, horns sounded, there were windshield wipers and splashes through a puddle. If you really thought about it, it was almost frighteningly mundane. But it was also exquisitely exciting, a fact that two continents' worth of record buyers were fast to pick up on.

Kraftwerk—hard driving men. (Everett Collection/Alamy Stock Photo)

Flür: "When we heard from America . . . one day Ralf called me, I was not so long in the band, maybe a year or so, and I was not a steady member of the band. But Karl [percussionist Bartos, replacing Klaus Roeder] had just joined the band, and Ralf called us up and said, 'Can we go for coffee and cakes somewhere, we have to tell you something.' So we got there, and he said 'what would you think about traveling to America?'

"We were young boys, we were twenty-three, twenty-five, green behind the ears. We didn't know anything, and Ralf told us our single was coming up in America, it's heading for number twenty, and we were invited to tour.

"America was so far away at that time, but we loved it. America was so modern and fast and exciting, and we were very proud to come over, very proud that our single was selling there. Some of the American stations were playing the short version, but some were playing the whole track. It sounded really good on car radios, I was told."

With both single and album storming the chart, Kraftwerk were one of the hot tickets that summer of 1975. The quartet played shows across both the United States and Europe, even making another rare TV appearance on the network concert show *Midnight Special*, and establishing themselves as one of the most memorable, if not visually exciting, live attractions around.

And they did it despite, not because of, the band's own apparent qualities. As journalist Simon Witter wrote a decade later, "In the glam era of glitter and guitars, Kraftwerk were four besuited squares playing keyboards. In the Germany of 'green' awakening they celebrated the ugly industrial network of motorways with which Hitler had defiled the country. At a time when 75% of German radio programmes were in English, they sang in German. . . ."

There was more. Reviewing a period live show, the *New Musical Express*'s Miles remarked, "Bryan Ferry might strive for this '40s decadent look but underneath everyone knows he's really a scruffy art student. But with these guys—they would actually look weird in a pair of jeans. Their music was blank too. The electronic melodies flowed as slowly as a piece of garbage floating down the polluted Rhine."

And back in Germany, Popol Vuh's Florian Fricke admired Kraftwerk's achievement from afar, but another song from a little closer up.

"One day as I was driving with the radio on, I heard a song that was almost as long as 'Autobahn,' except instead of driving, the singer sounded like she was having sex. I don't remember if I liked it, I think not. But then the disc jockey said who it was, and I thought, 'Oh, doesn't she work with Giorgio Moroder?' and that surprised me because I only knew Giorgio for the Schlager, the pop hits, 'Son of My Father,' things like that.

"But this was something very different, and then I discovered that just like 'Autobahn,' the record company had cut it down for a single, but the disc jockeys were playing the longer version as well.

"Which made me proud because maybe something new had started and it was another German record. But also, I thought people needed to start paying attention to what Giorgio was doing."

• • •

The problem with both "Autobahn" and "Love to Love You Baby" . . . which wasn't really a problem per se, so much as a conundrum disguised as an irritant . . . was that they *were* just so darned long.

Not for radio—or at least those corners of radio that felt they could get away with playing fifteen-, twenty-minute album tracks without interruption. FM stations in the States that habitually played lengthy LP cuts, and the late-night broadcasters in Europe that were cut from a similar cloth were destined to lap both performances up.

For kids, though, it posed a considerable dilemma.

Obviously, they needed to own the records; Kraftwerk because the excerpt made it sound so cool; Summer because anything that got the daytime broadcasters that riled up had to be worth hearing. All the more so as time went by, and rumor, reality, and apocrypha continued to mount up around her record.

True, there was never anything so dramatic as the ex-communication of a Catholic A&R man, as allegedly happened when "Je t'aime . . . moi non plus" was fresh. But, according to *Oui* magazine, "In London, Ladies Groups are picketing the BBC . . . and they haven't even played the song yet. In California some 'really heavy' people are claiming 'Love to Love You' has saved their marriages and changed their lives."

There was even a radio station in Wisconsin that didn't play the record, and was rewarded with "all the spot schedules from several of the largest radio advertisers in the town because its competitors did [play it]."

How could any rebellious teen resist buying such a record? Mom and pop would go *nuts*!

But how could they afford it? Singles at that time generally cost what one would call "pocket money prices": seventy-five cents or so in the USA, forty-five to fifty pence in the United Kingdom. LPs, correspondingly, were several weeks' worth of pocket money, and that was fine when you were getting ten, twelve, songs for your money, the latest hit single among them.

Love to Love You Baby, on the other hand, featured just five tracks, with the single spread across side one . . . all the way across . . . and then its B-side, plus three further tracks on side two. Kraftwerk's *Autobahn* album was just as frugal. In terms of actual playing time, you still got your money's worth. But the inescapable logic remained. You were putting out five bucks for a longer version of a regular hit single.

Jeffrey Morgan's review of *Love to Love You Baby* in *Creem* hit the nail on the head. "This album *is* to the disco scene what [Iron Butterfly's] *In-A-Gadda-Da-Vida* is to rock 'n' roll and what 'Autobahn' is to electronic drone . . . Just what you always wanted: music to read *Penthouse* by. You can forget about Side Two automatically."

Or what did *Black Music* say, again about Summer's offering? "Forget side two." This was "an album for people who can afford almost three quid for a single tune, and who like company when they get it on."

There really ought to be something in between.

On these occasions, there weren't. Either the more impecunious purchaser went with the short version and imagined the rest, or they went without everything else and finally sprang for the album. Both ways, sales were lost, and minds began to whirr.

Although they were scarcely a common occurrence, LP side-long singles were not exactly a rarity at that time. British prog bands, such as Yes, Genesis, and Jethro Tull, had all excerpted similarly expansive album tracks for 45s, although more for the benefit of radio disc jockeys than with any hope of scoring a hit.

But Motown rockers Rare Earth broke into the *Billboard* Top 5 when four minutes of "Get Ready" were cut from their latest album's behemothic title track in 1971. And then there was the aforementioned "In-a Gadda-Da-Vida," which was *probably* the first side-long album track to first, be trimmed of as much fat as possible, and then sent soaring chartward.

They were rock records, though, targeted at an audience whose main interest was LPs. Even Kraftwerk were covered by that clause.

"Love to Love You Baby," on the other hand, was a dance song, a pop song, a hear-it-at-the-youth-club song, which you wanted to take home with you. True, your parents would likely throw a fit somewhere around the eighth or ninth orgasm, but what do they know? Well, they knew what an orgasm was, which something that a good proportion of the song's youngest admirers had probably yet to fully determine, but that's beside the point. "Love to Love You Baby" sounded naughty and fun and all-tingly-inside spread over four minutes. Just *imagine* what it would be like at close to seventeen.

Except imagine was all you could do because it might take weeks to save up for the LP, and there'd be a whole lot more you'd want to buy in the meantime. Sometimes, life is *so* unfair.

Or is it? Because it wasn't just the kids who were feeling the pinch.

The preceding couple of years had seen the music industry laboring beneath first, the unprecedented strictures of a worldwide oil shortage, and then, once that was over, its aftereffects. An all-encompassing vinyl shortage.

Ignited when the oil-producing OPEC nations declared an embargo against those Western countries that supported Israel during the Yom Kippur War of October 1973, the six-month oil crisis saw the price of oil all but triple. Gas stations ran dry; lines that formed at those stations that did have the precious substance could stretch for miles. At the government's suggestion, many stations (anywhere up to 90 percent of them) did not even open on Sundays, which made the Saturday waiting lines even longer.

But it was not only motorists that were slammed by the crisis. Any industry that relied on oil, or its by-products, was also hit, and the music industry was one of the first in the firing line. Vinyl is petroleum based.

Retail prices did not, in general, increase. There were other ways of handling the crunch. Records became thinner. Those chunky discs of the sixties and early seventies were suddenly a thing of the past, as labels sought to cut corners in every direction they could, beginning at the manufacturing stage.

New releases were postponed unless there was a sure-fire guarantee that they would be a hit. New bands found themselves less likely to be signed, as labels concentrated on releases by the acts they already had (and many of those suddenly found themselves being dropped), rather than risking precious vinyl on unknowns. Where once a new release might be guaranteed a lavish gatefold sleeve, now it was more likely to be sleeved in a single cardboard cover.

It could even be surmised that that was another reason why dance music became so preeminent during those years; because it was a reliable seller. Unlike rock audiences, discotheque-goers would not get on or off the floor depending upon the artist that was being played at any given moment; their likes and dislikes were not predicated on being a fan of this or that act. Either a record was worth dancing to or it wasn't. It didn't matter who was singing on it, or playing the lead guitar.

So, with more dance records (or, perhaps, fewer rock records) being released, more dance records had a chance of being heard. First they'd get picked up by the discos, then local radio would hear the buzz. Word would spread, the record would get bigger. Leafing through back issues of *Record World*, studying the regional Top 10s that Vince Aletti published therein, you can follow the rise in dance music's popularity week by week. What was hot in the clubs one week would be nudging the charts the next.

Slowly, however, things began to return to normal; gradually, labels became willing to start taking chances again. And one of the first issues that needed to be addressed was the one that was raised by "Love to Love You Baby."

For Donna Summer was not the only artist whose masterpiece was sliced and diced for single success that year, only to find disc jockeys happy to play the full-length version instead.

Back in January, side one of Gloria Gaynor's upcoming new album, *Never Can Say Goodbye*, was handed to disc jockey Tom Moulton, an A&R man at Scepter Records, with instructions to make it sparkle on the dance floors.

Moulton was already a legend in discotheque circles, a DJ who specialized in creating his evening's repertoire on reel-to-reel tape *before* the show, and then let that play through the night. Most DJs at the time mixed their sets live.

It was a painstaking process, but Moulton had an impressive setup at his disposal; he could do things to records that his counterparts could only imagine, and as his reputation grew, labels began to pay attention. In 1973, Moulton created what is often described as the first dedicated extended dance mix ever to be released, across B.T. Express's "Do It ('Til You're Satisfied)"; now he was at work building the first-ever vinyl dance *show*, three separate Gaynor tracks, including the title song, mixed into an uninterrupted sixteen-minute dance set, a mini discotheque in its own frenzied right.

You still had to buy the album to hear it, though. What if there was a happy medium between the two?

The twelve-inch single would become the first significant new vinyl format to be introduced since the birth of both the single and album at the end of the 1940s. It was, as its name suggested, the size of an LP. But it would feature only the single (and its attendant B-side, of course), pegged at a price that certainly leaned closer to a regular 45 than an album, but extended way beyond both the time constraints and the sonic confines of the seven-inch.

It is, in hindsight, astonishing that nobody had thought of doing this before. Up to this point, it had been albums, not singles, which fueled the discotheque market. Some disc jockeys prided themselves on eschewing 45s altogether, and playing only album cuts. Any week in *Record World*, you would read Vince Aletti commenting upon the *albums* of the moment, and rarely even mentioning singles . . . which, in any case, were rarely the tracks that the DJs preferred and, even if they were, were often edited down from a longer album version. The best that one could hope was that a long song might be split, parts one and two, across both sides of the single.

The twelve-inch single could—and would—solve all of these issues; and it is for this reason that many American twelve-inch singles would revolve at 33 rpm (elsewhere around the world, 45 was the preferred option). It meant that disc jockeys, accustomed as they were to playing albums, would not have to keep changing the speed when they wanted to spin a twelve-inch.

From an artistic point of view, too, there were advantages to be found. For too long, hit records had largely been constrained by the amount of music that could be squeezed onto a seven-inch slab of wax. Now, if an artist wanted to stretch out across a few minutes more, the twelve-inch offered the perfect palette. Likewise, if a dance track was only just getting started after the first seven inches, those additional five would certainly take it as far as it needed to go.

As always, the hottest new ideas were not necessarily very new. Back in 1973, soul man Little Jerry Williams, recording now beneath the alias of Swamp Dogg, self-released advance copies of his latest single, "Straight from My Heart," as a twelve-inch platter. It was a great gimmick, but that's all it was.

The following year, Tom Moulton took the next step in the process, although he was quick to admit that it was not intentional. Rather, he was preparing an acetate of a new dance track, Al Downing's "I'll Be Holding On," when his assistant, José Rodriguez, informed him that they'd run out of seven-inch blanks.

Moulton wanted to get the job finished, so he asked for a twelve-inch blank. It was only when they played the pressing back, a six-minute song spread across twelve inches of plastic, that they realized just what they had stumbled upon. The music was louder, the bass was heavier, the entire performance had been aerated. No more squishy mumbles fighting to escape the tyranny of tightly packed grooves. And if it sounded this good on a regular stereo, imagine what would happen on the dance floor!

The twelve-inch did not take off there and then. It would take the success of "Love to Love You Baby" and "Autobahn" to really force the industry to pay attention. But slowly over the next year or so, the first twelve-inchers began to appear.

Initially they were promotional only, mailed out to disc jockeys who might have a use for the likes of Banzai's deeply dippy "Chinese Kung Fu," Gerri Granger's cover of the Four Seasons' "Can't Take My Eyes Off You," the Trammps' "That's Where the Happy People Go," and Tom Moulton's liquefying revision of Jesse Green's "Nice and Slow."

The format itself took a while to bed down, too. Calhoon's "Dance Dance Dance" was originally scheduled for release in June 1975 as a *ten*-inch disc (Warner Brothers), while Atlantic's newly launched Disco Disc series of promos appeared as 33 rpm seven-inchers.

These were little more than experiments, however. In May 1976, Double Exposure's "Ten Percent" became America's first commercially released twelve-inch (or "Giant 45," as they preferred to call it), a three-minute LP track that was suddenly transformed across nine glorious minutes by remixer Walter Gibbons.

The first commercially available 12-inch by Double Exposure. (Author Collection)

Almost simultaneously, Tavares's celestial "Heaven Must Be Missing an Angel" became the first release to confirm the commercial value of the twelve-inch, as it blasted into the chart.

It was a similar story across the Atlantic, where a reissue of the Who's eleven-year-old "Substitute" may not have been the United Kingdom's very first twelve-inch, but the format was certainly novel enough to make it a hit. German band Boney M's "Daddy Cool" quickly followed, the first in a succession of hits for producer Frank Farian's dream team. (If the name's familiar, Farian later put together Milli Vanilli.) By early 1977, anyone who set out to be a "twelve-inch collector" was already feeling the strain, both financially and musically.

Here a slab of soft rock Australiana from the Little River Band; there a "greatest hits" EP by Joe Walsh. Here, a cut from the new Steve Winwood album; there, the latest Ramones single, barely two and a half minutes of high-octane punk sprawled across so much vinyl that one joker joked, "It's like every note in the song has its own groove."

It was still a slow process. Jim Kerr of Simple Minds recalls the first time someone mentioned a twelve-inch single to him, that summer of 1977. "What the fuck's a twelve-inch single?" he demanded. "A single that's an album? What are you talking about?'"

Not every label jumped aboard the burgeoning bandwagon, at least for public consumption (disc jockey-only releases continued appearing with even greater alacrity). Motown certainly missed the boat when the full-length version of Thelma Houston's magnificent cover of the old Harold Melvin hit "Don't Leave Me This Way" remained confined to its parent LP alone.

Likewise Diana Ross's "Love Hangover," the 1976 hit that was a direct follow-up to "Love to Love You Baby" in everything but artist's name alone. Eight minutes long in its unabridged form; less than half that on the single, "Love Hangover" pulsated, pounded, and purred in a manner so far removed from the remainder of Ross's repertoire that it was hard to believe it really was her. "Baby Love" seemed far, far away, and yet it could have been even further.

Written by Pamela Sawyer and Marilyn McLeod, there was some uncertainty at the time whether Ross or Marvin Gaye should voice the instrumental track of "Love Hangover" that producer Hal David laid down.

He eventually went with Ross, reasoning that she would probably sound a lot sexier, and he was doubtless correct. One departure from "Love to Love You Baby" should be noted, however. When Summer went into the vocal booth, her producers turned down the lights and had her lie on her back on the floor, to put her in a more "sensuous" mood. When Ross recorded "Love Hangover," Davis installed a strobe light, to give her the discotheque vibe.

In marketing terms, neither "Don't Leave Me This Way" nor "Love Hangover" can be said to have suffered from the lack of a commercial twelve-inch—promotional copies were pressed for the clubs, and both records became effortless hits at home and abroad. But still there was a lingering sense of discontent among those fans who did buy the cruelly cut seven-inchers, having experienced the album versions on the dance floor first. Lessons were being learned.

Donna Summer, meanwhile, was having a dreadful time trying to follow up "Love to Love You Baby."

Further dance hits were certainly escaping Germany as the seventies flashed their cleavage. In early 1975, producers and songwriters Sylvester Levay and Michael Kunze saw Silverbird's "Save Me" become a club hit even before they were forced to change the band's name to Silver Convention, to avoid confusion with an already existing American Silverbird.

In April, readers of Vince Aletti's *Record World* column were being tipped off to Amon Düül II's "long, strange" "Da Guadeloop"; by the end of the year, Silver Convention's "Fly Robin Fly," was topping the *Billboard* chart for three weeks; the following summer, the reissued "Save Me" spent just as long at number 2.

Boney M launched their own half-decade long British chart domination later in 1976; even Can, hitherto regarded among the most impenetrable of all the Krautrock bands, scored a Christmas 1976 hit in the United Kingdom with the hypnotically sibilant "I Want More," a record that Holger Czukay subsequently mused was "the middle ground between 'Autobahn' and 'I Feel Love.'" "Although, of course, we did not know that at the time."

Claudja Barry's "Sweet Dynamite" lived up to its title in 1977, while German studio combo Lipstique's side-long disco medley "At the Discotheque" was getting feet on the floor even before DJs flipped it over and discovered a string-fried cover of Piero Umiliani's novelty nonsense chant "Mah Nà Mah Nà."

The original had been a British hit earlier in the year, although the Muppets produced the definitive, and very hairy, reading. Neither, however, was a patch on Lipstique's version, which imbibed the simple phrase "mah-na mah-na" with as much sweaty sexuality as Donna Summer unleashed on "Love to Love You Baby."

Summer, however, was foundering. No matter that the media was already referring to her as "the Queen of Disco" (that is, when they weren't describing her as "the Queen of the G Spot" or, excruciatingly, "the Black Panter"). In commercial terms, her crown was looking increasingly precarious.

A cover of Barry Manilow's "Could It Be Magic" proved not to be that magical at all. "Try Me, I Know We Can Make It," another ruthless edit of a side-long album track (from her 1976 *A Love Trilogy* album); "Spring Affair" and "Winter Melody," they all did reasonably well on the *Billboard* dance charts, but they failed to make a mark beyond that.

Donna Summer, 1970s. (Photofest)

Summer put a brave face on the situation. "'Love to Love You' was a jumping board into what we want to do," she told Britain's *National Rock Star* newspaper. "But first of all you have to get someone's attention before you can make them listen. I'm not going to let 'Love to Love You Baby' confine me, except that I have to take things slower. Mind you if I hadn't had a hit I would have had to take things even slower. I can't complain."

As a genuine commercial proposition, in the countries where success was measured strictly in terms of Top 40 impact . . . the United States, Britain, Germany . . . and even in Holland, where she was a chart regular before "Love to Love You Baby," Summer was fading.

Thankfully, Moroder and Bellotte had an idea that might arrest the decline.

8

AND ENO SAID TO BOWIE . . .

Listening to Moroder's *Einzelgänger* today, in the light of the next three Kraftwerk LPs (1976's *Radio-Activity*, 1977's *Trans-Europe Express*, and 1978's *Man Machine*), is an instructive experience.

Personal taste, critical insistence, and history itself have conditioned us to regard that trilogy as a universe unto itself, a seamless sequence of unparalleled innovation in the world of electronic music.

Yet, in terms of the actual materials that Kraftwerk had at hand—not just the machines that they were utilizing, but also the capabilities of those machines—they were playing with much the same deck as any other musician of the time, Moroder included.

Relenting on his post–"Son of My Father" disdain for the synthesizer as simply something that made weird noises, Moroder now chose to make a record that was almost exclusively weird noises, and the fascinating aspect of that is, how much of Kraftwerk's future he predicted.

The robotic burble over the intro and outro of *Einzelgänger*'s opening title track. The insistent synth rhythms that underpin the nine tracks. The metronomic electronic heartbeat of "Aus (The End)." The metal-on-metal clatter of "Percussiv." There are tones and frequencies cut so obviously from the Kraftwerk playbook that you could almost believe that you're listening to their outtakes. As opposed to an album that both predates the trilogy, and was recorded contemporaneously with the album that preceded it, *Autobahn*.

Which is not to say there was any element of mimicry at work, any more than two separate rock albums, based around guitar, drums, and bass, can be said to have copied each other. Every musical form has its limitations, technical if not creative, and if two people happen to be working within the same extreme, then they are going to butt musical heads at some point. Particularly in the realm of mid-'70s electronics,

The Dutch 7-inch edit of "Try Me, I Know We Can Make It." (Author Collection)

where every synth on the market had effectively the same preset sounds and rhythms, and most synth players of the time knew exactly where and what they were.

The tricky part lay in learning how to utilize them to the music's greatest advantage, and adding personal (usually homemade) touches. Which is why there were many more ambient-sounding whooshes and impressionistic swoops being spilled onto the market than there were propulsive beats. Why there was a lot more synthesized space rock floating around than electronic dance music.

Kraftwerk's studio, now named Kling Klang, was almost wholly electronic. The group purchased their first commercial synthesizers, a Mini Moog and an EMS Synthi AKS, in 1973, and by 1976 they had added the Synthonorma, two sixteen-step sequencers custom-built by the Bonn-based Synthesizerstudio. Other equipment was designed and built by the band itself, according to the demands (or possibilities) of the music they were working on at the time.

Kling Klang was a purely private concern, utilized by Kraftwerk alone. Musicland, on the other hand, was thriving. Widely regarded as the only mainstream recording studio between Paris and Tokyo, the studio was now host to a dazzling array of visitors. In 1975, the Rolling Stones recorded the bulk of their *Black and Blue* album in that Munich basement. The Sweet, T. Rex, and Led Zeppelin all passed through, too.

Moroder remained the studio's most frequent user, though, his engineer Reinhold Mack and the ever-faithful Pete Bellotte completing a formidable, and increasingly ambitious team. Yet *Einzelgänger* remained a largely untapped opportunity, an experiment whose outcome they had yet to fully appreciate.

Indeed, Giorgio's next album, 1976's LP *Knights in White Satin*, was an almost regressive step. Still reliant on the strings-and-things tropes that were familiar from so many other dance records of the time, the album revolved around a painfully extended revision of the Moody Blues' (misspelled) title track that did little more than plod behind Moroder's best come-to-bed vocal for fourteen minutes—and that despite the insertion of a completely different song, "In the Middle of the Night," halfway through. There were some nice synthesizer flourishes, but "Love to Love You Baby" it most certainly was not.

It did, however, inspire Casablanca toward a move that Moroder seems still to regard with a certain bemused munificence.

Donna Summer had unquestionably been taken to the heart of the gay community, whose own most public outlet were the discotheques. Now, Casablanca was marketing *Knights in White Satin* toward the same audience, beginning with a front cover that is startlingly homoerotic, the magnificently mustached Moroder poised within what certainly looks like a steamy bathhouse, while five open-shirted males kneel before him, gazing up in adoration.

He told *Out* magazine's Jason Lamphier, "[Neil Bogart] was pushing me to be 'gay,' I think he recognized quite fast that disco could appeal to gays."

Could? At least on the East and West Coasts, most observers agree that the gay community had been the discos' most voracious consumers for five years by that time. If anything, their stranglehold on the culture was loosening by 1976, not strengthening, as "disco music" increased in mainstream popularity.

Bogart was correct, regardless. In strict marketing terms, if you could "crack the gay market," as a bland, clueless salesman might have put it, you were on to a winner.

At the same time, however, Moroder's output was not going to make it easy for them. Still loyal to the string-driven flourishes that characterized "Love to Love You Baby," *Knights in White Satin* was a major step backward in every respect, and his next release, the single "I Want to Funk with You" was little better.

This time, Moroder was accompanied by a breathy female vocal that seemed delighted by the titular double entendre. Unfortunately, the song itself was little more than standard dance floor fare . . . nothing at all to get excited by.

More interesting was his production of Dino Solera and the Munich Machine's storming take on Beethoven's "Für Elise," retitled "Classically Elise." Of course, it was Moroder's second attempt at the piece, but now it was the latest and greatest in what was becoming a stream of reworked classics from various dance producers. (Coincidentally, the British-based Philharmonics' latest single was their own disco-fied version of the same melody.)

A familiar piece of music taken to unfamiliar lengths had both novelty value and ear appeal, and "Classically Elise" was at least as inventive as Walter Murphy's similarly danceable take on Beethoven's Fifth Symphony—the famous bit, of course. (Hence the title "A Fifth of Beethoven.") Maybe even more so.

If any lesson whatsoever had been learned from the success of "Love to Love You Baby," however, it was one that contemporary critics believed Moroder had no intention of heeding. Dance music was great if you actually knew what you wanted to do with it, and too little of Moroder's output seemed to care.

Roberta Kelly's *Troublemaker* was a terrific album, it is true, and it spun off three solid floor-fillers (the title track, "The Family," and "Love Power"). But still there was something generic about it, nothing to distinguish Moroder from any of the host of rival European disco producers emerging around the mid-1970s. And now, fresh competition was emerging from some most unlikely directions.

When Kraftwerk's follow-up to "Autobahn," "Radio-Activity," first materialized on dance floors, a lot of people didn't know what to do with it. Slow, metronomic, monotonous, it took a skilled DJ to successfully work it into his set, and skilled dancers to figure out how to take advantage of it. Particularly when its competition on the floor included the likes of "Love Hangover," Vickie Sue Robinson's "Turn That Beat Around," Andrea True Connection's "More More More" and, astonishingly, a disco-fied translation of one of the melodies from Mike Oldfield's "Tubular Bells," by the French combine Champ's Boys Orchestra. Imagine the main theme from *The Exorcist* meeting the bass line from "Love to Love You Baby" and you'll be close.

But "Radio-Activity" *did* work, and electronics were fizzing elsewhere, too, until a good portion of an evening's dance card could be made up from nothing else—Passport's "Ju Ju Man," the title track from Mort Garson and Ataraxia's sci-fi sound effects–infused *The Unexplained* album, . . . and hitting the floors out of nowhere, Frenchman Jean-Michel Jarre, enjoying a surprise club hit with the synth instrumental "Oxygène Part Four"—a surprise because sporadic releases over the past seven years, and only a modicum of success and recognition, had never afforded Jarre the extravagance of a fully equipped professional studio.

Rather, like Joe Meek before him, he built his own at home, a Scully eight-track recorder, a Korgs Minipops drum machine, a VCS3 synthesizer, an ARP 2600, an Eminent 310 Unique electric organ; and there he recorded *Oxygène*, the breathlessly beautiful electronic symphony that established him as an international star, beginning in the most unexpected arena of them all.

The *Oxygène* suite is so much a part of the symphonic electronic furniture today that it's hard to believe that the first time many people heard it, it was beneath the mirror balls of myriad discotheques.

Such pieces, such adventure, seemed a world away from the cookie-cutter dance records that Musicland was pumping out. But Moroder and company were paying attention. Because they possessed the answer to both their critics' complaints and their own ambitions, a synthesis that was quite unlike anything anyone had heard, or even dreamed of, before.

Donna Summer had returned to the United States to live, on a five acre estate in Benedict Canyon in Hollywood. She was still selling records; her last two albums, *A Love Trilogy* and *Four Seasons of Love*, had both gone gold, despite neither coming close to recapturing the impact of "Love to Love You Baby."

Certainly Casablanca behaved as though nothing was amiss. Released in October 1976, *Four Seasons of Love* was feted with a Hollywood-style launch party, the album serenading the industry guests first as they ate a vast Chinese meal, and again at an after-dinner discotheque.

Not only that, but a single precious acetate of the set was then taken around Los Angeles by Casablanca promo man Marc Paul Simon, who then waited as it was played in its entirety at four different discotheques across town. By comparison, Stevie Wonder's latest offering, the four-sided *Songs in the Key of Life* was launched that same week with a low-key afternoon spent at a studio outside Worcester, Massachusetts.

On the road, too, Summer was now beginning to take on the mantle of a headliner.

Early US tours (during which, much to her surprise, the more excitable elements in the audience took to throwing their underwear at her) saw Summer opening for the likes of the Spinners and the Temptations. Now, however, she was topping the bill at venues on the level of New York's Roseland ballroom, and was both adjusting to her fame and hoping, by avoiding any return to "Love to Love You Baby" territory, to fashion it more to her own liking.

Still discomforted by the sexual nature of her biggest hit, and by people's reaction to it, she was talking with Moroder about a new album, a conceptual piece that would embrace the history of late-twentieth-century music so far. It was an ambitious project, especially with Casablanca already asking when the pair would have new music ready for launch.

Label head Neil Bogart firmly believed that a major artist should never be allowed to slip from the public eye; that there should always be fresh music for people to buy. At other companies, many artists were permitted a year or so between new LPs. Bogart had no time for such pampering. He considered himself lenient if he gave them six months.

I Remember Yesterday, as it was pieced together in Musicland, would feature just seven songs, each one referring back to a specific era. Across side one, the 1940s (the title track), the 1950s ("Love's Unkind") and the 1960s ("Back in Love Again"); across side two, the dance-pop sound of the present day would account for "Black Lady" and "Take Me." English songwriter Tony McCauley's "Can't We Just Sit Down (And Talk It Over)," the only nonoriginal on the album, would offer up a timeless ballad. Finally the closing number, "I Feel Love," would take a look into the future. For added authenticity, every song on the album would feature Summer singing through a suitable period microphone.

It was an ambitious project, conceptually beholden, perhaps, to the Carpenters' 1973 *Now and Then* LP, but far removed from that too, as Summer drew upon every aspect of her theatrical background to take on the roles of a big band showgirl, a Brill Building songstress; a Motown-esque pop idol and so on.

Indeed, so bound up in the overall concept were the team—Summer and Moroder, Mack and Bellotte—that the concluding number really didn't feel especially dramatic to any of them. Just a quick slice of electronic pop that predicted people might be using more synthesizers in the future.

Even Neil Bogart, when he heard it for the first time, did little more than listen, nod, and suggest Moroder remix the track.

So far as Moroder was concerned, "I Feel Love" was just the last brick in the conceptual wall, and nobody at the record label was disposed to disagree. When it came time to pick a single from the finished album, "Can't We Just Sit Down (And Talk It Over)" appeared to be everybody's tip for the top. "I Feel Love," on the other hand, was chosen as the B-side. Nothing to see here, folks, move along please.

The record company's lack of what we would now call foresight, vision, *common sense* even, should not be condemned. In the context of the times, and the audience toward which Casablanca Records and Summer alike were aiming, "I Feel Love" was a long shot by any standards.

It worked in the context of the album's overall concept, of course, but few people imagined that Moroder and his machines genuinely represented the "future" of music. *A* future, perhaps, but not *the*.

Neither was it an especially impressive technological achievement. Looking back from 2019, Todd Rundgren recalled his initial impressions of "I Feel Love":

"[It] struck me as lazy, uncreative. You take the first sound you get out of [the synthesizer], and that's it. I don't remember the first time I heard it, where I was, but I do remember that my reaction to it was—'you know, I do this stuff in my living room with my little Putney synth, and now people are making records out of it?'

"I was mystified that something so dumb would be such a big hit! There's no words to it, just some mumbling, and it's just 'I Feel Love' over and over again."

He is, perhaps, a little harsh, but he's not wrong, either. "I Feel Love" was recorded using a Moog Modular 3P synthesizer that Moroder had recently borrowed from Eberhard Schoener—the same person who loaned him the Moog for "Son of My Father" five years earlier.

Indeed, to illustrate just how new this latest instrument was to Moroder, he also borrowed Schoener's assistant Robby Wedel, to show him how to synchronize the various elements into the song by the use of an internal click track. "I needed him because, even if I'd owned one, I wouldn't have been able to get any sound out of it," Moroder later admitted to *Mix Mag*.

Pete Bellotte continued, "We got the first line down. So then Robby says, 'OK, do you want to synch the next track?' We didn't even know what that meant. So he says, 'I've laid down a synch tone from this Moog so that anything we record on the next track is going to lock it into that.' When we put in the next track, it was absolutely spot-on. It was a revelation for us."

Dutch picture sleeve for the ill-fated "Can't We Just Sit Down" single. The B-side would do far better. (Author Collection)

Bellotte later described Wedel as "the unsung hero of all of this," not only for what he did for the recording, but because Robert Moog himself wasn't aware that "synching was even possible."

Composer Mel Wesson—an ambient music designer known today for his collaborations with Hollywood composer Hans Zimmer, and the synth group Node, but just a teen at the time—elaborates on the actual machine that was used.

"I still use an old Moog modular, pretty much identical to the one used on 'I Feel Love.' These were monster musical telephone exchanges, the stuff of sci-fi movies. These days, that sort of musical power comes with an app on your phone but. . . . those old machines were far more than a box of noises. It's all about the way those machines make you to think, especially when you're talking about sequencers, the part of the system that allows you to loop simple patterns of notes.

"Forget today's computers with endless tracks at your disposal. The heart of 'I Feel Love' was the Moog sequencer, a very simplistic device by today's standards, allowing the user to loop three rows of eight notes . . . the root of 'I Feel Love' is one of those rows of knobs and just couldn't have been created without that machine."

The process was slow. Moroder usually composed at the piano, but not this time. He had to start with the tracks, not the melody, so his first layer was the bass line.

He detailed that element for *Time Out* in 2013. "It was a big, big job. . . . I recorded a click, the tempo, about four notes in [and] looped them. I got the sound I wanted by holding one note—let's say C—and holding it, then moving it to F and G. . . ."

The Moog sequencer had a nasty habit of going out of tune very quickly; Edgar Froese of Tangerine Dream once complained of spending eleven days in the studio, and emerging with just six minutes of usable material. Now it was Moroder's turn to discover that the elements sought could be recorded in no more than thirty second bursts, and sometimes even fewer. Talking to the Library of Congress almost forty years later, Moroder remembered having to take breaks every seven or eight seconds!

Gradually, however, the piece took shape, not only the sequencer parts, but other elements, too—the bursts of white noise that the Moog generated, and which Moroder processed to replicate the sound of the hi-hat; and the one organic instrument on the entire backing track, the kick drum that was supplied by session drummer (and future producer in his own right) Keith Forsey.

Summer, for her part, recorded her vocals in a single take, instinctively aligning her voice with whatever the backing tape required. "Sometimes Donna would do crazy things just for the fun of it," Moroder recalled. "Most of the time we would take no notice, but the way she sang 'I Feel Love' was kind of okay."

Moroder knew from the outset what he wanted from the song, "a sound that was of the future," and he used synthesizers "because I thought it was the instrument that would be used in the future—be the instrument of the future. We used it, and only it, to create all the sounds. I wanted to try to imitate what people would do in twenty or thirty years."

He knew, too, that he had succeeded. In a 2015 interview with the DJ Moby in *Interview* magazine, Moroder said, "I thought I had something special, the concept of having just a machine or a computer to do all the tracks, like hi-hat and all that stuff."

Mel Wesson, onstage with TV *Smith's Explorers* in 1980. (Photo by Dave Thompson)

What he did not foresee, as he told the talks.com in 2014, was just how special it would prove to be.

"I only realized that a few months later, when Brian Eno told David Bowie that he heard the sound of the future in 'I Feel Love.' I would have never thought that something like that would come out of Brian Eno."

There was just one element that even Moroder's customary perfectionism could not remedy. The team decided to add some delay to the bass line, knowing that that would truly "change . . . the whole feel of the song."

Unfortunately, "at that time, it was really difficult to get the exact tempo so that the bass line would double like that; nowadays, you [can]. [But] then, you really had to guess. It took several hours to get it right."

In fact, they didn't get it right. Not quite. If you want to be technical about it, the process split the downbeat between the two speakers, the beat on the left, the delay on the right with the result, as Moroder explained, that "if you were dancing . . . next to the left speaker, then it was alright. But if you were next to the right . . . you only heard the delay."

Midge Ure, future front man of Ultravox, immediately noticed that split-second dislocation.

"If you listen to 'I Feel Love,' you'll hear that the sequence and the bass drum constantly slip. They're not tied in, because there was no way of doing it. So the bass drum keeps slipping around, it's not locked in because everything had to be done manually and played manually because of that sequence."

Even Summer, after hearing her record played at a club one night, returned to the studio to tell Moroder, "You know, something is wrong with this recording."

But it was so wrong, that it was perfect, a genius finishing touch. Or, as Ure concluded, "a real breakthrough!"

So there it was, the final track on the album, the B-side to Summer's new single and, for a short while, it looked as if that was all "I Feel Love" would ever accomplish.

Released in the United States on May 1, 1977, "Can't We Just Sit Down (And Talk It Over)" was sent out to the radio stations and began to pick up airplay. It entered *Billboard*'s R&B chart at the beginning of June, and for a moment there was hope that it might inch higher.

Casablanca was certainly banking on it. As Larry Harris wrote in his memoir of the label's golden years, *And Party Every Day*, Casablanca was seriously hemorrhaging cash as costs and expenses soared, but only one band, KISS, offered a reliable return. Its *KISS—Alive!* concert spectacular had finally broken them big on the charts, and the upcoming *Destroyer* was expected to echo that.

"But with Donna, panic was beginning to set in. Since her debut, she had won a tremendous amount of peer acceptance, as well as industry awards too numerous to mention. But those accolades couldn't save her flatlining career."

There was a little dance floor action for her theme to the movie *The Deep*, "Down, Deep Inside (Theme from *The Deep*)," when the soundtrack was released in June, 1977; and a little for her collaboration with Paul Jabara, "Shut Out." But that was all. With the new single also set to sink, it was time for some serious talking.

Harris continued, "*I Remember Yesterday* was the final LP we would do with Donna under the terms of our original agreement, and we knew if we didn't hit it out of the park, then Donna would be shopping for a new record company."

That possibility was growing closer all the time. While Casablanca's latest signing, the French act Love & Kisses, was storming dance, pop, and R&B charts alike, "Can't We Just Sit Down (And Talk It Over)" was receiving less R&B station airplay every day, and pop radio simply wasn't responding.

Even more ironically, after two years of so many people trying, somebody had finally come up with a record to match "Love to Love You Baby" in terms of extended sex appeal. Summer's ballad could not escape its slipstream.

Saint Tropez were a French act (*another* French act!) whose debut album, *Je t'aime*, was little short of sex nonstop, heavy breathing, and seductive whispers, and a version of the Jane Birkin/Serge Gainsbourg title track that made the original sound positively celibate.

Fronted by singers Ida Boros, Louis Aldebert, Monique D'Ozo, and Suzanne Mireille, and produced by Frenchman Laurin Rinder and American W. Michael Lewis, Saint Tropez weren't quite hard-core pornography.

But in musical terms, it would be difficult for it to have been more torrid. Or, as Vince Aletti put it that summer, "Sex always sounds more chic in a foreign language . . . and this is definitely high-fashion passion." Had Saint Tropez only expanded their American appeal beyond the discotheques, Donna Summer might have seen her ongoing status as disco's number 1 sex goddess dissipate as unexpectedly as her commercial crown had apparently slipped.

Might have. Yes, first impressions were adamant that the clubs were as unimpressed by Summer's latest single as everybody else was. In fact, it simply took a while before somebody noticed that they were paying attention after all. Just not in the way that anybody expected.

They'd flipped the record over.

Déjà vu? Back in 1969, when Dick Hyman scored that first ever Moog hit with "The Minotaur," that song too had initially been released as a B-side, to the alluringly titled "Topless Dancers of Corfu." On that occasion, however, the A-side, too, was Moog driven, so it was less a case of the label's not appreciating what it had, than it was simply the wrong decision.

"I Feel Love" was different. "I Feel Love" was the clubs throwing Casablanca's offering back in its face; ignoring the sales reps, the A&R men, the artist. This was mutiny. And how sweet it was, even if Moroder himself professed to be baffled by the entire phenomenon.

Donna Summer recording "Down, Deep Inside," 1977.
(Columbia Pictures/Photofest © Columbia Pictures)

A stubborn nondancer himself, as late as a *Guardian* interview in 2019, he was still insisting "You can't dance to 'I Feel Love'! It's not very good to dance to." He cited a couple of his other, subsequent productions, Blondie's "Call Me" and a later Summer single, "Hot Stuff," as infinitely more suited to the dance floor.

And perhaps they were. But context is everything, and in terms of what was happening on the chart, on the dance floor, on the overall record market that summer of 1977, "I Feel Love" wasn't simply revolutionary. It was utterly unique.

By the end of May, clubs as far afield as New York City, Philadelphia, and San Francisco were reporting overwhelming demand for "I Feel Love." By mid-June, there was scarcely a discotheque in the country where you could avoid hearing the song . . . and not just the edited 3.45-minute B-side version. They were spinning the full, almost six-minute album track, and Vince Aletti, in *Record World*, could barely contain his enthusiasm.

"A brilliant combination of whipped-up synthesizer and . . . dreamy, ecstatic vocals. The pace is fierce and utterly gripping with the synthesizer effects particularly aggressive and emotionally charged."

Faced with a record that even the influential Aletti confirmed was "unlike anything" that the Summer-Moroder-Bellotte team had ever produced in the past . . . something that was "nearly as innovative as 'Love to Love You Baby,'" Casablanca had no choice but to elevate "I Feel Love" to the A-side of the single.

Aletti, meanwhile, had just one point of reference to offer to his weekly readers. Compare it, he suggested, to "Kraftwerk's 'Metal on Metal,'" a cut from their only recently released sixth album, *Trans-Europe Express.*

9

THE HALL OF MIRRORS

Kraftwerk had a difficult time adapting to the sudden spotlight that "Autobahn" and, to a lesser extent, "Radio-Activity," focused in their direction.

"They called us innovators and asked us what we were thinking of when we made our records," Wolfgang Flür lamented. "But we didn't know what we were doing. It was just fun for us. Others decided what it meant later, and told us. You are so involved in the work, in the happiness and the joy of that, the friendship and the traveling, you have no time to think about what it might mean to other people.

"If you are working, you cannot change your position into a listener who is far away from you, it is impossible. Of course an artist has his own ideas and his own special tracks, but when we recorded, I really cannot remember what we felt, it was just work, and every time, we tried to do our best."

Kraftwerk had completely refurbished Kling Klang by now, pouring the proceeds from "Autobahn" into outfitting it with the latest technology, and setting to work on their next LP.

By the end of April 1977, one track from these latest sessions, "Europe Endless," was already drawing them in for New York disc jockey Tom Savarese at Harrah (on Broadway and Sixty-Second, not to be confused with the ultimately better-known Hurrah) in New York City. A couple of weeks later, the new album's slow merge of its title track, "Trans-Europe Express," and the succeeding "Metal on Metal" was high up Sharon White's playlist at the same city's Sahara.

The world into which *Trans-Europe Express* and, a couple of months later, "I Feel Love," were released, however, was a very different one to that which had greeted "Autobahn" and "Love to Love You Baby" with such open, welcoming limbs.

Dance music was changing, and it is difficult to pinpoint exactly when that started. The why, on the other hand, is easy. It changed because, finally, America had shrugged off the successive hangovers and recriminations that scarred the first half of the decade. The recession was over, the economy was getting back on its feet. But the mood remained pessimistic. Things might get better, but they could also get worse.

So, why not have fun while you wait for the handcarts to take the whole world to hell?

More discos were opening in more towns; more whites and more straights were flooding in through the doors. More hit sounds from the current Top 40 were booming out of the speakers, and if the influx of new disco dancers seemed to subsume the so-called minority societies that had hitherto been the discotheque's most loyal customers, the man collecting money at the door wasn't complaining.

By early 1977, dance music had the nation in such a tight grip that "disco" was indeed accepted as the generic term for anything that made people want to get up and boogie . . . the movement even had its own brick-and-mortar superstar as Studio 54 opened for business in the old Gallo Opera House at 254 West Fifty-Fourth Street in Manhattan, on April 26, 1977.

But if somebody wanted even greater evidence of the inroads that disco-dancing was making into straight society, they needed look no further than President Jimmy Carter's inaugural ball on January 30, that same year.

All the way from Atlanta, Georgia, Scott Woodside and Barry Chase's Portable Peach mobile disco came to town, to intrigue revelers with what journalist Andrew Kopkind described, somewhat disbelievingly, as "disco dancers in peanut costumes dancing to the music of [Harry T Booker's] 'Bicentennial Disco Mix.'" Almost forty-five years later, historian Dominic Sandbrook still found that a "terrifying spectacle."

Things were a little different in the United Kingdom.

If the tabloid press and music media was any kind of reliable barometer, it was punk rock that held sway in that country, the disaffected roar of myriad bored teenagers snatching up instruments they (in some cases, anyway) could barely play, and making as much noise as they could.

It was a two pronged assault. Politically, punk lashed out at a system that had abjectly failed them. Youth unemployment was high; homelessness and hopelessness were the decade's sole gift to kids growing up in the seventies, while a toothless government flailed futilely against militant unions and mounting national debt.

In the United States, people were outraged when New York City declared bankruptcy. In Britain, were it not for the largesse of the International Monetary Fund, the entire country might well have gone down that same pan.

Musically, punk's targets were equally well chosen—all that was old and tired in pop's past. When the Clash insisted there would be "no Elvis [Presley], Beatles, or the

Rolling Stones in 1977," it was not intended as a statement of fact. It was a rallying cry.

They could have easily have added Pink Floyd, Barclay James Harvest, and Gentle Giant, although as the year unfolded, it transpired that the Clash had been (almost) right in the first place. It was the year in which Presley died; the Stones' Keith Richard only narrowly avoided serious jail time after a drugs bust in Canada; and Paul McCartney committed what many observers considered career suicide by releasing "Mull of Kintyre."

Overnight, it seemed, rock's obsession with moneyed superstars frittering away their royalties on extravagant stage presentations, obscenely expensive instruments, and lifestyles that made Bacchanalia look cheap. was held up as the profligate sham it was.

In 1975, Rick Wakeman's retelling of the legends of King Arthur album cost around £50,000 to take on the road. By comparison, the average annual wage in the United Kingdom that same year was £2,556.

Of course progressive rock would not go away; neither would any other genre. Punk did not *change* the music scene, it merely offered a more affordable alternative to what was already out there. Besides, punk itself was only one string on the new revolutionaries' guitar. The other was the fact that some of them weren't that crazy about guitars to begin with.

One album old before punk ever hit, John Foxx's Ultravox! were already postulating the kind of dystopias that could emerge from the ever-gloomier political climate. No scorched earth vocal nor coruscating guitars, Ultravox! schemed a landscape of twitching sinew and dangerous rhythm, encased within Foxx's epic sagas of alienation and darkness, mourning the ruins of western civilization even as the songs themselves swaggered triumphantly through its detritus.

"The Wild, the Beautiful and the Damned," and "Saturday Night in the City of the Dead" gripped the rudiments of that collapse years before *Blade Runner* saw the same message; "I Want to Be a Machine" both warned of and yearned for technology's triumph, while *The Terminator* was still in short trousers. And it was from those sessions, with Ultravox!'s youthful enthusiasm and angular electricity still ringing in his ears, that producer Brian Eno hot-footed it over to the French countryside to meet up with David Bowie.

There they schemed Bowie's latest album, *Low*—one side, the first, a series of synthesized vignettes that raced past, as the opening track might have put it, at the

Ultravox!'s 1977 live EP. (Author Collection)

"Speed of Life"; the other, the second, vast paintings in sound, instrumental notions, and passages that would now be expanded beyond the simple riff or chord sequence that Bowie originally envisioned, into a side-long symphony of wordless atmospherics, impressions of places he'd passed through in recent months.

"I had no statement to make," Bowie told *ZigZag* magazine at the time. "It was a very indulgent album for me to find out what I wanted to do musically.

"The strange thing that came out of *Low* is that in my meanderings in new processes and new methods of writing, when Eno and I listened back to it, we realized we had created new information without even realizing it, and that by not trying to write about anything, we had written more about something or other that one couldn't quite put one's finger on. It was quite remarkable."

It was also utterly dislocating.

Bowie's record label of the time hated the album, famously refusing even to release it unless Bowie extended his contract by one further LP, effectively giving the company *Low* for nothing.

He agreed, but admitted that even he was surprised when both the album and the single "Sound and Vision" became massive hits. And even more surprised when he learned that Britain's punk community had embraced it as readily as *whoever* it was that he'd targeted it at in the first place. Apparently, he wasn't sure who they were, either.

Although there were little direct correlations between the two, it was clear from listening to *Low* that Bowie was no stranger to electronic music—"Sound and Vision," in particular, rode a compulsively danceable rhythm and certainly took off in European discotheques. (It had less of an impact in America.)

He'd already told Brian Eno of his love for *(No Pussyfooting)*; his 1976 tour then saw him tell the world of his love for Kraftwerk, when he compiled a tape of favorite tracks from their albums so far, to be played before he took the stage. (Kraftwerk would return the favor by name-checking Bowie and his friend Iggy Pop in the title track of their new album; Bowie would then title a track from his next album, *"Heroes,"* after Florian Schneider.)

Neither was Bowie alone in his admiration. Among the so-called punk rockers, both the Buzzcocks' Pete Shelley (who had been recording electronic music in his bedroom as far back as 1974) and the Sex Pistols' Johnny Rotten cited Kraftwerk as an influence. And, as much as the savage yowling of the Sex Pistols, or the monolithic mood shifts of *Low*; no less than the deaths of Elvis Presley and Marc Bolan; and, of course, "I Feel Love," *Trans-Europe Express* remains locked forever within the curious musical melting pot that was 1977; is, in turn, symptomatic of all that was to be wrought during that tumultuous year.

Not since the peak of psychedelia, precisely ten years before, had musical tastes seemed so ripe for experimentation and, with serendipitous consequence, for change and transformation. *Low* unlocked the doors through which so many people would eventually pour. *Trans-Europe Express* cracked them open and looked outside. All in readiness for "I Feel Love" to blow them off their hinges.

Released in March, 1977, *Trans-Europe Express* was greeted, initially, with disbelief. To many people, Kraftwerk were still those same old Teutonic Beach Boys, and first impressions were of that earlier hit having simply been rerouted down a railroad track, with clattering metal replacing hissing rubber, and the travelogue dictated not by the freedom of the road, but by the iron discipline of the rails.

Paring rhythm and melody to their lowest common denominator, a frigid delivery against which the vocals sounded almost tuneful, *Trans-Europe Express* was bright, brutal, bitter, brittle, a robotic dismissal not only of humanity, but of humankind itself.

Neither was the title track alone in dictating the gulf that lay between rock'n'roll and Kraftwerk's *idea* of rock'n'roll; "Showroom Dummies," the tale of shop window mannequins who come to life and go dancing, spoke volumes for that same dislocation, even when translated into French for a major club hit on both sides of the English Channel.

"*Nous sommes les mannequins*" may not sound particularly threatening, but when the strobe hit you right, and the volume started to hurt, that's when the glass would shatter and *les mannequin* escaped their storefront window prison. (Coincidentally, to the delight of everyone who recalled "Autobahn" as "*Doctor Who* music," that same television show had predicted that precise scenario in the story *Spearhead from Space*, back in 1970. Only these mannequins didn't go clubbing.)

Yet *Trans-Europe Express* was not a cold record. Flür explained, "We loved the feel and the rhythm, and it became a very big part of ourselves. We knew we had transplanted European culture into our music. It is my greatest delight of the Kraftwerk time, because of its romanticism and its beautiful sounding melodies."

He is correct. Whereas other Kraftwerk albums have a futuristic sense to them, *Trans-Europe Express* looked back as well as well as forward. It was a nostalgic album, one which evoked images of an age long past, when there really were places like the Hall of Mirrors, where Franz Schubert played, and the showroom dummies posed. When railroads really were the arteries through which civilization's blood coursed.

Flür continued. "All of us in the group are children who were born straight after World War Two. So, we had no musical or pop culture of our own, there was nothing behind us. There was the war, and, before the war, we had only the German folk music.

"In the 1920s or 1930s, melodies were developed and these became the culture which we worked from. So, I think it was in us, ever since we were born. It is romantic, childish, and maybe it is naive, but I cannot do anything about it. It's in me."

He acknowledged a parallel . . . a possible parallel . . . between *Trans-Europe Express* and the music of the Kinks, a band whose own magic was similarly rooted

The German language version of Kraftwerk's *Trans Europe Express*. (Author Collection)

in an awareness of a lost past. "Maybe. The Kinks have something special, they are very special, and they use very English pop melody lines, which was always in them.

"So yes, I think it is the same thing. There is something you cannot put your finger on, which is very English, in the Kinks' music, which I could not do, which is their own style. There was something very German, but equally indefinable, on *Trans-Europe Express*."

Trans-Europe Express was not an immediate hit, nor was it expected to become one, even by the people charged with promoting it—the EMI sales rep, for example, who toured north London's record stores with a copy, and spent the entire record making cheap cracks and lame jokes about the music. "This one's called 'Metal on Metal,'" he'd quip, "and listen. That's all it is. They're just banging things together."

Haha.

Rising to number 56 in Britain, number 119 in the United States, *Trans-Europe Express* did little more than any reasonably successful cult band could expect. It did better on the continent, and in France, journalists were even offered a promotional ride from Paris to Rheims aboard a restored 1930s locomotive. It was an interesting irony; the ultimate antirock group holding court within that most typical rock setting, the free press junket.

But, as the cliché goes, the people who needed to hear *Trans-Europe Express* were the people who heard it; who filed it alongside *Low* among the records that spoke the loudest to the exploding new world. And now they were joined by another, and not only would it hail from the most unexpected arena of all, it would also reveal its own fascination with the past, and the ways in which it could blend with the present to create something that was not of either age.

• • •

Punk rock's stranglehold on the British music scene continued to tighten as 1977 marched on, but there were factions within the factions within the factions.

Ultravox! and, in their wake, Rikki and the Last Days of Earth, proved that not every "punk" act was three chords and a snarl. The Buzzcocks demonstrated that not every band wanted to beat the living daylights out of its audience, while bathing in a hail of flying spittle. The Damned were evidence that not every lyricist wanted to destroy the system.

And not every record buyer gave two hoots for punk rock. Ultimately, punk rock would merit its historically unassailable place among the key turning points in the development of twentieth century rock. Through the first half of 1977, however, the evidence was somewhat scantier.

By June 1977, only the Sex Pistols had truly cracked the national chart, when their second single, "God Save the Queen," soared either to number 1 or number 2, depending upon which conspiracy theory you subscribed to. (Banned by the BBC in the run-up to the Queen's Silver Jubilee, and even omitted from some retailers' Top 20 chart displays, the Pistols record was odds-on to take the top spot, only for the latest Rod Stewart 45 to mystifyingly overtake it at the last moment.)

Other bands—the Stranglers, the Adverts, and the Jam—would not be far behind them as the summer heated up. But, right now, you could count on two hands the number of punk bands that scored anything close to being a major (Top 10, Top

20 at a pinch) hit single. You could count on one hand those that were capable of selling out a venue much larger than a scout hut. And you could count on one finger the number of groups whose name would actually be recognized by the populace at large.

And why? Because even in 1977, most people bought the records they liked because they liked them, not out of some kind of misbegotten form of brand loyalty. It's always been that way, but the point is worth making here because there is so much hindsight heaped onto punk that sometimes, it feels as though everyone in the country, from babes in arms to grannies in bath chairs, must have been sporting a safety pin and spitting at the Queen.

They weren't. What they were doing was, dispatching old prog rockers like ELP ("Fanfare for the Common Man") and Yes ("Wondrous Stories") into the Top 20 for the first time ever. Extracting every ounce of enjoyment they could from the soft rock sounds of *Starsky and Hutch* TV star David Soul ("Don't Give Up On Us" and "Silver Lady"). Sending Andrew Lloyd Weber to number 1 ("Don't Cry for Me, Argentina," mercifully voiced by Julie Covington); and buying both American- and British-made disco records in ever vaster proportions, until it was nigh on impossible to move without being pushed in the bush or feeling the need, while the Floaters floated on and the disco inferno raged.

Because, when it came down to it, the kids in Britain wanted to dance as well.

Among the biggest UK club hits that spring of 1977, which in turn translated into a major chart success, was "Magic Fly," a synthesized instrumental by Space—a French act that sounded as good on the dance floor as the band, all decked out in spacesuits, looked on TV.

Front man Didier Marouani's embrace of electronica was a surprise. Just a few years earlier, he was an impassioned would-be heart throb emoting the gloriously bombastic likes of "Le Pays de Ce Grand Amour," "Si Tu M'avais Vraiment Aimé," and "Je Suis Ton Chevalier" on French television.

Now he was calling himself Ecama, and performing dynamically quirky electro-pop confections with names like "Velvet Rape," "Flying Nightmare," and "Ballad for Space Lovers." *Plus ça change*, indeed.

In tandem with Jean-Michel Jarre's *Oxygène*, and the unexpected disco success of Bowie's lurching "Sound and Vision," the popularity of "Magic Fly" makes it clear that British dancers were taking a very pointed turn away from their American cousins.

Most towns and cities had at least a handful of regular discotheques, with such venues as Tiffany's, Crackers, and the Mecca coming close to household name status. As early as 1974, there was reckoned to be upward of twenty-five thousand mobile discos operating in the United Kingdom, setting up everywhere from youth clubs and church halls to holiday camps and pubs, and manned by some forty thousand professional disc jockeys.

Nor were such events restricted to smaller clubs and venues. The massively successful Radio One Roadshows grew out of the popularity of these affairs, a touring company of top BBC disc jockeys that went around the coastal resorts throughout the summer every year, broadcasting their own set live to the rest of the nation, in front of crowds that often numbered in the thousands.

Just as in America, it is impossible to overestimate the impact that these operations had on the success (or otherwise) of the records that the DJs chose to play. Soon . . . too soon, some might say . . . their hegemonic rule as the arbiters of the dance floor's tastes would be utterly upended by the emergence of the veteran British Bee Gees as the new public face of disco music across the globe, and the commercial side of the disco machine's drive for international supremacy.

But for now, as 1977 moved toward its midriff, British disco was just as feral a beast as punk rock, and—in terms of media exposure—even more underground than that.

It was equally influential, too. Jimmy Somerville, of 1980s hit-makers Bronski Beat, is not the only young teen who recalls their first nights at a discotheque (in his case, Shuffles, in a suitably darkened Glasgow basement) as a rite of passage that would change his life.

Somerville was so nervous as he made his way there for the first time that he almost threw up. But he had scarcely been on the dance floor for fifteen minutes (devoted in their entirety to Donna Summer's "Love Trilogy") before he realized that this was where he had always wanted to be.

Nor was he the only teen who discovered his own sexuality on those dance floors, nor the only one who learned the value of that discovery. Somerville told *Quietus*, "There was one man who would introduce me to some incredible music . . . he would basically give me money for sex, and I would go and buy records with the money. He would even tell me which records to buy."

And the lights kept flashing and the beat kept pounding, and the room kept swirling and the crowd kept sweating, and the band kept playing, and it was in the heart of this fevered, febrile atmosphere of opportunity and anticipation that the disc jockeys learned to respect the crowds. That they truly understood that one false move, a record that broke the mood, was the cue not merely for a hail of abuse and projectiles, but an entire night out to be shattered. Never to recover from one moment of mad inattention.

But a record that no one had heard before, or was nothing like anything anyone *had* heard before . . . that was different. That could make a man immortal and a night unforgettable.

As the calendar clicked down to the beginning of July 1977, that record was coming closer every day.

10

CAUSE AND FX

Every urban sprawl has one . . . or, at least, it used to. A rundown, seedy bar perched unobtrusively between the dry cleaner and the deli, a makeshift you-could-barely-call-it-a-stage, and an exotic dancer going through the motions for an audience that is far more excited than she is.

It could be anywhere, in Yonkers or York, Wuppertal or Wilmington, Calais or Calgary. Any bar in any place, just so long as it is seedy.

For example, were one to have been visiting the south side of the River Thames, a not especially salubrious corner of Elephant and Castle, on a summer Sunday afternoon in 1977, one might have chosen to stop off at a certain neighborhood hostelry.

The exotic dancer on the makeshift stage is . . . ah. It's so easy to be judgmental over strippers. Author and producer Diablo Cody, who was an exotic dancer herself, says as much in her memoir *Candy Girl: A Year in the Life of an Unlikely Stripper.*

"Most girls I knew hated strippers with the tenor of fury best reserved for serial rapists. They used 'stripper' as an adjective to dismiss anything that was crass, blowsy or distasteful."

The girl onstage is none of those things. She is pretty, even with the glazed expression of someone who was clearly wishing they were elsewhere, even with an unmistakable overtone of "move any closer and I'll eviscerate you," that she directs toward her audience.

She's probably in her late teens; and yes, she's bored, so much so that any new arrival in the room gets a smile, as long as he's not old enough to be her father. Or, at least, a very dubious friend of his. The sort that suggest you call them uncle, and who hang around pool halls with people named Frank. In truth, however, it's probably just a reflex action. Butts on seats means banknotes in thong, and that's why she's there.

Her dancing is as nondescript as the music she was dancing to. Or maybe her dancing just makes it seem nondescript. Nothing sticks out, everything just drifts past as she disinterestedly gyrates and jiggles.

And then "I Feel Love" comes on. The twelve-inch, of course.

Everything shifts. No more the listless brunette wriggling to a pack of men in overalls. Suddenly she is Hannibal crossing the alps, she is Newton discovering gravity, she is whatever grandiose analogy you want.

The stage fades to gray, the audience to invisibility. It is just the dancer and the music, and it is becoming increasingly difficult to distinguish the two; to determine where one began and the other ended.

That was the magic of "I Feel Love." It got under the skin, transformed the listener, and made the whole world seem sexy again.

People talk a lot . . . *this book* talk a lot . . . about how "I Feel Love" changed music, how it grafted fresh ears onto old heads and planted new ideas into hidebound imaginations.

But that's not all that it did. "I Feel Love" made people dance, and it made them danc*ers*. You went out clubbing with your friends and you saw people hop around who had never so much twitched to the beat in the past.

Punk rockers forgot to pogo, square dancers abandoned the do-si-do. Or, as Pete Burns of Dead or Alive once said, "If 'Love to Love You Baby' was a record that made you want to fuck, 'I Feel Love' made you want to fuck harder. And snort sulfate off her tits while you did it."

For too many people, the kind of dance music . . . disco music . . . that was now infiltrating the mainstream possessed something approaching anesthetic quality, literally numbing the parts that other genres effortlessly reached. Even its fans, even the disc jockeys, would soon be tiring of the sheer bulk of bad beats, generic songs, and facile rhythms that were being flung at them on a weekly basis.

"I Feel Love" had the opposite effect entirely. That slow fade into a startled insect beat. The grace with Summer's voice that floated in out of nowhere. The sense that so much was happening within that most minimalistic framework. It was as if Moroder had taken everything people loved about music, be it disco, electronic, new wave, old fart, *whatever*, and stripped it back. Exposed the wiring. And then challenged us to lick a finger and touch it.

For several years now, journalists had bandied around the term *motorik* as shorthand for the relentless beat that was a characteristic of so many Krautrock artists. The electronic rhythm of "I Feel Love" was motorik-plus.

How many actual words are there in the song? Twenty-one, three per verse, and three more in the chorus. And that's only if you count the syllables, as opposed to the actual words, that make up the third ("fallin' free") verse. It's still almost twice as many words as Silver Convention squeezed into their two US hits (six apiece), but it was minimalist all the same.

"Musically, it's essentially a chant based around a drone that has a couple of changes, and very few lyrics," explained John Foxx. "But what is so wonderful about it is the entwined rhythms of synth, sequencer, and drums.

"The nearest songs are the chorus of 'For Your Love,' by the Yardbirds—elements of a Catholic chant. But it was that combination of a superb female singer and Germanic electronic instrumentation that seemed totally original at the time, and it went straight to the heart (and feet) immediately. It was played in every club you went to."

Kevin Bond, "the Big K," deejayed around southeast England's Medway Towns in the midseventies. "I don't know if I was the first person to play 'I Feel Love' around there, but I know I was one of the first to actually get a copy."

He was visiting the London offices of Donna Summer's UK label GTO when he was handed an advance copy of *I Remember Yesterday*, just as the first pressing of the American release arrived there. Playing the full album once he got home, he then dropped three of the songs into his set that same evening, beginning with "I Feel Love."

"People just didn't know what to make of it. The first few moments, I thought I'd made a terrible mistake—nobody even moved. There was something about the beat, the rhythm, the way it sounded and the way it made them want to move, that nobody could make any sense of. It could only have been a few seconds, but it felt like forever. Suddenly the whole place went crazy. I think I played that record half a dozen times that night, and I could probably have played it even more."

Other first impressions may not have been so profound, but they were certainly just as memorable.

In New York, photographer Bob Gruen remembers the twelve-inch "I Feel Love" among the only disco records he ever bought. "There may have been five altogether, and that was one of them."

In London, Alan Lee Shaw, guitarist and vocalist with the punk band the Maniacs, reflected, "For myself and my ilk, punk rock was blazing a scorched earth trail through the ears and minds of youth, commanding the style, fashion and energy of all that was young hip and snotty in the UK and beyond. But, if truth, be known, it was Donna Summer and the electronic disco sound of Giorgio Moroder that unequivocally ruled the airwaves. Disco . . . may have been anathema to punk, but 'I Feel Love' would arguably be the true soundtrack of 1977."

Cut from a somewhat similar musical cloth, the first time New York new wave band the Feelies heard the song, they were in a car on their way to a mall in New Jersey with friend Roger Nelson.

"We heard it on the radio and all of us said nothing," recalled Nelson. "Went into mall and found a record shop. Bought a copy and stuffed it under my T-shirt. Went back to car and one of us sheepishly admitted they had just bought it. Whereupon the other four of us whipped out our copies."

Teenaged keyboard player Mel Wesson spent his summer of 1977 "working on a building site to get the cash to buy my first synth. A building site full of beer-bellied, ass-flashing, [construction workers], catcalling stuff like 'Are those your mum's shoes?' etc. It paid off though, I bought my synth for £199 from the back pages of *Melody Maker.* I then got thrown out of my band because of it . . . then it broke.

"To add insult to injury, every time I walked into the bar of the Croydon Greyhound (i.e., most days), 'I Feel Love' was on the jukebox. It was disco, so I wasn't supposed to like it, but it had synthesizers . . .

"The track was so familiar. That sequencer bass was the preserve of Tangerine Dream and Klaus Schultz who served it up in twenty-minute portions before Giorgio microwaved the idea, removed all the goodness and served it up as a three-minute ready meal. A truly genius idea."

Neil Arthur, later the front man with eighties new wavers Blancmange, heard "I Feel Love" for the first time "on [British television's] *Top of the Pops*, I would imagine. I don't remember the performance, but what I do remember is the incessant sequencer. I thought that was absolutely amazing.

"Of course it's still being referenced, it's up there. I don't know all the details of the history, but if you think about how the club scene developed, disco being slammed and then coming back, you put that song in a club today, it still gets people moving. It slips in so easily.

"It's a wonderful, wonderful groove and it seems so simple. But in my experience, 'simple' is the most difficult thing to achieve. To strip away to the bare bones and not disguise it with other things, that's very hard.

"I remember when [Blancmange] were first messing around with sequencers, 'let's get the delay going,' you have to really work hard to make that happen and that's one of the most beautiful things about that song, it's so bloody difficult to get right.

"I remember . . . 'That's Love' on Blancmange's second album; we spent ages trying to get sequencers to work, to sync up, a couple of days. Suddenly we got something going and got the tape running. 'Let's hope this stays in sequence!' We've done that . . . on [other] songs and it's 'oh my goodness, if we put the delay on that right. . . .'"

He invoked the song again forty years later, while working on "Distant Storms," the opening track to Blancmange's next album (2018's *Wanderlust*). "'I Feel Love' was on our mind when we were molding the shape, the groove element of what the sequencers were doing. The sequencers involved on that particular song were the same era, a Moog Modular."

For Keren Woodward, now one-half of eighties chart toppers Bananarama, hearing "I Feel Love" transports her straight back to her local ice-skating rink in Bristol, sixteen years old and tearing around the ice with her best friend Sara Dallin (the other half of Bananarama).

"Growing up, Sara and I absolutely loved disco. Proper disco. We used to have discos at school and it would be 'Funkin' for Jamaica' by Tom Browne, James Brown . . . when we have a kitchen disco now, which we frequently do, with Sara's daughter and her mates over, it's always seventies stuff, seventies funk and disco.

"The first time I heard 'I Feel Love,' it was at the ice-skating. Sara and I used to go on a weekend; it was an ice-skating disco, you just skated round and round to music and flashing lights, and we absolutely loved that." So much so that Bananarama, too, slipped a tribute to "I Feel Love" onto their 2019 album, *In Stereo*, "Dance Music." "It's a modern version of it," continued Woodward. "Such a nice funky groove, electro, I love that song. It's got a really nice feel to it."

Lush bassist Phil King—later to attain electronic glory as compiler of a fine series of early seventies Moog pop singles—was also teenaged at the time. "Although I was going to a lot of punk shows [at the time], 'I Feel Love' was the soundtrack to my summer, lying in the back garden in Morden. . . ." He liked it ("of course"), but admits, "it always reminds me of the smell of [suntan lotion]!"

John Foxx: "I first heard 'I Feel Love' on the radio and was entranced. I could hear the bass line was lifted from a piece on Jean-Michel Jarre's *Oxygène* album (part five, about five and a half minutes in), as was some of the sequencing. But it was all very well done and completely cohesive.

"At first, I thought it actually was Kraftwerk with a great singer—I thought it was remorseless and beautiful, all those simple elements making a great complexity of rhythm, well psychedelic, as well as functional dance. Perfect combination and a precursor of acid and rave and everything since.

"Donna Summer with synths—what a great idea. That's what really made it. Moroder's taste is often questionable, but that combination was absolutely immaculate—a woman surrounded by synthesizers—spot on, Gorgio.

"It changed black music and white music forever. A kind of instant reunification happened. There were very few black punk bands, but here was a form that included everybody. And women singers—especially black women singers—were center stage."

Everybody who heard that record, it seems, was struck by it in some way. But some introductions proved to be nothing short of life changing.

In the summer of 1977, Glasgow-born and -bred friends Jim Kerr and Charlie Burchill were maybe three months into the life span of their first "real" group together, Johnny & the Self Abusers. It was, as the name suggests, a punk band, and the band's career echoed that of innumerable others.

Johnny & the Self Abusers played their first-ever gig at a pub on April 11, 1977; two weeks later, they were opening for first wave punkers Generation X in Edinburgh. They were picked up the London independent label Chiswick Records, and their debut single was scheduled for release in November. On the very day the wax hit the racks, the band broke up.

It was, vocalist Kerr implies, Donna Summer's fault.

"I remember the first time hearing 'I Feel Love.' We were playing Glasgow that night. It was quite a violent discotheque and we weren't looking forward to it because there was always [fighting and violence], so we're getting fueled up on cheap wine and getting some Dutch courage, and I think we'd done some interviews earlier that day with various fanzines, talking about how punk was the be-all and end-all and 'punk this' and 'punk that.' . . .

"I remember this as clearly as anything. We were about to go on and the disc jockey came in and he said to us, 'Okay, you're on after the next single, but it's okay, because you get eight minutes.' So we're sitting at the side of the stage and he played 'I Feel Love,' the twelve-inch version [available only as a US import at that time], and it was the first time we'd ever heard it.

"And fueled with the cheap wine and whatever else we were taking, it was pretty amazing. Donna Summer was wailing like . . . it sounded kind of Arabic, and Charlie and I looked at each other; we could hear the machines behind her, and we were already aware of Kraftwerk and that; we could hear the machines and we thought: 'Punk is over.' Before we knew it, we just had to track down someone with a synthesizer and, lo and behold, that became Simple Minds."

Donna Summer onstage. (Photofest)

Was "I Feel Love" an influence on Simple Minds, then? "Big time, absolutely big time."

Across the Atlantic, the young Thomas Thorn, a decade away from his career with Electric Hellfire Club, was similarly impressed, and similarly influenced.

"I lived in a small rural town with no record store or anywhere else to hear new or cutting-edge music. You had to go to mall in the nearest big city for that. My dad certainly wasn't about to squander money on something as extravagant as cable TV, so I had to content myself reading about punk rock and new wave in *CREEM* and

Hit Parader. I was fascinated by the styles and ideologies, but wasn't quite ready to risk wasting cash I made mowing lawns or detasseling corn on something that might completely suck. Besides, I wasn't quite done buying KISS records yet.

"And then this crazy song came on the radio. I knew it was a synthesizer but it was being used in a way I'd never heard: to create a driving, throbbing rhythm that was simultaneously mechanical sounding but also somehow organic at the same time.

"In later years I would gravitate toward using analog synthesizers for bass lines because they created these huge sounds you could feel in your teeth. The chittering metallic arpeggios of 'I Feel Love' had that same effect when I jacked the volume on the seven-inch 45 I'd bought at the dime store and kept secret from my friends. It was on the same label as KISS was, so it was easy to camouflage.

"The slightly atonal synthetic strings sweeping across the intro gave the song an otherworldly feel—speaking the same language Vangelis used five years later to conjure a sonic dystopia for the *Blade Runner* soundtrack. That juxtaposition of seemingly incongruous sonic elements continued throughout the song, but somehow it worked. It was supposed to be disco, but it was really in a genre by itself.

"Donna Summer's voice was ethereal—like that haunting warble in 'Good Vibrations' . . . it would take me years to realize that was a theremin and not some processed female vocal. Haunting, eerie even . . . yet oozing sexuality at the same time. Looking back, I have to believe the song touched a lot of [future industrial musicians] the same way, because we all integrated those elements (or at least tried) into our own songs over a decade later. She was the siren that lured us toward our synthetic destinies."

"I Feel Love" was released in the UK on July 2, 1977, but—just as it had in the United States—prerelease plays in the clubs, and interest in the album, had already primed the pump.

Advance orders were so high that it took "I Feel Love" just one week to enter the British chart, straight in at number 15. There was one week when half the nightclubs in the country were playing it incessantly; a second week as the rest caught up. Now it was number 3. And the week after that, with "I Feel Love" pounding out of every radio, every bed-sit, every dance club, every shop, Donna Summer was number 1.

She remained there for the next three weeks, through the height of that glorious summer, swatting back Boney M, home-grown hit-makers Hot Chocolate and the Brotherhood of Man, just as she would repel all boarders elsewhere around the world.

Top of the charts in Australia, Austria, Belgium, Holland; number 2 in New Zealand and Switzerland; Top 5 in Canada, Germany, Italy, Spain, Sweden; number 6 in South Africa and on the *Billboard* Top 100 . . . incredibly and still inexplicably, the record even registered on *Billboard*'s Easy Listening chart, where it could have done nothing for any heart conditions that may have ailed that particular audience. There you are, after all, settling down with a nice mug of cocoa, James Taylor on the radio, Henry Gross, Seals and Croft, and fading in from another planet . . . here come the machines.

Here come the showroom dummies.

11

THE COURSE OF THE CRIMSON KING

John Foxx: "I Feel Love" "hit the zeitgeist perfectly," that curious, indefinable moment when time and place, mood and momentum, culture, and taste come together, piece by piece, bit by bit, just waiting for the last component to slide into place.

First punk, then Bowie, then Kraftwerk, each of them inverting the norm and abandoning convention to push music and, hand in hand with it, youth culture to ever further extremes. A sense that *something* was coming, something, big, something bad . . . something like the end of the world?

The gloves were off.

The timing continued serendipitous. "I Feel Love" was released on July 2 and, if you were paying attention to roots reggae music, you would know that it was just five days until Armageddon.

All year long, people had been poised in a state of suspended animation, awaiting the events of July 7, 1977. The seventh day of the seventh month of the seventy-seventh year. The day that the two sevens clashed.

Nobody seemed quite certain of who made the prophecy in the first place, but that was beside the point. Ever since the band Culture released their single "Two Sevens Clash" in 1976, the word had been spreading. On January 1, 1977, the countdown to Armageddon would begin.

The panic started in Jamaica, but it spread. Anyplace where there was a sizable Jamaican population . . . New York and London included . . . the warnings appeared on walls and conversation was dominated by nothing else. In the United Kingdom, where reggae and punk had long since been bound by a sense of shared destiny, the fear even spread into the white youth community. Hindsight assures us that it was never as pervasive a panic as the Y2K millennium fever, but it was something else to worry about, all the same.

With every passing day, the end drew closer. January, February . . . March, April . . . May, June . . . now the first week of July was upon us, and the tension was palpable.

In London, an unearthly silence settled over the streets, hushing even the sound systems that had hitherto soundtracked the summer. In Jamaica, the government placed the Jamaica Defense Force on alert, and private citizens began arming themselves for the apocalypse And on July 7, itself, many businesses closed for the day and there was scarcely a soul on the street.

Of course, the world did not end. Indeed, in a display of the most remarkable political theater, Prime Minister Manley chose to unveil a new Jamaican constitution at precisely seven p.m. that evening—adding one more seven to the pile. And it was several years before Culture front man Joseph Hill admitted that nowhere in Rastafarian lore were the two (or any other quantity of) sevens imbibed with such powerful significance. The whole affair had been one massive, mighty hoax.

"I Feel Love" soundtracked the entire affair, and would continue pounding out as the British year continued to tumble into the abyss.

There, that fall of 1977, the fire service went on strike for the first time in its history, at more or less the same time as the electricity grid went down, and candles were lit when the sun set. A foundering government was probably doing its best to cope (the jury was out on that), but even its supporters . . . strike that; even its own *members* . . . were aware that its best was simply not good enough.

On streets still black with a century of soot, like an overdeveloped photograph of the morning after the Blitz before; where wasted youth squatted in derelict houses, happy only to have a roof above its head, and sufficient speed to keep them awake late enough to avoid closing their eyes to the darkness, racism was on the rise, street violence endemic, police brutality the law.

Roaming gangs of ne'er-do-wells scoured the darkness in search of punks to beat up, and when their victims went to the police for support, they were more likely to be asked, in all seriousness, "Well, what do you expect if you go around dressed like that?"

The two sevens may not have been clashing anymore. But sometimes, it didn't feel that way and, though nobody with any part to play in the success of "I Feel Love" could ever have dreamed such perceptions could arise, the fact that such a summer and fall of rampant discontent should be soundtracked by the inhuman throb of Moroder's machines was an irony that few could ignore.

Neither was that irony confined to Britain. America felt it, too.

New York City had dodged the bullet of bankruptcy, but the city was not yet out of the woods. *New York Times* journalist Jonathan Mahler gave a taste of the city as seen through the eyes of an eight-year-old, visiting the metropolis for the first time in 1977.

"When we climbed into a taxi, my parents would immediately roll up the windows and lock the doors. When we took the No. 4 train to Yankee Stadium, my father kept a tight grip on my arm as I tried to decipher the anarchic swirls of graffiti that covered nearly every inch of our airless car."

The city had been dicing with schizophrenia for years. You could walk down Fifth Avenue and not see a soul with a hair out of place. Then, you'd turn left or right alongside any flagship department store, and you would enter a different world. If you were lucky, you might even leave it again, unmolested.

Times Square, so famously the most glittering jewel in theater land, was a maze of cheapo porn theaters, drug dealers, and hookers. Take one step too far as you exited your Broadway night out, and it was Bruce Wayne's parents all over again, gunned down in an alley by a man they barely saw. Except there was no Batman around to avenge them and, even if there had been, he'd have had other things on his plate.

Of the best-known music venues in the city, CBGBs was down on the Bowery, decades before gentrification finally cleansed the area of the homeless, the alcoholics, the junkies, and ultimately, CBGBs itself; and Max's Kansas City was reputedly (although not actually) the most sexually and morally degenerate hole you could fall into, without physically plunging into an underbelly that polite company could not even think about.

Even Studio 54, already a legend in the world of discotheques, was still battling to come to grips with New York State's liquor laws, and was raided and closed just months after opening. It reopened the following evening, but only fruit juice and soda were on sale. So, people smuggled their own hooch in, or necked it on the street outside. So much for the liquor laws.

Everywhere, the dichotomy of the greatest city in the world roared aloud, the feral and the furriers marching cheek by jowl toward oblivion. And on the night of July 13 . . . that is, six days after the sevens did (or didn't do) their thing . . . a lightning strike fifty miles north in Buchanan ignited a succession of failures that culminated in plunging the entire city into darkness.

Heartbreakers guitarist Walter Lure, flying home from his band's extended residency in London, landed in New York at the height of the blackout. "The whole city was in darkness. No lights, no signals, no subway . . . no air-conditioning.

"What there was, was rioting, looting and, nine months later, a massive surge in births. It was also desperately hot—104 degrees Fahrenheit, with not a breath of fresh air to be found. But hey, New York's New York. We just go on with things."

Things that, as the night wore on, included over a thousand fires, and as many stores damaged or looted. In excess of three thousand people were arrested. Television stations were down, radio too, but still the reports of violence and assaults skyrocketed.

Rumor ran rampant. For a year now, a serial killer known as the Son of Sam had held hostage the city's already diminished sense of security, picking off his victims—courting couples, mostly—with what appeared to be supernatural impunity.

What a night this would be for him to continue his murderous spree! "Hello from the gutters of N.Y.C.," the Son of Sam wrote in one much publicized missive, ". . . filled with dog manure, vomit, stale wine, urine and blood."

It wasn't really that bad, of course it wasn't. And he remained silent that night. But, like Britain, New York—and, by extension, all those cities that looked up to New York—was in a bad way.

"I Feel Love" would not be their salvation. But it was at least a gorgeous distraction from all of life's little problems. BBC broadcaster Mark Radcliffe once called "I Feel Love" "almost a world in itself."

Maybe it's not so incredible that it should help forge a new world as well. At least in musical terms.

John Foxx: "The timing of 'I Feel Love' was immaculate. A generation was clearly hungry for something fresh." Punk had shown that "there was a huge gap to be filled, [but] this new thing was much more agile and fascinating. 'I Feel Love' completely cleared the table." The first phase of British punk ended "not with a bang, but with a bleep."

Not immediately. In commercial terms, punk would only gather speed over the next six months, while the notoriety that adhered to it in media and establishment eyes would never go away.

Even today, discussing punk's merits (or lack thereof) with fans of other musical styles, one is more likely to be regaled with a tired recitation of yellowed tabloid lies than any measured understanding of what the music meant. Disco, too, labors beneath a Sisyphean burden of reactionary disdain and uninformed prejudice . . . it "sucks" and that's the end of it.

Robert Fripp, Brian Eno, and David Bowie in the studio in Berlin, 1977. (Photofest)

Yet "old" ears were open to "new music," in these and every other musical field, and some people were prepared to take their fascinations even further. And, in so doing, they helped lay the foundations upon which an entire generation would soundtrack their own interpretation of the state of their respective nations.

Robert Fripp, former mainstay with art rockers King Crimson, had been living in New York City's Hell's Kitchen neighborhood since March 1977. He was there when he heard "I Feel Love" for the first time, and immediately he was excited.

Throughout Crimson's career, reaching back to 1969's *In the Court of the Crimson King* LP, and then onward through a sequence of increasingly dramatic, and diverse ventures into experimental sound, Fripp's distinctive guitar had woven wholly unique textures from the instrument's traditional palette. Away from the band, in cohorts with Brian Eno, he had released two utterly compulsive albums of electronically treated, tape-delayed and looping drone, as *(No Pussyfooting)* was followed, in 1975, by *Evening Star*.

As much as any musician of his generation, and a lot more than most, Fripp was fascinated more by the guitar's possibilities than its capabilities; for Fripp, any technique that could disguise the essential guitar-ness of the guitar was one that was worth investigating.

When he heard "I Feel Love," then, he did not hear an electronic disco song. He saw a new sonic frontier. He named it Frippertronics.

He did not muse alone. That same summer, Fripp was in Berlin with Eno and Bowie, working on the latter's *"Heroes"* album—Bowie's second new LP of 1977 and, if you count the pair that he cocreated with Iggy Pop, *The Idiot* and *Lust for Life*, his fourth in just nine months.

Fripp would have been party to his hosts' ruminations on Moroder and Summer's sonic achievement; he would have shared his own thoughts on what it portended. And, after returning to New York City, he set about locating suitable collaborators for his own investigation.

Blondie were a punk band birthed in the same downtown Manhattan melting pot as the Ramones, Television, Patti Smith, and so forth; and, like them, swiftly locating their own unique sound—which itself was somewhere between teen-angst-driven sixties girl group pop, and edgy, almost danceable rock. Their debut album, *Blondie*, had certainly fallen into that first category; their now imminent second, *Plastic Letters*, evidenced their transition toward the second.

By 1979, and the worldwide hit single "Heart of Glass," the process would be complete but for now, that number was still largely unformed—a demo, ironically titled "Disco Song," that Blondie had been toying with for a couple of years, but which never quite seemed to click. But they, too, had heard "I Feel Love," and "Disco Song"'s final form was suddenly in reach.

Fripp was already a firm fan and friend of the band. Although Blondie were certainly the product of a very different musical generation than King Crimson, which had already lived out their career while Blondie's members were still scrabbling

Blondie's Debbie Harry. (Photofest)

around a succession of local acts, Fripp was in fact a year younger than Debbie Harry, the band's so-photogenic vocalist.

When the pair talked of the music they'd grown up with and loved, it was geography, not years, that separated their tastes. In fact, in stark and vivid contrast to the teenaged/early twenties nexus around which the best of British punk assembled, the New York variety was more likely to be approaching, or even breaching, their thirties, and the wisdom and experience that they'd amassed in those extra years was always to be the great divide between the two nations' musical strivings.

Superficially, there were few points of contact between Blondie's music and Fripp's. Beneath the surface, however, there was a vast reservoir of shared experiences and beliefs. According to *Rolling Stone* in summer 1979, Fripp, Harry, and her partner Chris Stein even formed a movie production company together, planning to remake French New Wave director Jean-Luc Godard's *Alphaville.*

That never happened. But other collaborations would soon be in place.

Freed from the weight of expectation that clung to King Crimson, Fripp was stretching his musical wings. In addition to the Bowie album, where he gleefully acceded to Bowie's demand for "some burning rock'n'roll guitar," he would also work with Peter Gabriel, Daryl Hall, and another New York band, the Roches, over the next year or so. But he was also gathering ideas and inspirations for his solo debut album.

Fripp made his live solo debut in New York in February, shortly before he relocated to the city, and the audience that awaited him had no idea what to expect. And still what he delivered was a shock: one man and the array of pedals, boxes, and tapes that were part and parcel of the fast-gestating Frippertronics . . . there would be no old Crimson favorites when Fripp performed, just the haunting, mesmerizing, hum and drone of what felt like an incalculable number of impossible guitars.

Harry and Stein were in the audience that night, and Stein was there, too, whenever Fripp appeared on journalist Glenn O'Brien's public access cable show *TV Party.* Indeed, the Blondie man was the program's cohost, and a mainstay, too, of the TV Party Orchestra, an ever-changing roster of players and guests who simply made whatever noises seemed appropriate. Fripp, of course, contributed Frippertronics.

Nevertheless, a lot of people were shaken when word spread that Fripp was planning to appear onstage with Blondie at an upcoming benefit concert at CBGBs.

The gig was a benefit for Johnny Blitz, drummer with the punk band the Dead Boys, as he recovered from the near-fatal stab wounds he received in an altercation in the East Village. Spread across four days (May 4–7, 1978), and with thirty bands scheduled to appear, any number of unexpected guest appearances were in store—both comedian John Belushi and John Waters's movie star Divine would be guesting with the Dead Boys themselves at the show.

Blondie were appearing on the final night, with Fripp joining them for an eclectic blend of numbers that included the New York Dolls' "Jet Boy," Iggy Pop's "Sister Midnight" . . . and, to the astonishment of all, "I Feel Love."

The *New York Times*' John Rockwell provides the details: "Miss Harry cooing erotically and the band punching out tense, hypnotic disco trance-rock, show[ing] that there need be no gulf between punk and disco after all."

Furthermore, Rockwell continued, Fripp's "own solos were spectacular, but what was equally interesting was the new directions for Blondie that his collaboration suggested."

Indeed.

Fripp continued to guest occasionally with Blondie across the next couple of years, with their repertoire eventually settling down to just two fiery performances, "I Feel Love" and Bowie's "Heroes."

Away from the public glare, too, matters were moving on, as Fripp invited Harry and Blondie to join him at the Hit Factory studios in New York, to appear on his still gestating solo album, provisionally titled *The Last Great New York Heartthrob*. Perhaps inevitably, they would be performing "I Feel Love."

Live recordings had already captured at least the frisson of the vision, anything up to eight minutes of relentless beat, a rapturous audience clapping along, and the sudden realization that whatever Moroder had done with synths, Fripp was . . . not replicating, but readdressing with a guitar that really didn't sound like a guitar. "Twisting the synthesizer shapes," as *Melody Maker*'s James Truman put it, while Harry "plausibly but undramatically" sang alongside him. The studio would allow the partnership to take things even further.

Blondie were not the only band experimenting in electronics in New York at this time. Suicide—the unearthly pairing of Martin Rev's unearthly electronics and Alan Vega's performance art Elvis—had been kicking around Manhattan since the early 1970s, predating any of New York's loftier seventies icons. There was more than one observer who put their longevity down to sheer stubbornness and bloody-minded spite.

Suicide were the band that Max's owner Tommy Dean sent on at three in the morning, to clear the club of New York Dolls fans. Suicide were the band that toured the United Kingdom with the Clash and were howled out of earshot by

Robert Fripp. (Atlantic Records/Photofest © Atlantic Records)

every audience they met. Suicide were the band that critic Jon Savage described as "a match/mismatch of Donna Summer and Lou Reed's *Berlin*."

And still nothing could prepare the unsuspecting onlooker for the full Suicide live experience (the band did not release an album until their self-titled debut album in 1978); Vega an inhuman yowl, a manic blur that teleported itself across the stage to scream in another direction, Rev locked behind keyboards from which he coaxed unearthly washes of sound that sometimes, you thought you could almost dance to. But few people actually tried.

Still, Alan Vega remembered encountering a British journalist on that Clash tour, in 1978, who asked him whether Suicide were influenced by Giorgio Moroder. "Definitely," Vega replied. "I'm growing a mustache right now."

More seriously, he remarked, "Our audience did begin to change at that time, I think as the old disco crowd, from before it was disco, abandoned the dance places and started coming to places like Max's instead. Not so much CBGBs, that was too much. But the places that had the reputation for a more arty atmosphere, they'd come and hang out, and it was funny because I met a few people who'd seen us back when we started, at the Mercer Arts Center, who then drifted away to go dancing.

"It had come full circle. People became more interested in electronic music, and you can hear a little of that, just a nod of the head, on [Suicide's] first album. Then

Debbie [Harry] took it a lot further, although not as far as it could have gone if she'd been able to do that Fripp thing."

That Fripp thing. Tentatively titled *The Last Great New York Heartthrob*, Fripp's solo LP was gestating slowly. It was, its maker mused, intended to be the first installment of a trilogy of records, each one dedicated to a different aspect of Frippertronics.

Opening the sequence, *The Last Great New York Heartthrob* would expose Frippertronics to the world of (largely conventional) song. Then would come *Frippertronics*, focused on the sound at its purest; the third, *Discotronics*, would "expand the possibilities of disco music as a vehicle for carrying a wider range of propositions than normally one would expect." He told *Melody Maker*, "[It] is officially defined as the musical experience resulting at the interstice of disco and Frippertronics."

The trilogy, ultimately, did not happen. *Frippertronics* and *Discotronics* would be combined, one side apiece, across the 1981 album *God Save the Queen/Under Heavy Manners*; while the first in the series, now retitled *Exposure*, would be cruelly sabotaged when Blondie's record company, Chrysalis, refused to allow them to appear on the record.

Fripp responded by dropping plans to record "I Feel Love," and calling in Peter Hammill, sometime front man of Van Der Graaf Generator, to deliver a new song, "Disengage." In a parallel universe, however, perhaps Fripp would have stubbornly adhered to his original blueprint, and Hammill—himself possessor of one of rock's most expressive, dynamic, voices—might have vocalized "I Feel Love" in Harry's stead. That *would* have been worth hearing.

In the event, Chrysalis Records did . . . if not repent, at least revise its opinion of Blondie's collaborating with Fripp, first when he guested on their next album, *Parallel Lines*, to contribute some signature guitar to the avant-ish "Fade Away and Radiate," and then when a live recording of "I Feel Love," recorded at London's Hammersmith Odeon in January 1980, made it out as the B-side to Blondie's "Union City Blue" single.

In addition, Chris Stein was responsible for *Exposure*'s sleeve photograph, a picture of Fripp taken at Radio City Music Hall. Apropos to very little, *Exposure* was apparently the first album ever to use a color Xerox for its cover artwork.

If "I Feel Love" was cruelly excluded from one off-shoot of the late 1970s New York underground, it would play a major role in another.

German-born countertenor Klaus Nomi moved to New York City in 1972, immediately slipping into the East Village art scene of the day with an appearance at the Ridiculous Theater's performance of Wagner's *Das Rheingold*.

The inimitable Klaus Nomi. (Photofest)

The self-described "bastard love child of Elvis Presley and Maria Callas," Nomi was blessed with the ability to hit notes that most mortals can only flinch at, while delivering them in an operatic tone that forever left listeners wondering just how seriously they were meant to things before the stage exploded in lights, smoke, and discordant electronics.

Nomi's appeal remained firmly encased in the novelty tradition over the next few years. In 1978, however, he appeared alongside new wave TV personality Lance Loud, electro performer Man Parrish, a singing dog, and some thirty other performers at the New Wave Vaudeville Show at Irving Plaza, artist David McDermott's four-day extravaganza of the city's wild, weird, and wonderful.

The evening was moving toward its close when McDermott took the stage to announce, "Ladies and gentlemen, what you are about to hear is not a recording! This is real!"

Attitude journalist Rupert Smith described what happened next. "The lights went down, thunderous music began and Klaus stepped onto the stage wearing a space suit, his hair sculpted into a point. While [dancer Boy] Adrian performed his robot dance, Klaus sang 'Mon coeur s'ouvre a ta voix' from Saint-Saens' *Samson et*

Dalila. The performance finished with bombs and strobes as Klaus backed off the stage, disappearing into the smoke."

The New Wave Vaudeville Show was Nomi's entrance into Manhattan's new wave club circuit. Appearances at Max's Kansas City, the Mudd Club, and so on saw his astonished audiences swell to include an ever-broadening coterie of superstar admirers; it was at the Mudd Club that Nomi met David Bowie, and was invited to appear alongside him on *Saturday Night Live* in December 1979.

Nomi would add his most distinctive backing vocals to three Bowie classics, "The Man Who Sold the World," "Boys Keep Swinging," and "TVC15"—the latter further illuminated by Nomi and musical partner Joey Arias walking a large pink stuffed poodle around the stage. The poodle's mouth was a television screen.

In between times, however, Nomi's own live show was growing ever more extravagant, setting down at some of New York's most legendary watering holes for a night of utter madness—one show, at Hurrah in 1979, was recorded and, though the tapes did not see release until 1986, three years after Nomi's death, it is there that we find a performance that his fan base had been enjoying for over a year at that point.

Closing the main show (Nomi would encore with the Saint-Saëns aria), a frenzied version of "I Feel Love" pursues the performance to the outer limits of the sonic imagination, both vocally and instrumentally, the frothing rhythm and apparently improvised lyrics collapsing into feedback, synth screams, and trumpet-led chaos about halfway through.

The singer reasserts his dominance, but now he is masterminding an ever-less faithful rendering of words and music. It remains the most audacious, but nevertheless delightful, approach that has ever been made to the song.

12

DISCO INFERNAL

Now we can trot out the clichés.

A sweaty club, a miserable night. Sordid souls milling, quaffing warm cocktails, none of which resembles anything their names are supposed to convey, but they have the little umbrella, and a cherry on a stick, and ooooh, aren't *you* fancy?

Cigarettes still damp from the night air outside choke the oxygen from the room and, as "In the Bush" sends the stroboscope into Morse message mayhem, so the boys from the suburbs mime the lyric's intent, arms outstretched as though clutching willing hips, and their own groin thrusting as they push . . . push . . . push.

Maybe, they're thinking, they'll do the pushing for real later. Maybe, any watching girls shudder, "getting lucky" will mean slipping out without being accosted.

How swiftly everything changed. How quickly our world was discovered and colonized. Here today, theirs tomorrow.

What had once been gritty now was garish. What had once been taut was now being taught . . . people were opening disco dancing schools, for goodness' sake. The gay underworld became gray overall, and yes, some people wore them as well.

Saturday Night Fever had its New York premiere on December 12, 1977, then opened nationwide four days later. Five weeks after that, its soundtrack album would go to number 1 in America, and remain there for the next six months.

Boney M now, and whoever imagined a time when a czar's mystic madman could become the topic of a pop song. "Ra, ra, Rasputin . . ." and then it's Michael Zager's "Let's All Chant" and the kids from the suburbs are growing rowdier.

The music was becoming commodified, and with it, the venues that had sustained it. A culture that had once been open to any kind of sound, so long as it had a good rhythm, was now being tyrannized by the beat. Songs, lyrics, melodies, all the things that were once as much a part of the experience as the way they made you want to move, had suddenly slipped into irrelevance.

Anointed a genre in its own right, "disco music" was all about the production. Somebody came up with the idea of counting a song's bpm . . . beats per minute . . . and suddenly that information became as much a part of a record's appeal as anything else.

The sensational Boney M. (Photofest)

It allowed disc jockeys to maintain a certain set pulse on the dance floor for as long as they wanted, but it stripped away the talent that had once been a good discaire's greatest ability, knowing how each record *felt*, and designing sets that rose and fell and slipped and slid as the evening wore on. As opposed to just heaping together a slew of otherwise unrelated floor fillers, on the grounds that they all made your foot tap at the same speed.

Individual records still stood out, of course: Alicia Bridge's "I Love the Nightlife," Anita Ward's "Ring My Bell," Lipps Inc.'s "Funkytown," Karen Young's "Hot Shot," Sarah Brightman's "I Lost My Heart to a Starship Trooper" . . .

A flood of discofied oldies that did strange and wonderful things to "I Can't Stand the Rain" (Eruption), "House of the Rising Sun" (the flamenco-flavored Santa Esmeralda), "Knock on Wood" (Amii Stewart), "Tobacco Road" (Bob-a-Rela), "Bridge over Troubled Water" (Linda Clifford), "Black Is Black" (Spain's La Belle Epoque).

A German band called Rosebud released an entire LP of danced-up Pink Floyd covers, while David Bowie even disco-fied his own glam anthem "John, I'm Only Dancing" for a twelve-inch single in 1979. (Although, in fairness to him, he recorded it in 1974, then hid it away for five years.)

Then there were the records that followed Moroder's lead into "the music of the future." Sylvester's "You Make Me Feel (Mighty Real)," introduced the tragically short-lived genius of disc jockey and producer Patrick Cowley to the mainstream. Sylvia's cover of Dee Dee Jackson's "Automatic Lover" was a glorious mash of Kraftwerk and Moroder, the electro throb of one, the robotic voice ("I am your automatic lover") of the other, and squeezing every last iota of passion out of the chorus's pleading "see me, feel me, touch me. . . ."

And finally, Frenchman Marc Cerrone, whose epic "Supernature" melding of synths, orchestration, and the ghost of John Forde's "Stardance" went on to sell over eight million copies worldwide. Forty-three years later, *Electronic Sound* magazine described it as "the unsung hero of 1977's electro trinity, alongside 'I Feel Love' and 'Trans Europe Express.'"

Cowritten with the then unknown Lene Lovich, "Supernature" was unlike anything Cerrone had recorded across two previous, and not unsuccessful, albums over the past couple of years. There he focused on the string-driven dance, to the extent that his lushly orchestrated side-long "Love in C Minor" was widely viewed as a male response to "Love to Love You Baby" (and received as avid a reception on American dance floors).

Which means "Supernature" might well have been his response to "I Feel Love," a solid synth backing drawn out across ten minutes that his US label, Atlantic, launched with a spectacular release party at Studio 54 in November 1977. The following June, at *Billboard*'s annual Disco awards, Cerrone and Supernature took home the gongs for Male Disco Artist of the Year, Disco Music Arranger of the Year, Disco Instrumentalist (Musician) of the Year, Disco Composer of the Year, and Best Producer of a Disco Record.

Moroder and Summer's response to that was not recorded.

"Supernature" would be among the last halfway innovative synthesized disco records of the age, so swiftly were electronics embraced by the producers behind both the greatest and the grisliest dance records. Besides, by the end of 1978, Rose Royce's "Love Don't Live Here Anymore" had introduced everyone to a brand-new sound, the pinging "boop" of the electronic syndrum, and now *that* was the flavor of the month.

Indeed, rather than encourage other artists to rise to the same glorious heights, the success of such records merely encouraged the volume of the crowd to soar to absorb them. To suck them down to the same leaden depths as everything else. Soon,

Sylvia's "Automatic Lover" 12-inch single. (Author Collection)

in fact, synthesizers were barely even noticed any longer, just one more wave of sound to fill the floor.

Someone's brought some party poppers, a raspberry squeal and the paper snake uncoils. What fun. A girl slides by, her face a mask of glitter and mascara, her boyfriend self-consciously splashed in tight tee and cheap Lurex, because she wouldn't be seen dead with a man who went out wearing anything less.

Here a hard-core tit shaker; there a tight-trousered cock jockey. Here a drunken real estate agent, shaking it for ladies who are barely half his age; there a latex Lothario, convinced that his leopard-print pants make him look like Rod Stewart, while the blonde on his arm grinds her teeth in pure panic.

Rose Royce, circa 1977. (Tribune Entertainment/Photofest © WGBH)

At least in Paris, at the trendsetting Le Palace, the waitresses are dressed as astronauts.

Where did all these people come from? And how do we make them leave?

According to a story in *Life* magazine, within a year of *Saturday Night Fever*'s hitting the theater circuit, there were over ten thousand solid brick-and-mortar discotheques in operation across the United States, with twenty more throwing open their doors every week. The percentages weren't much different in Britain, in France, in West Germany, across the Low Countries and Scandinavia.

Disco even infiltrated the Iron Curtain that then divided East from West, despite the litany of punishments that the alarmed Communist authorities meted out to dancers and disc jockeys alike.

The music would, eventually, filter into official channels in East Germany—by the end of the 1970s, there were even a few East German disco bands, including the three sisters of Die Caufner-Schwestern, and the funk-driven Gruppe Kreis. Prior to that, however, and preempting the warehouse raves of the late eighties West, discos themselves were deeply underground affairs staged in abandoned industrial buildings, or in the basements of World War Two–era ruins.

In East Berlin in 1972, activist Aljoscha Rompe was visited by the Stasi secret police for operating an illegal discotheque (in the original sense of the word); a decade later, in 1983, two DJs from Cottbus received five months in jail for playing a record that the government considered subversive (West German rocker Udo Lindenberg's "Sonderzug nach Pankow").

Western music lovers—not just disco kids, but punks, jazz heads, bluesmen, the lot—risked midnight raids, brutal interrogation, and days in detention simply for listening to the decadent sounds of America and its allies. In Poland, DJ Jan "Yahu" Pawul recalled being "repeatedly stopped and interrogated by the Political Secret Police," the SB, for the crime of promoting "misguided imperialist tricks hostile to the socialist homeland."

In that latter instance, however, the authorities may have had a point. For, in the United States, those same "imperialist tricks" were responsible for the most widespread and lucrative musical boom the country had seen since Beatlemania.

The Hilton hotel chain was considering converting its now-unfashionable bars into trendy new discos. Vidal Sassoon had created a twenty-five dollar Travolta-style haircut, sideburns optional. Designer Ray Halston was launching a new line of disco wear in loose and clingy styles.

In Beverly Hills, Zeidler and Zeidler complained it couldn't even keep black shirts and Cuban heels in stock anymore, so vast was the demand. In Brooklyn, Abraham & Strauss announced plans to open a Night Fever menswear boutique. Somebody even floated the notion that airports should attach discotheques to their passenger terminals, for the benefit of travelers with time on their hands.

Once, if an old bar or tavern felt it needed a face-lift, it ordered new ad signs for its regulars' favorite beers. If it *really* needed to make a change, it hired a dancer.

Now, its longtime regulars were scattered to the winds, pushed out to make way for mirror balls and turntables, and another horde of trendy twenty-somethings flowed out to out-Manero and Stephanie on the nightlife disco round. Add a traffic light light show and a worn-out strobe, a drunk with big hair singing the wrong lyrics loudly, and your evening was complete. Travolta doubles played clone wars on the sidelines, and it suddenly became fashionable to wear sunglasses after dark. Sunglasses indoors. Sunglasses indoors, in the dark.

They'll be hiring out roller skates next.

Don't knock it. Even as Donna Summer's own career eased out of disco music's increasingly cloying, opportunistic embrace, she remained adamant. "I don't think disco is bad," she told *Smash Hits*. "As the years go on, more and more artists are making disco records. People wanna dance . . . they wanna move. They're tired of being tied down. To me, discos are indoor playgrounds where people go to wind down from their frustrations."

She wasn't wrong. Rockers began paying attention. The Rolling Stones' "Miss You," in 1978, was a genuinely brilliant move; Paul McCartney's "Goodnight Tonight" was sheer class; and Rod Stewart's "Do Ya Think I'm Sexy?" was a blow-by-blow document of a typical night on the town that only the most simple-minded of listeners could believe was meant to be taken seriously.

Dan Hartman went even further, not just hijacking disco for a solitary hit, but rebuilding his career around it. Early 1978 saw him working toward the follow-up to his 1976 *Images* album, pure pop propelled by a band comprising drummer Hilly Michaels, fresh from a stint with Sparks; and guitarists Vincent Cusano and G. E. Smith—respectively, future members of KISS and the *Saturday Night Live* house band.

Several months of rehearsal had already gone into the project. But behind the scenes, as drummer Michaels recalls, Hartman "was a passionate closet disco freak!" By day, Hartman and Michaels would be "talking about searching out players for the new super pop Dan Hartman Band"; by night, "he was secretly visiting disco clubs in New York. He loved ABBA, the disco tracks. Donna Summer. . . ."

Michaels himself was a fan. The very first time he heard "I Feel Love," he says, "I loved it, thought, Genius!!! Never ever tired of listening to it, rare. Seemed to put a big smile vibe across New York City. Sexy song, sexy sounds." Indeed, later in his career, into the early 1980s, he was making his own experiments with electronics.

"[Record producer] Roy Thomas Baker came over and was raving about the Roland TR-707 drum machine, I should buy it. Next day got it, hooked it into my modulator analog mini moog or Korg black box with dials. The hi-hat output triggered the countless bass sounds. Had a small Roland keyboard. The second I pressed one or four keys on the keyboard, an amazing syncopated bass pulse which could be controlled fiddling with a few dials.

"The trick of course was to sing a catchy melody along with a rig/sound like that. Listening to 'I Feel Love' [recently], I was able to count four synchronized pulse parts going on."

But even Michaels was unprepared for the day when Hartman turned up at a band rehearsal, clutching a tape. "Look what I recorded last night," he said. "Instant Replay," one of *the* disco smashes of 1978, was born.

Dan Hartman's "Instant Replay" 12-inch. (Author Collection)

Michaels: "Dan played every instrument! Then he ran it right over to [Studio] 54, asked the DJ to spin it, and the place went nuts. 'Hey guys, now we're gonna do a disco album!' And we did, much to the chagrin of GE and Vinnie. . . ."

Yes, KISS took a serious misstep when "I Was Made for Loving You" turned them into temporary disco fodder, and the Electric Light Orchestra's "Shine a Light" was fairly unforgivable, as well. But neither was alone in that. As Summer said, "Musicians have realized that if disco is what people want, that they'll give it to them."

Still it was difficult not to be disappointed, not only by much of the music that Summer was championing, but also by the work of its champion herself, aching over the cake she was baking, and how it melted in "MacArthur Park." How she let us down. Eighteen months earlier, Donna Summer had the world at her feet. Now she was reworking an idea (and a song) that Camouflage's "A Disco Symphony" had already exhausted six months earlier.

But we should not have been surprised. For, even as "I Feel Love" stormed our brains and turned everything upside down; even as Eno murmured to Bowie about how it was going to change dance music for years to come; even as John Lennon allegedly locked himself away, playing "I Feel Love" over and over on repeat, and insisting "this is the future" . . . even as all those things were taking place, Summer, Moroder, and Bellotte were shuttered away, back in the basement of the Arabella complex, working on yet another new album. A double album, this time, befitting an artist of Summer's new stature.

The workload that the three of them, but Moroder and Bellotte in particular, had assumed seems incredible. With Summer turning out a new album as soon as the last was complete, Moroder maintaining his own solo drive, and Bellotte writing for both of them, they could barely have had a moment to draw breath.

But that's what they did. Summer's new album was under way, but Bellotte and Musicland drummer Keith Forsey were already overseeing a project of their own, *Watch Out* (under the name of Trax), a pounding electro monster highlighted by the side-long shouter "Watch Out for the Boogie Man." They were scheming a new album with veteran singer Marsha Hunt. And they were plotting the soundtrack for Summer's movie debut, Casablanca's newly inaugurated film division's own *Thank God It's Friday*—including, in a flash of jaw-dropping synchronicity, the song that started it all for her, the ballad she wanted to emulate when she first started dreaming of "Love to Love You Baby," a fifteen-minute cover of "Je t'aime . . . moi non plus."

Summer and Moroder had already recorded the song once, at the end of 1976, intending it for release on Valentine's Day 1977. In the end, they canned it, only to see Saint Tropez then ride in with their own supersexed rendition of the same song.

They returned to the song later in the year, viewing it as a potential follow-up to "I Feel Love." A handful of promo twelve-inchers were pressed and distributed around key DJs, only to be ignored by almost all of them. The Saint Tropez version remained so much better.

Now they were to try again—and, in the event, they failed quite spectacularly to muster even a lightly smoldering version.

Hopes were, understandably, higher for Summer's next LP.

Released barely five months after *I Remember Yesterday*, *Once Upon a Time* was her most ambitious project yet. Summer had sown up the disco world. Now her sights were set on something far vaster, a Diana Ross/Barbra Streisand–shaped superstardom in which she could turn her attention to whatever she chose, and pull it off with ease.

She wasn't wrong, either. Those years of theater had taught her well; as a singer, just as an actress, Summer could slough off one guise and adopt another, and her voice and range were so unflinchingly vast that you could not even see the costume change.

Summer told the *Austin American-Statesman*, "In the beginning, I had an 'image,' and the image was not quite the person. And what I have tried to do is combine the person that I am with the person they want me to be and become a person they will accept. And it works.

"That's what made a person like Judy Garland so immensely acceptable and so incredibly great, because even when she was a drunk and was, like, way over the line, she was able to just absorb people through sympathy. They looked at her not only as an entertainer but as a human being." That was what she was working toward, and that is what she would eventually achieve.

Moroder, too, reveled in the freedom that Summer's talent and ambition brought him. Yes, he remained experimental at heart. But he was experimenting within the broadest arena imaginable, within the full glare of fame and success and popularity.

Again, *Once Upon a Time* was a concept album; the story of a land where unreality was the only thing that was real, and the girl . . . whose life, some said, might have mirrored Summer's own . . . who picks her way through it.

Each of the four sides was presented as a fresh "act," the full production bookended by a single titular theme, and although there were no immediate hits from the album, that scarcely mattered now. In less than one month, *Once Upon a Time* had gone gold, and Europe went crazy for the final act's "I Love You."

There was even, for those who expected such a thing, a suite of electronica, eleven minutes punching from the motorized chorale of "Now I Need You" into the ethereal robotics of "Working the Midnight Shift," and if it was never destined to enjoy even a fraction of the impact that "I Feel Love" demanded, that's because it was never intended to.

It was a reminder, not a rehash, and certainly not a reinvention. Across *Once Upon a Time*, the story was the message and the singer was the messenger. "I Feel Love," of course, had inverted that equation completely.

It continued to do so, too. Just not in any arena that might have been expected.

The first suggestion that "I Feel Love" had not yet run its course came later that summer of 1978, when Moroder welcomed movie director Alan Parker into Musicland, to record the soundtrack to his upcoming movie *Midnight Express*.

Parker "loved" "I Feel Love," Moroder told *Time*, and when it came to the crucial chase scene in the film, that was the mood he wanted to recapture, the punishing bass line, the constant throb.

"There's a scene at the beginning of the movie where the guy escapes and Parker said, 'Give me something in the style of "I Feel Love."' So, I composed the song and he loved it. He said to do whatever I wanted with the rest of the movie, so I did—and he didn't want to change anything. And we mixed it in one Sunday afternoon."

"Chase" emerged an eight-minute instrumental that built from a Mini Moog bass line beneath a Roland SH-2000 synthesizer melody. The resultant piece opened what Moroder later described as the first fully electronic movie soundtrack ever released and, almost inevitably it was also released as a single . . . intriguing in seven-inch form, and unstoppable across twelve. Anyone caught on the dance floor as that leviathan commenced its remorseless journey had no alternative but to remain there until it was over. It was, Mel Wesson quipped, "pretty much the same formula as 'I Feel Love,' but feeling the love of a Turkish jail."

• • •

Jim Kerr and Charlie Burchill's excitement that night they heard "I Feel Love" for the first time, and promptly headed out in search of a synth player, was not unique.

All over Europe and the United States, but particularly in the United Kingdom, it seemed, musicians who had been perfectly content to scream the punk rock odds atop a barrage of guitar chords and trashcan percussion were suddenly looking, and listening, elsewhere.

You can hear the influence of "I Feel Love" in Thomas Leer's first single, a solo electronic piece released in 1978, following the demise of his punk band Pressure. "Private Plane" was rudimentary, recorded with just a Watkins Copycat for loops and echoes, a Roland organ drum machine, and a handful of pedals at his disposal, alongside guitar and bass.

But the motorik throb and the white noise percussion swept straight out of Musicland, and though subsequent Leer exercises were to stray far from that prototype (beginning with longtime friend and Pressure bandmate Robert Rental's "Paralysis," later that year), the linkage was established.

Other pioneers were a little slower off the mark. Six months after "I Feel Love" left the chart, in January 1978, Gary Numan and his Tubeway Army were still thrashing out hyperspeed covers of the Velvet Underground as concert encores. Their first single, "That's Too Bad," had just been released, to be described by the *New Musical Express* as "a feeble Johnny Rotten."

But then he discovered a synthesizer waiting in a corner of a recording studio, asked if he could have a go . . . and the old Tubeway Army sound was swept from his mind.

Looking back, he doesn't seem to see the big deal. Only slowly did Numan find himself listening more to Moroder and Ultravox! than to his other musical pleasures; only gradually did he transition from one thing to another.

"I was just a guitarist that played keyboards, I just turned punk songs into electronic songs." But his "Are Friends Electric?" became one of the biggest hits of 1979, and the floodgates would soon be straining behind him.

The landscape was changing all over. When Bob Geldof and the Boomtown Rats followed up the adrenaline punk crash of "Mary of the 4th Form" with spring 1978's metronomic "Like Clockwork," at least one reviewer was moved to knowingly pun "'like Kraftwerk,' more like," and he wouldn't be wrong. They didn't even need a synthesizer to do it. But the mood was managed regardless.

Bands armed themselves with whatever they could, and suddenly they had a lot of options. Neil Arthur recalls how Blancmange's first release, the *Irene & Mavis* EP, "was all done on an eighteen pounds sterling guitar, an amp I made at school, and Stephen [bandmate Stephen Luscombe] had an organ that he bought, a cheap one that we put through delays and distortion pedals and came up with some noises. We were trying to get our instruments to sound like synths."

They did not have long to wait. Synthesizers, once the preserve only of those wealthiest enough to have money to burn, were suddenly plummeting in price. There was a growing movement toward building your own equipment, from the charts and diagrams being published in a wealth of electronics magazines. There was even a buoyant market in used equipment.

Californian Edward Stapleton, whose band Nervous Gender were among the first LA punks to synthesize their savagery, recalled for PostPunk.com, "a ton of . . . recording studios with synths that were starting to go out of business. . . . There were some cut-rate synths on the market from failed studios. That's how [I] got [mine]."

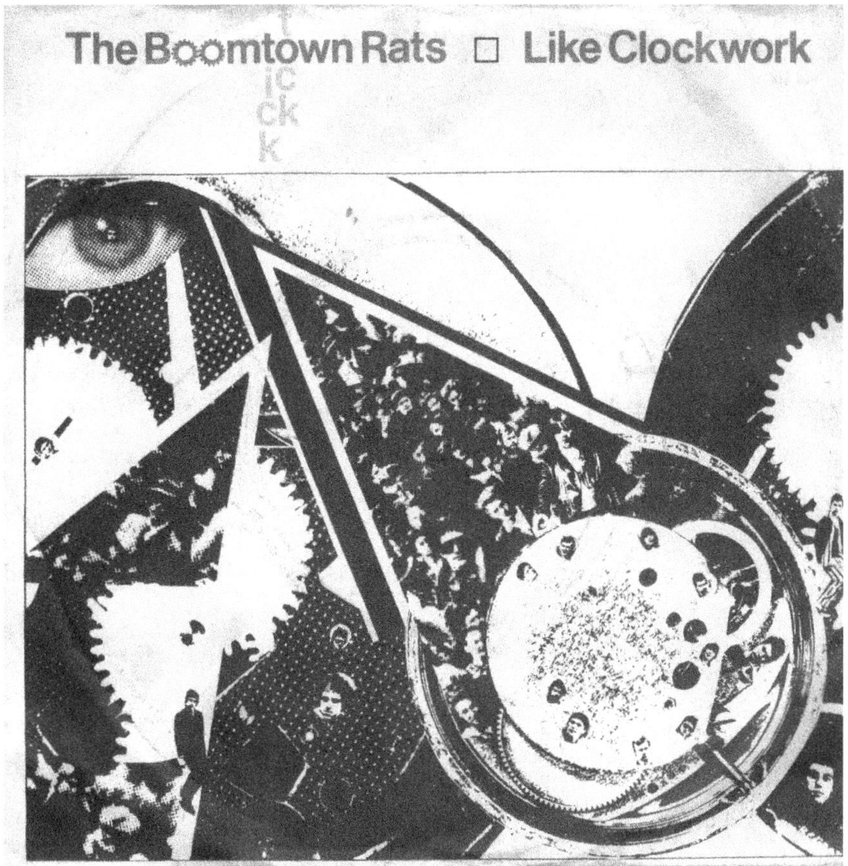

The Boomtown Rats—like Kraftwerk? (Author Collection)

Daniel Miller, whose 1978 single "TVOD" (released under the utterly unsuitable name of The Normal) is generally cited as year zero for independent electronica, made the record with a Korg 700s that he picked up used, and if Miller was one of the pioneering handful of practitioners who *didn't* need Donna Summer to tell them how to flick a switch, his audience, largely, wasn't. With their curiosity piqued by one, and reinforced by another, a steady stream of would-be synth mavens made a beeline to the nearest equipment store.

The Wasp was awaiting when they got there.

Named for its distinctive black-and-yellow livery, the Wasp synthesizer was launched in 1978 by Electronic Dream Plant (EDP), a newly established company founded by musician Adrian Wagner (the great-great-grandson of composer Richard Wagner) and designer Chris Huggett.

With a retail price of under £200, it was scarcely more expensive than a decent guitar, and while it was—compared to the titans of the breed—both tiny and primitive, it was also astonishingly versatile. The original two-octave Wasp boasted two digital oscillators supported by analog filters, envelopes, and controls; the battery-operated Deluxe that appeared the following year featured a three-octave keyboard, an oscillator mixer, and an external audio-input. Both had their own built-in speaker, and both were endearingly temperamental.

Even relatively minor fluctuations in temperature (the stage in a small, hot club, for example) could set the Wasp off into a fury of sounds without anybody even touching the device Its name and the venue long forgotten, one hapless band found itself so fascinated by its Wasp's selfish performance that its members laid their own instruments on the stage and joined the audience in watching the synth itself.

Neither was the Wasp the zenith of EDP's quest. By 1981, you could pick up a Gnat synthesizer for just ninety-nine pounds, and a Spider sequencer for a hundred more. Suddenly, even the most impecunious would-be performer seemed to be sporting their own brand-new synth, and the mysterious noise maker of just a few years before was now beeping and burping everywhere one turned.

One of the first albums ever to feature the Wasp (if not *the* first) was released within months of the instrument's appearance. *The Bridge*, by Thomas Leer and Robert Rental, was recorded in just two weeks early in the summer of 1979, with a pair of Wasps accompanied, as the sleeve notes put it, by "blips clicks & unseemly noises . . . generated by refrigerators [and] other domestic appliances." All "are intrinsic to the music."

Others were swift to follow. Blancmange started their electronic life, recalls Neil Arthur, with a "borrowed Wasp and an ARP Odyssey," before "Stephen borrowed a VCS3, and did some stuff."

Birmingham band Fashion were an early supporter, with a Wasp in full view when they appeared on the BBC TV music show *Look Hear!*, while another Birmingham band, future Duran Duran guitarist John Taylor's Dada, also got in early. So did teenaged electro-fans William Bennett and Philip Best, who used a Wasp throughout the early days of their band, Whitehouse, exponents of what they termed "extreme electronic music." Ricky Wilde, son of sixties pop idol Ricky, used a Wasp to write the song "Kids in America," a hit for his sister Kim.

Other equipment, too, suddenly became available. The Tascam Portastudio 144 was introduced in 1979 as the first genuinely affordable four-track tape recorder, one that could be set up in even the smallest space—ideal for budding home studio enthusiasts.

Roland's Dr. Rhythm DR-55 was a cut-price (in a good way) version of the CR-78 CompuRhythm, the percussive base of both John Foxx's *Metamatic* debut album, and Blondie's "Heart of Glass."

Korg's M500 Micro Preset attracted bargain hunters from 1977 on; and the Moog Prodigy, introduced in 1979, allowed even the most parsimonious purchaser to play behind the most recognizable logo in electronica. There was even a build-it-yourself synthesizer kit on the market, the magnificently named Powertran Transcendent 2000.

Not every band was starting from scratch. In the English city of Sheffield, Cabaret Voltaire had been experimenting and recording together since 1973, relying on homemade equipment until the prices started to drop.

Ultravox!, with major label Island Records behind them, were also suited and booted by the time "I Feel Love" came along. "I never actually got to grips with building anything myself," conceded John Foxx. "I never got on with soldering. Even though Tony Bassett was still at it.

"The synths we used were ARP Odyssey, Mini-Moog, Micro-Korg, and the British AMS. They were the first generation of reasonably affordable synthesizers, being scaled-down versions of the big, unattainably expensive modular synths. The drum machines were the TR77 and the Bentley Rhythm Ace—mainly used for cocktail lounge music, but we recognized they could be kidnapped and customized.

"The synths could all make a vast range of beautifully grungy, strange and ethereal noises and new rhythms."

But they could also go in the opposite extreme. "We had synths and drum machines and we used them to make a sort of sonic terror, as well as rhythm and atmospherics. We knew we could make bigger, filthier noises than any band around.

"We also considered the guitar to be an electronic instrument, working with feedback, distortion—even interjecting huge explosive sounds by simply kicking the spring reverb in the guitar amp. So, it was a mix of refined and debauched. That's what appealed to all of us.

"It was great fun putting everything through cheap MXR effects boxes to mutate the sounds even more. They made us sound very different from any other band—and that was precisely the idea. We were non-generic at a time when generic punk was in the ascent, and just before some writer coined the New Wave and Post Punk tag."

They were at work on their second album, *Ha! Ha! Ha!*, when "I Feel Love" first burst onto the radio. It immediately had an impact; not musically, but in terms of personal satisfaction.

Foxx: "We loved the record, [although] we'd already found our own voice, which was partly aligned with that kind of European electronica, but also with other elements we were developing.

"But it was an absolute validation of what I'd felt about the potential of electronica, and everyone involved with that was galvanized, of course. It also made record companies sit up and become very interested in bands with a synth, so this encouraged an entire movement to grow."

13

REMIX, REMODEL

To begin with, it didn't seem any different. The abrupt fade-in, the motorik rhythm, the opening "oooooh" . . . a year, give or take, since we first heard "I Feel Love," the record still sounded brand new, still sounded utterly unlike anything else that filled the floor.

But, this time, there was something else going on. We're still in seven-inch territory, edging toward the twelve-inch mix. And then, just past the three-and-a-half minute mark, the familiar began feeling strange. New rhythms. New effects, and even newer ones building on top.

Beneath, the sequencers maintained their metronomic pace. But above and around, even after Summer came back into earshot, layer upon layer of fresh robotics. Whip-crack rhythms, a whole new melody. Past the twelve-inch single's limit and still it goes on. Nine minutes, ten minutes . . . by the time it was finished, we'd been dancing for sixteen minutes, and still *nobody* knew what they'd been moving to. The disc jockey wasn't saying, either. Not until the night was over, and a few curious souls finally cornered him to ask . . .

What was that?

He picked up a plain white label single, with just a randomly affixed typewritten sticker to give the barest of details: "I Feel Love (Synthesized)," the record speed (thirty-three and a third) and the total duration, 16.04. Forty-six seconds shorter than "Love to Love You Baby," but how many more times the speed?

The search was on.

First the facts. "I Feel Love (Synthesized)" was a bootleg—that is, an unauthorized release of a record that someone had taken upon themselves to "remix."

Bootlegs weren't common back then, but they weren't exactly unusual, either. Later, into the early 1980s hip-hop era, such releases enjoyed a massive boom, but right now, the very-nascent movement's chosen media was still cassette tapes, just as its chosen sound source was the boom box.

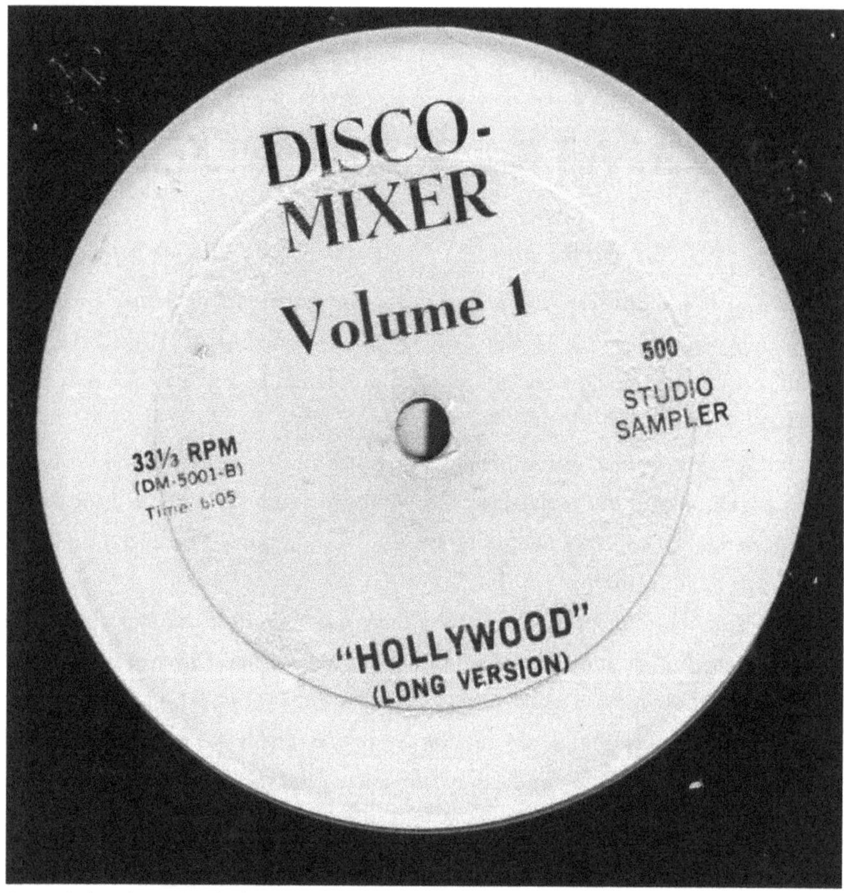

An early bootleg 12-inch disco medley. (Author Collection)

Vinyl, however, held sway in the discotheques, and with so many disc jockeys falling over one another to catch the next wave before anyone else was aware of it, there were a lot of pressing plants around the United States and Europe that were happy to slip out the odd "limited edition," of material that had either been illegally sourced, or unofficially tampered with. Remixed, in other words.

The vast majority of widely circulated bootleg releases tended to be medleys—special edits of songs that faded into one another across each side of a twelve-inch single.

The Hollywood Mix crew were among the first to get into the game, with their series of "Special Disco Mixers." The Disco 79 label unveiled the aptly named "Bits and Pieces," and so forth. A snatch of "I Feel Love" debuted in this world on the very first release by the Fusion label, alongside half a dozen other Moroder/Summer cuts.

These were a later development, however, slipping into sight around 1978. One of the very first bootlegs to appear on the dance scene was a straightforward repressing of Cameroon saxophonist Manu Dibango's "Soul Makossa," after a few copies of the French original arrived in New York as a French import in 1972.

A few copies found their way onto the dance floor and uncaged such a furor that *everybody* had to have a copy. Unfortunately, the sole importer in town, a company in Brooklyn, had long since sold out of its original stock, and it was weeks away from a larger consignment arriving.

The song that launched a thousand bootlegs. (Author Collection)

The bootleggers stepped in, a wave of pirate pressings that at least scratched the disc jockeys' itch. Cover versions began to appear . . . Afrique, the Lafayette Afro Rock Band, All Dyrections (on Neil Bogart's Buddah label), the Ghana Soul Explosion.

Finally, Atlantic Records put everybody out of their misery and gave Dibango's original record a US release. Its subsequent chart success would never have happened without the demands of the dance clubs.

A couple of years later, while the whole world was dancing to the Tymes' "You Little Trustmaker," a handful of DJs were able to air a version that no one had heard. Some enterprising soul had got their hands on an acetate copy of an earlier, unreleased, version, recorded in Philadelphia with the Three Degrees, and decided to bootleg that.

The New York Community Choir's "Express Yourself" was bootlegged in 1977, and Prince's "Sexy Dancer" in 1979. The mysterious Syster Slege was credited on a bootleg pressing of the somewhat better-known (and better-spelled) Sister Sledge's "Got to Love Somebody." A thirteen-minute "Mega Mix" of Michelle's "Disco Dance" was a must-have staple of the scene in early 1978. And now "I Feel Love" had fallen prey to the bootleggers.

As it turned out, that earlier Michelle mix, and this new assault on "I Feel Love" were both the work of the same man, a twenty-nine-year-old San Francisco-based disc jockey named Patrick Cowley. And, as much as Tom Moulton was regarded among the kings of the East Coast disco remix scene, so Cowley would soon establish himself as its West Coast counterpart.

More so, in fact. Indeed, it is often said, and hard to disagree, that Patrick Cowley was the nearest American disco ever came to having its own Giorgio Moroder.

Certainly nobody else in the field had such an intimate understanding of electronic dance as he, a point that he proved with his visionary extension of "I Feel Love." How, after all, do you improve upon a record that many listeners already regarded as perfect?

The fact is, he didn't. Listened to in cold isolation, away from the dance floor, the lights, and the bodies, a lot of Cowley's additions to the original record come across more as impositions, unnecessary additions to the stark simplicity of Moroder's initial creation.

But that is the case with a lot of "official" remixes, too, and when one remembers that Cowley was effectively working from home, with nothing more than the same pressing of the record as anyone could buy from any store (for, of course, he did not have access to the original master tapes), then his achievement becomes even greater.

In 2017, *MixMag* was still describing his 1978 bootleg as "the seminal track's finest rework" topping out, then, over efforts by such nineties-and-beyond masterminds as Danny Howells, Afrojack, and Masters at Work, and it wasn't surpassed, either, by Qattara, who reworked the song for inclusion in 2018's DC *Titans* television series.

Lauren Martin, who worked with Cowley for a time, recalled his working methods for Mixmag.com. "I used to stand there and watch over Patrick's shoulder while he worked on these electronic boxes and patch-boards and I just had no idea what he could be doing. . . . he didn't have sequencers and he didn't have MIDI. He was doing it the hardest way possible: by hand."

His mix complete, Cowley then needed to find an outlet for it. In the introduction to the published edition of Crowley's journal, another of his collaborators, Jorge Socarrás, recalled the night that "I Feel Love" debuted, at San Francisco's Trocadero Transfer.

"All those hundreds of sexy men dancing, mostly shirtless, throwing their arms up in the air in blissful abandon, pumping up the menergy—I'd not seen anything like it."

Cowley initially envisioned approaching Summer's own label to see whether it would be interested in doing something with the remix. His journal for October 16, 1977, reported "Casablanca Records possesses the extended, augmented version of 'I Feel Love' and I await their judgment."

The label ultimately passed on it, at least for now, and Cowley decided to take the underground route, instead. He had heard of a company out of a tiny New York office by mastering engineer Frank Trimarco, called Sunshine Sound. He had heard, too, that the firm tended not to ask questions about the discs it was pressing up.

It's unclear how many copies of "I Feel Love" were produced by Sunshine Sound; nor how many bootlegs of the bootleg might have followed in the wake of its initial success. But, by the time the Disconet remix company picked it up in 1980 for release on a subscription-only twelve-inch compilation of the hottest remixes around, Cowley's "I Feel Love" was already a legend on two continents. And two years after that, he finally received the official stamp of approval when his effort was released by Casablanca Records itself.

Cowley himself was considerably better-known by then. Early in 1979, with his "augmented" "I Feel Love" still knocking dancers dead in the discos, Cowley ran into a local San Francisco musician named Sylvester James Jr., at that time working toward his second album for the Fantasy label.

A limited edition 12-inch promo release for Cowley's "I Feel Love." (Author Collection)

Long a fixture on the San Francisco club scene, Sylvester's past included a couple of years (1970–1972) performing as part of the Chocolate Cockettes, an avant-garde African American gay troupe whose acclaim won admirers as far apart as Andy Warhol and Al Goldstein (publisher of *Screw* magazine), and saw them headline the Anderson Theater in New York.

From there, he moved on to his own blues-rocking Sylvester and the Hot Band, followed by the more dance-oriented Sylvester and Two Tons o'Fun—the latter subsequently better known as the Weather Girls.

That led him to former Motown producer Harvey Fuqua, and a deal with Fantasy, but while Sylvester's eponymous first album, in 1977, had been entertaining

The 7-inch edit of Cowley's remix, given an official Casablanca release in 1982. (Author Collection)

enough, it remained barely distinguishable from a lot of the other party-themed, strings and horn-driven records that were beginning to flood out.

Only the soaring falsetto Sylvester voice stood out, and it did so like a beacon in the dark. A talent like that demanded far more from the music than the musicians seemed capable of offering, and Sylvester knew it.

That was why he sought out Cowley. Perhaps he had heard "I Feel Love." Maybe he was already familiar with Cowley's work—the remix, after all, was simply Cowley's breakthrough record. He'd been making electronic music for five years or more, self-releasing it on limited-edition cassettes that he distributed around his friends, or loaning it to the soundtracks for locally produced gay porn films.

Feeling mighty real—Sylvester. (Photofest)

That latter was a course that many early bedroom synth pioneers found themselves turning to during the early to mid-1970s (and probably beyond) and, while history remains tight-lipped over who a lot of these people were, Cowley didn't care. His music was getting out there, and it was getting heard. Now Sylvester was promising to make it even louder.

By the time the pair got into the studio and started work on *Step II*, it was clear that the newcomer was bringing more than fresh ears to the sessions. "Pat" Cowley would ultimately be credited with adding synthesizer (String, Electro-comp 101 and 200 Models, Oberheim Ds-2 Sequencer) and "Special Effects" to the seven songs within, but the difference that he made to the Sylvester sound can never be reduced to a few brand names and model numbers.

From the moment the opening "You Make Me Feel (Mighty Real)" kicked in on a wave of adrenalined synth, it was clear that Sylvester had found his Tweety-Pie. Cowley's electronics subjugated every other instrument on the track, transforming it into dizzying symphony for voice and machine alone, a single side-long suite shifting seamlessly into (the admittedly inferior) "Dance (Disco Heat)," before moving back to back to "You Make Me Feel (Mighty Real)," as if realizing its mistake.

Released in mid-June 1978, *Step II* was, according to *Rolling Stone*, "as good as disco gets"—which may or may not have been damning with faint praise, but it was a quote-worthy clip regardless. Not that the record needed such things. "You Make Me Feel (Mighty Real)" topped the *Billboard* dance chart, stormed up the UK Top 10, and was just one of three, four, more Sylvester tracks you might hear on a night out that particular summer. Or, just as often, the one song you might hear three or four times a night.

Cowley would remain an integral component within Sylvester's band for the next couple of years, composer of both the title track and "I Need Somebody to Love Tonight" on the singer's next album, *Stars*, and an unmistakable presence across the three in-concert sides of the live *Living Proof* LP.

But Cowley also branched out in other directions. He produced the debut EP by a local new wave band, Indoor Life—the startling eponymous disc opens with "Voodoo," a thirteen-minute slab of edgy, jerky, mutant funk. In his own right, he ran up a clutch of killer singles that included the title tracks to his first two solo albums, *Menergy* and *Megatron Man*; he produced Paul Parker's 1982 dance smash "Right On Target," and Sylvester's "Do You Wanna Funk" that same year.

He was also responsible for a titanic fourteen-minute megamix of Tantra's "Hills of Katmandu," scything and excitable—reminiscent, in places, of what he'd done with "I Feel Love," but charged with an energy that even that had not packed. The instrumental intro alone is longer than many conventional singles, close to four minutes of building riffery and rhythm, and while it could be pointed out that Cowley's mix was in fact some two minutes *shorter* than Tantra's original album-side long vision, the difference lies in what happens during those minutes.

Cowley's own music, too, was dynamic—and, confrontational. "The boys in the back room, laughin' it up," he sings in "Menergy." "The guys in the street talk

Sylvester's Patrick Cowley-powered breakthrough hit. (Author Collection)

checkin' you out . . ." and then a sudden drop, a bass drum returning after a few beats' absence, an electronic orgasm as it hit the floor.

Few who heard it doubted that they were in on the ground floor of a talent that might dominate dance floors for years to come; even today, artists as far apart as the Pet Shop Boys and New Order credit Cowley with singlehandedly pioneering the Hi-NRG dance scene. Other ears have pointed to the more traditional electronic sounds he was recording earlier in life, and posit fresh dimensions there as well.

But Cowley himself was ill, laid low by a succession of minor ailments that, a few years later, would be readily recognizable among the early signs of HIV, but which, in 1982, simply baffled the medical community.

One doctor diagnosed food poisoning; others simply shrugged and sent him home.

Yet even as he lay dying, and *knowing* that he was doing so, Cowley remained indefatigable, recording his third and final album, *Mind Warp*, while reclining on a couch in the studio. According to author Joshua Gamson, "People propped him up by the synthesizer so he could work."

Cowley even referred to the work-in-progress as "my death record," and gawker.com would later describe *Mind Warp* as "the earliest full musical statement on [HIV's] invasion and takeover of the human body.

"By merely meditating on a disease that no one cared about, that no one of power would talk about, Cowley's disco was more political than most. It is a tough listen . . . it's hard to imagine anyone dancing to it today."

Mindwarp was released in October 1982, just as Cowley approached his thirty-second birthday. Weeks later, on November 12, he passed away, one of the first high-profile victims of the disease.

• • •

If Patrick Cowley is frequently described as America's first "modern-style DJ," Rusty Egan fulfilled that same role in the United Kingdom. As John Foxx puts it, "He set the pace in London, and this fed into lots of ensuing movements, right around the country."

Disc jockeys were already a power in the clubs, but hitherto their role had been to *play* music. Now, thanks to Egan's pioneering efforts, says Foxx, "they're a significant part of music-making itself.

"That's another change precipitated by the era begun by 'I Feel Love.'"

Egan first came to attention as the drummer with former Sex Pistol Glen Matlock's new band, the Rich Kids. Destined to cut just one album before disintegrating in December 1978, the Rich Kids specialized in what the UK music press had just began to term *power-pop*—which, it transpired, was a long way from the music that Egan personally preferred.

Bowie, Krautrock, dance music, those were the topics that Egan happily waxed rhapsodically on when talking to fans at Rich Kids gigs. He may not have been marking musical time during his tenure with the Rich Kids, but he was certainly keeping his eyes open elsewhere.

It was guitarist Jim "Midge" Ure who finally lit the touch paper that ignited Egan's ambitions.

Mighty mixer Patrick Cowley. (© Dark Entries Records)

Having first come to attention as a member of the short-lived teenybop sensation Slik, Ure had only recently been lured into the Rich Kids when he first heard "I Feel Love."

"That running sequence was just mesmeric. It was the palatable end of electronics, it was a huge commercial hit. 'Autobahn' was a hit, but it was still seen as a novelty, these weird guys from Germany. 'I Feel Love' was by Donna Summer."

He would not have the opportunity to act upon the song's inspiration. But in bandmate Egan, he swiftly discovered a kindred spirit.

Egan had recently linked with friends Dave Claridge and the flamboyant vision that was Steve Strange as founders of, and disc jockeys at regular Tuesday evening Bowie Nights, hosted at a somewhat sleazy Soho niterie called Billy's.

There, the night would be devoted to the music of Bowie, Roxy Music, Kraftwerk, and anything else that took their fancy, and fit the mood. Including "I Feel Love" and, that fall, Giorgio Moroder's newly released "Chase." Interviewed by Radio London DJ Gary Crowley some four decades later, Egan's enthusiasm for that track, and its effect on the dance floors, remained fresh and fulsome.

Billy's was not a unique venture. Crackers, a discotheque a few doors down from the Marquee Club on Wardour Street, was staging similar ventures as far back as 1975, with the introduction of its Bowie Nights. There, too, the city's young and beautiful would while away nights dancing to and dressing as their heroes—for Bowie's music was not all that was played there; much of Egan's later playlist could have been borrowed from the Bowie Nights fare.

Other venues, too, catered for a similar crowd, the Club Louise on Poland Street, where a red door with gold plates was guarded by Louise herself, an old French lady with heaped gray hair; and Chaguerama's . . . Shaggers . . . on Neal Street, a basement gay club secreted beneath the bustling Covent Garden wholesale produce market.

But Billy's was different. Perhaps because it was operated by people who shared their audience's musical tastes; perhaps because the DJ dug deeper for delights; or perhaps, simply, because Shaggers had closed (the space was swiftly reborn as the Roxy Club of punk renown), Louise's had changed and Crackers had fallen from fashion. Where else was there to go?

It doesn't matter. The fact was, Billy's one night a week quickly became *the* night of the week for a growing horde of . . . first, young Londoners, but soon people pouring in from other parts of the country, simply because the grapevine had whispered its name in their ear.

Midge Ure: "You could go down there on whatever night it was, and [Egan] was pumping out Telex or La Düsseldorf or Can or Kraftwerk or whatever, 'I Feel Love,' Moroder, all this electronic stuff, early Ultravox! . . .

"There was this thing happening and all this stuff was sounding fantastic on dance floors, and none of it came from jazz or blues or soul or America. It all came from cold middle Europe, and it was different. Every other form of music seems to have come from the blues, but this hadn't, it had come from Berlin or Düsseldorf, disaffection and vision, these austere, dystopian atmospherics. But it sounded fantastic, and all the sounds were being generated by an electronic instrument."

Quickly, and likewise inspired by word of mouth, similar clubs sprung up in other towns and cities. Some 230 miles north of the capital, Neil Arthur of Blancmange fondly recalls, "The Lodestar in Ribchester, right in the middle of nowhere. Saturday nights, where the oddities from my area of Lancashire used to drift and meet up, those who weren't necessarily into the mainstream.

"When I started going there, it was Roxy and Bowie, the Velvets, Lou Reed, and every so often the disc jockey would succumb and play an Eno track for me. They'd sometimes put Kraftwerk on, that kind of stuff, and people used to really dress up.

"My lot—my girlfriend and I, my mate and his girlfriend—were more into the Roxy thing, a tie and shirt, smart trousers, Oxford shoes, trying to look nice. Some of the other lot used to do more of a Bowie look, and you'd have the tall Bowie, the fat Bowie, the blond Bryan Ferry, it was interesting. It was a place full of oddities, whereas you wouldn't have been able to do that in the more conventional clubs."

That was the appeal. A place to be different . . . different even from the shock headed distortions of punk. But with that, there came a problem, too. Once past the obvious artists and records, there was very little music around that *did* fit the mood. Krautrock as a whole made sense in small doses, but audiences were never going to spend too long dancing to much of it. Play them often enough and even old favorites will soon be merely old.

No less than their counterparts in the mainstream discos, the disc jockeys working in clubs like this spent far more time auditioning *possible* inclusions into their set, than actually playing the ones that passed muster, because while a lot of *names* could be bandied around the average audience's "must-hear" wish list, the number of songs that actually worked was surprisingly small.

An ear bent to the conversations that drifted around the room was encouraging. A lot of ideas were floating around at the time; a lot of unknown would-be musicians were talking about taking their first steps into music. But just as the first punk disc jockeys, a couple of years earlier, had found it extraordinarily difficult to actually fill an evening with bona fide punk rock music, because so little had then been recorded or released, so this new wave of DJs found their options, too, were harshly limited.

Their punk predecessors got around the dilemma by introducing roots reggae to the brew, instinctively comprehending how the intention, if not the delivery, of the music dovetailed perfectly with punk's antiestablishment stance.

For Rusty Egan and Steve Strange, as they surveyed the growing success of Billy's, it was not so easy. They could delve deeper into the catalogs of the artists they were regularly playing, but only at the risk of alienating those audiences that only wanted to dance. So, that's a yes to "Trans-Europe Express," but a big no, for example, to "Ananas Symphonie."

And an awful lot of hope and faith placed in the news, early in the new year, that Kraftwerk themselves had a new album lined up, and it would be appearing in just a couple of months.

Giorgio Moroder, 1979. (INTERFOTO/Personalities/Alamy Stock Photo)

14

SPARKS IN THE DARK

Released in 1978, Kraftwerk's seventh album, *Die Mensch-Maschine* (*The Man Machine* for English-speaking markets) had its roots in the group's 1975 American tour, the band members' enthusiasm for the outing dulled by the mindless routine of traveling, performing, and being interviewed every day.

They began to dream—and, to begin with, it was only a dream—of replacing themselves with look-alike robots. Automata that would be able to play the music, conduct themselves at press conferences, do everything, in fact, that a functioning band needed to do once the music had been recorded.

It was a brilliant concept, particularly as it once again contained those elements of irony and double meaning that so appealed to the group's sense of humor: *worker*, in Russian, translates as "robotic."

Once they returned to Kling Klang, therefore, they set about having some built. And if these original creations were little more than carefully adapted showroom dummies, Kraftwerk's latest song would breathe in the life that they so obviously yearned for. "The Robots," the self-defining opening cut on *The Man Machine*, not only includes a reference to the "dancing mekanik." It also choruses with the most unequivocal lyric of all: "We are the robots."

A hit across Europe, Top 10 in the United Kingdom, *The Man Machine* would be played in its entirety on more than one occasion at the clubs that cared most for the music, and compete with (of all things!) an imported French novelty album of robot disco performed by, of course, the Robots, on the dance floors of America.

The difference was, Kraftwerk were believable. Again and again as *The Man Machine* unfolded, it really was credible that the music was the product of robotic energies alone, a testament not only to the power of Kraftwerk's music, but also to their powers of suggestion.

Wolfgang Flür: "We changed, time changed, and the music changed because of the developing of other tools, more technical things. The sequencer which we used for the first time on *Trans-Europe Express*, we developed more. We got more into

Kraftwerk—we are the robots, 1978. (Everett Collection/Alamy Stock Photo)

machinery. We were bound to that, and the machine handled us, we handled the machines, and we were getting together."

Ultimately, this union would prompt Flür to leave the band. "I noticed, two or three years later, what was happening to us. I was becoming a robot in my own personality, more and more speechless, until I wondered, who was directing who? And it made me sad because what was going on was not so nice. It was, in the end, the reason for my leaving Kraftwerk."

Yet, *The Man Machine* did contain some moments of stunning beauty, and none more so than the wistful "The Model." Indeed, three years (and one new album) later, that song would finally give Kraftwerk their second major hit, when it soared to number 1 on the British chart.

That, however, would be at the height of what the media termed the New Romantic movement, at a time when, if anything, simply *too much* electronic music was being thrown into this particular marketplace. For now, as 1978 marched on, the paucity was such that Rusty Egan finally decided that, if he wanted even more new music to play, then he would need to make it himself.

He would not be operating in a complete vacuum. Across the United Kingdom, noises were being made, tapes recorded, sounds manipulated. In New Cross, London, Little Bob Minor was recording his own compositions with a VCS3, a sequencer, and a tape delay, and hoping for a home on the cassette label Snatch Tapes.

In Manchester, Gerry and the Holograms (in actuality, CP Lee of the comedy troupe Albertos y Lost Trios Paranoias) were recording a self-titled piece as a response to the local Absurd label's recent demand for more unusual tapes—years later, on a U. radio interview, Frank Zappa proclaimed "Gerry and the Holograms" one of his twenty favorite records of all time.

In Liverpool, Orchestral Manoeuvres in the Dark were stirring. In Cabaret Voltaire's hometown of Sheffield, the Human League were taking their first steps out with the single "Being Boiled." In west London, DTTC were mourning "A Pixie Nicked My Girlfriend." All electronic, all heeding the siren call of electronica's sudden awakening.

Now the Rich Kids, too, were considering making a similar shift. Or, at least, half the band was. Midge Ure, wholly entranced by the music that Egan was playing, announced that he wanted to incorporate this new technology into the group. "So I bought a synthesizer, a Yamaha, and half the band loved it, which was Rusty and I, and the other half—Glen [Matlock] and Steve [New]—absolutely hated it."

Ure's choice of instrument was limited in its capabilities, "a four-note polyphonic thing. It wasn't particularly good, but it got me in there, got me interested and trying to copy what I was hearing.

"For me it was the punk ethos: if you can't play, you pick up a guitar and learn three chords and form a band. Well, it was the same thing with electronics, you bought a synth, you didn't have a clue what to do, and then you start recording in your bedroom. That's how the Human League were born, or Depeche Mode, or any

The Human League's debut single, "Being Boiled." (Author Collection)

of those bands. Up to that point, synthesizers were synonymous with Rick Wakeman; you had to be a boffin and a billionaire to buy one. But the technological revolution that happened in 1978 was astonishing."

Nervous Gender's Edward Stapleton agreed, happily reflecting for PostPunk.com upon "the punk aesthetic of non-musicians taking to the stage. . . . The idea of an instrument that could make other-worldly noise with the push of buttons and the turn of knobs was very appealing."

Ure remained limited in his abilities. But he was fascinated by his acquisition, and Rusty Egan happily encouraged him, no matter what consequence it might have for the continued survival of the Rich Kids.

"The synth certainly put cracks in the band," Ure reflected. Even as the musicians discussed recording a second album, it was clear that "we were in the final throes of the Rich Kids," and that was when "Rusty suddenly came up with the idea of 'wouldn't it be great to put together a studio band of all our favorite musicians,' and I said 'right, okay, stop. Let's do that.'"

The Rich Kids shattered, "and we started working on Visage. Rusty said 'my mate Steve Strange wants to be a singer, so he can do that,' and we just begged borrowed and stole studio time."

Visage would later be termed a supergroup, although at the time, such designations were far from anyone's mind. The bulk of the lineup that would record Visage's initial three song demo was borrowed from Magazine, a jerky, aggressive Manchester act formed by Howard Devoto after leaving the Buzzcocks. Egan and Ure respectively played drums and guitar, Billy Currie was drawn in from Ultravox (they had now dropped the ! from their name), Strange took lead vocals, and all concerned offered up a remarkable cover of Zager and Evans' 1969 hit "In the Year 2525" as their statement of intent.

A slow countdown intro, a vocoder overture, driving percussion, swooping synths, the tape swiftly found its way onto Egan's club play list; swiftly, too, producer Martin Rushent took one listen and agreed to finance further recordings. By September 1979, Visage's first single, "Tar," was hitting the dance floors.

Sessions for what would become Visage's debut album would eventually spread out over a year, primarily because of their parent bands' own touring and recording schedules. It was at the end of one of these enforced breaks, in fact, that Midge Ure's immediate future appeared before him.

"Ultravox come back from their American tour a broken band, and dropped by their record label, and that's how I ended up joining." John Foxx had departed for a solo career and, for a time, Ultravox lay moribund. In April 1979, however, the band regrouped with Ure at the forefront, and a ready-made audience at the club.

As with Visage, it would be another year or more before Ultravox finally made their move into the LP bins; their *Vienna* album, and the single of the same name, commenced moving up the UK chart just as Visage's "Fade to Grey" commenced its downward slide. Ure appeared on both, and if both bands were late in arriving at the party they had effectively thrown, it only meant that the festivities were in full swing. There was no need to break any ice.

"My mate Steve wants to be a singer . . . " Steve Strange. (Photofest)

Egan and Strange's club nights had moved on by now. After three months at Billy's, disagreements with the club's owner saw them shift their base to Blitz, a wine bar in Great Queen Street significantly equidistant from the two great central London art schools, St Martin's School and Central School.

Naturally, the audience that had developed at Billy's followed them, a self-styled exclusive (although less so every week) gathering of post punks, fashion designers, artists, and androgynies, all lining at the door to be policed by Strange in his role as club doorman. As much as the music being played within, it was Strange's oft-times unpredictable insistence upon what was and was not "appropriate dress" that contributed the most to the audience's flavor.

Ultravox with Midge Ure (second left). (Photofest)

His attitude was not unwelcome. Just as music becomes formulaic once the industry scents a "scene," so its uniforms become . . . well, *uniform*. Certainly it happened with punk, as the original welter of anything and everything was narrowed down to a numbing regimen of bondage pants, torn T-shirts, and lashings of safety pins.

Blitz went in the opposite direction entirely, an ocean of posing, preening, prancing, beautiful people in beautiful . . . *clothes* was the wrong word, for some turned up near naked, while others extemporized from whatever they found in the linen closet.

The movement was exclusive—right now, it didn't even have a name, which is probably why *The Face*, the newly launched music and fashion magazine whose birth coincided almost precisely with the movement, favored "the Cult with No Name." The traditional music press coined "the Now Crowd," and "the Futurists" was bounced around for a time, even titling a weekly Top 10 in *Sounds* newspaper,

Visage's maiden hit "Fade to Grey." (Author Collection)

compiled from Billy's own playlist. They were the "New Europeans" for a time, looking back to a golden age of pre–Great War decadence and style, and forward to the utopian federalization with the continent that lay at the end of the European Union rainbow. Thirty-five years later, many of those now-middle-aged New Europeans were doubtless numbered among the millions of Britons who voted not to be European after all. Is there a time limit on irony?

Ultimately, history would settle on "the New Romantics" as a suitable name for the weekly gatherings, although as Steve Strange once wearily remarked, "Why do we even have to have a name? It's only so they can shift newspapers, after all."

What did matter was the sheer volume of new music (and it was new) that was suddenly pouring out. As Ure put it, "It was a time when you were allowed to experiment, you were given the space, you were given enough rope to hang yourself, and thankfully the industry at the time had the wherewithal to let you experiment and not break the bank."

Not only at Blitz, not only across the United Kingdom. Throughout Europe, the United States, and farther afield, too, synthesizers were set to become the predominant musical instrument of the now-imminent new decade.

John Foxx: "It was a moment when there was a great hunger for ideas and new style. Punk had blown the doors open and radical style mutated out of that into many other forms.

"Through all these, various kinds of electronic dance music made the soundtrack . . . vindicating the earliest and more recognizably electronic outfits—The Human League, Orchestral Manoeuvres, etc.,—[but] also [feeding] into the punk inspired bands that had potential to evolve.

"It allowed a space for great bands like Joy Division, the Cure, and the Fall. There were the fringe artists spearheading the wilder side of synths—from Daniel Miller to Thomas Leer and Robert Rental and even Suicide. The clearing of the table achieved by 'I Feel Love' made a space for all that—and gave it all some commercial viability."

And, in the midst of this, that summer of 1979, Gary Numan soared to number 1 in Britain with the sublimely minimal "Are Friends Electric?" and even the synth's reputation for making novelty noises became redundant. Numan was a star and the Nu-men were taking over. By the end of the season, even David Bowie was taking heed.

First, he dropped by to document the impressions that would be poured forth in his spring 1979 hit "Boys Keep Swinging," filming the accompanying video at Billy's one day, and playing tribute, too, to one of West Berlin's most fabled nightclubs, dancer and singer Romy Haag's Chez Romy Haag. The sequence in which Bowie wipes his mouth and smears vivid lipstick across his face was a move that he'd witnessed Haag herself enact, during the time in which he lived in West Berlin.

The following year, Bowie was back at Blitz, this time to scoop up a clutch of the club's most distinguished regulars to appear in another video, "Ashes to Ashes." And suddenly there they all were, Steve Strange and co. on *Top of the Pops*, being pursued down a beach by a bulldozer.

David Bowie was not the only so-called veteran paying close attention to the new world, however. Ron and Russell Mael, the startlingly dissimilar siblings who fronted the California band Sparks, too, were paying attention.

In 1974, Sparks were enormous in more or less every major record buying market in the world bar America. By 1978, they'd not only departed the label they scored so many hits with, they were no longer with the one they'd signed to afterward. Two successive albums, *Big Beat* and *Introducing Sparks*, had vanished without trace, and the days of "This Town Ain't Big Enough for Both of Us" (a number 2 UK hit in 1974), "Something for the Girl with Everything" (Top 10 later that same year), and the epochal *Kimono My House*, *Propaganda*, and *Indiscreet* albums seemed far, far away.

It had been a good run, but a mercurial one. Nobody really expected to hear the duo's names, or front man Russell's angelic falsetto ever again. Sparks may not have been completely forgotten, because oldies radio would always have time for the oldies. But they were certainly gone.

Fortunately, nobody told them any of that.

The brothers were at home in Los Angeles the first time they heard "I Feel Love," and their ears pricked up immediately. Neither Ron nor Russell can remember who heard it first; only that, as it sank deeper into their consciousness, a radical notion began to form.

Sparks had always prided themselves, even before fame came along . . . and certainly after it departed again . . . of never allowing their last album to influence the sound of their next. In fact, that was probably why they'd fallen from grace in the first place.

Their audience wanted another "This Town Ain't Big Enough for Both of Us"; Sparks offered them "Tits" instead. Few people, the pair agreed, knew what they might do next. And absolutely no one, as Russell put it, "had any idea of what a disco producer working with an eccentric rock band would end up sounding like.

"We were really excited about 'I Feel Love.' We'd been bored with working with bands, thinking we'd tapped out all we could at that particular point from the traditional band context and format. We wanted to try some other approach . . . we were doing as we do every so often, just journeying to find some new kind of context in which to place what we're doing.

"We'd heard 'I Feel Love,' and thought that this was something amazing, and that it might be interesting for us to see if there would be a way to put Ron's songwriting and lyrics, and my singing, into a completely different framework than we'd been working in the past."

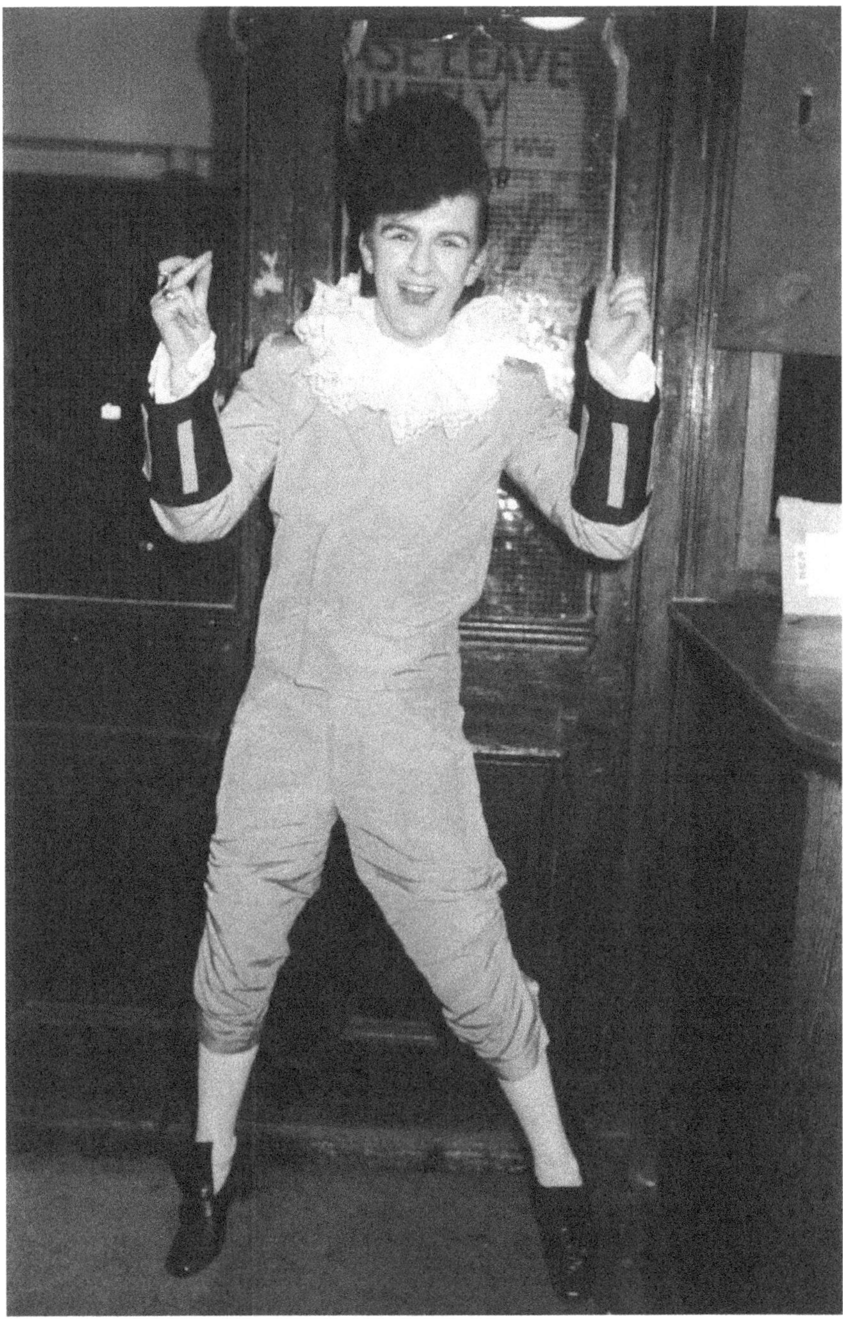

Welcome to Blitz—it's 1980! (Mirrorpix/Alamy Stock Photo)

Comeback of the year—Sparks and *The Number 1 Song in Heaven.* (Author Collection)

In fact, they were so enthusiastic that they actually told a visiting German journalist that Moroder would be overseeing their next project, before they had even tried to approach him.

"We told her and, of course, of all the people living in LA, she happened to be close friends with Giorgio.

"But she was instrumental in helping us to reach him, and he was really keen to work with us, too, because he'd not worked with a proper band and a band sensibility. So, he was up for the challenge. He thought it would be interesting for him to branch out in another area. It was a really interesting collaboration."

The brothers admitted that they were flying blind. No matter that "I Feel Love" was the song that drew them into Moroder's orbit, still they went into the studio with no idea what might emerge.

They had already started working toward a new Sparks album, but the sessions were going nowhere—that was one of the reasons they wanted to contact Moroder in the first place. Neither was Moroder especially impressed by the songs they had to play him—a couple of numbers left over from the last album, and half a dozen more that had been recorded as demos (and rejected by every label that heard them). He would green-light just two of them, "Academy Award Performance" and "Beat the Clock," and both of those would be dramatically reconfigured by the time they saw vinyl.

Indeed, all of Sparks' traditional working methods would be flung out, as Moroder even shattered what had hitherto been Ron Mael's inviolable domination of Sparks' songwriting. No less than four of the eight songs on what became Sparks' *No. 1 in Heaven* album were written by Moroder and Russell Mael alone.

It was still a hard slog. Even with Moroder firmly at the helm (the duo signed to his production company as the sessions commenced), the music industry in general seemed to have no interest in the project. In Europe and the United Kingdom, the Maels were regarded as has-beens; in America, they were never-weres.

Weeks turned to months and the rejections continued piling up; almost a year after the album, *No. 1 in Heaven*, was finished, Virgin Records' UK office finally agreed to take a chance on the band, and even then, there was what Russell described as "some head scratching. . . .

"People understood Sparks to be a band, a rock band with a slightly different sensibility. So, when you throw into the mix that it's now not got guitars and it's icy electronic music. . . . The irony is, there were more hit singles on that album than on any of the ones before it."

Things continued moving slowly. "Number One Song in Heaven," truly the one song on the album that absolutely established how vastly different this new Sparks was from those that preceded it, was released as a single in February 1979, and, for eight long weeks, it stubbornly refused to sell.

The clubs were playing it, though, especially those that had sprung up in the wake of Blitz, and whose denizens remembered Sparks for all the glorious records that soundtracked the glam rock era. In late April, the single finally drifted into the UK Top 40; by mid-June, it had become Sparks' biggest British hit in five years.

Sparks' "Beat the Clock" hit single. (Author Collection)

By which time, ironically, Sparks' idea of turning conventional rock/pop notions on their head by bringing to that genre all that "I Feel Love" had brought to disco was not such a revolutionary idea after all.

The very same week that Sparks appeared on *Top of the Pops* with their second Virgin single, the now hyperventilated "Beat the Clock," the duo was joined in the television studios by not one, but two fellow purveyors of the suddenly unleashed electro beat, M performing the irresistibly overexcitable "Pop Musik," and Mike Oldfield, the latest rock artist to "go disco," with the pounding "Guilty."

Gary Numan's "Are Friends Electric?" was sitting on the top of the charts; the Flying Lizards' harshly computerized revision of the old R&B staple "Money" was girding its loins for its own chartward thrust. Had *No. 1 in Heaven* only come out when it was actually finished, Sparks would have had the entire field to themselves.

Climbing four places higher than its predecessor, "Beat the Clock" made it to number 10 on the UK chart; a third single, "Tryouts for the Human Race" (a song about sperm, Ron acknowledged later, although the video depicted the brothers transforming into werewolves) made it to number 45. As comebacks go, it was rather impressive.

The album from which all three came, however, did not do so well.

While Sparks were certainly cleaning up on the dance floors, the critical establishment was less certain about their rejuvenation. Indeed, while the media could not get enough of the erstwhile Johnny & the Self Abusers, whose *Life in a Day* LP self-confessedly owed much to the Sparks of old (Simple Minds kept their Damascene conversion at the hands of Donna Summer to themselves), Sparks were treated like pariahs.

Disco sucked as hard in the United Kingdom as it did in the United States; harder, in fact, in the eyes of the establishment critics, for whom all this newfangled electronica was scarcely even worth referring to as a musical genre. Nobody asked about the technology that created the record; nobody praised Sparks (and Moroder)'s ingenuity. All they wanted to know was, "Why did you make a disco album?"

Sparks had no answer. They'd not even been expecting the question. Ron acknowledged that yes, maybe the record did have a disco element. But they'd hoped people would see past that, and applaud them for their true achievement. A full album that combined that element with so many others.

Neither was the band's original fan base especially impressed. The electro-nerds liked the record; the boffins in their bedrooms, too; and collectors of exotically colored and sleeved singles were overjoyed as Virgin pulled out all the marketing stops for the three singles.

But others, and that included great swathes of Sparks' original fan base, were utterly nonplussed. Neither the Rolling Stones nor Rod Stewart had yet been forgiven for "going disco," as their critics accused, and Sparks weren't going to be allowed to get away with it, either.

"*No. 1 in Heaven* was blasted by fans," Russell reflected in a 1983 interview. "They called us disco traitors, when in fact we saw it as a chance to work with Moroder who was into electronics with a neat beat like nobody else. It wasn't the pejorative 'disco music'—call it 'dance music' today and it's cool again!"

Besides, although they may not have been traditional Sparks fans, the people who did understand *No. 1 in Heaven* really understood it.

Sounds journalist Sandy Robertson was one of those who were quick to applaud the brothers' guile. Moroder, his review declared, was "the best filter for their ideas since [Todd] Rundgren," while Sparks themselves "have exhibited a laudable talent for survival and staying on top of the heap (something I thought was quite beyond them these days). Ethereal vocals and shimmering tunes and wires come across like a mating of Popol Vuh and music for dancing fools."

He doubted, he admitted, whether *No. 1 in Heaven* "will go down in history as one of the all-time hot one-hundred albums, but it's icy sharp and fresh. 'Beat the Clock,' Sparks sing. They've done it, too."

"Moroder's finest achievement," agreed another UK magazine, *Smash Hits*, "must be in picking up the shambolic, played-out remains of the once fine Sparks, plugging the dubious twosome into the mains and making them what the music business would term a 'viable proposition' once more."

• • •

Making his first television appearance alongside Mike Oldfield that night, when Oldfield's "Guilty" and Sparks' "Beat the Clock" were both tearing up the UK chart, was keyboardist Tim Cross.

From his own back room studio in London's Baron's Court, where a copy of the "I Feel Love" twelve-inch was conspicuous within his record collection, Cross had already been experimenting with electronic pop for some months before he was introduced to Oldfield. He would remain a mainstay of Oldfield's band for much of the next three years, while he also recorded and gigged with punk icons the Adverts. But any additional downtime was devoted to a projected solo album.

Hello would never see release . . . indeed, by the time of Cross's death in 2012, he no longer even knew where the tapes to the album might be. In the context of the era in which it was made, however, it was a remarkable collection.

Entirely self-composed and -performed, *Hello* comprised a succession of short, two- to four-minute pop songs that sparked and startled their way out of Cross's newly purchased Crumar DS-2 synthesizer.

Hitherto better known for manufacturing organs (and, prior to that, accordions), Crumar introduced the DS-2 to the market in 1979, one of the first synths to feature digitally controlled oscillators. Never ranked among the most fashionable

Tim Cross at home, 1979. (Photo by Dave Thompson)

makes, it was a versatile beast regardless and it was certainly ideal for Cross's purposes, both onstage and in the studio, and at home, too, where it was allied with a wealth of other, treated (or treat*able*), instruments—guitar, voice, and in lieu of percussion, a collection of empty cardboard boxes that Cross arranged and played like a xylophone.

One track, "Tube," rerouted "Trans-Europe Express" along a London underground rail line; another, "Silent Heartbeat in the Night" (later to be covered by blues singer Dana Gillespie) conjured both a heartbeat and the night from the electronics. Indeed, a fanzine of the time described it as what might happen "if Squeeze and Simple Minds met David Bowie in an 8-track studio in [Hammersmith] . . . and if you can imagine that, well that's a tribute to the originality of the music."

Today, *Hello* is a reminder of just how much music was being made at this time that did not see daylight; that either remains buried away on forgotten cassette tapes, or was finally scraped out on some future compilation. How much great music.

Like Cross, the late Rikki Sylvan was another largely unsung hero of this singular moment in time. His band, Rikki and the Last Days of Earth, were—like Ultravox!—already brewing their own gloriously doom-laden drama when "I Feel Love" first impacted upon them. Indeed, their *For the Last Days* album stands alongside Ultravox's debut as an early pinnacle of punk's relationship with electronics.

The Summer hit did not pass Sylvan by, however. Last Days bassist Andy Prince recalls, "Moroder's use of a sequencer did have an influence on Rikki, although his solo Moog album, *Radio Mercury*, was more indicative of this than *For the Last Days*." Already heavily influenced by Wendy Carlos and Kraftwerk ("of course," adds Prince), Sylvan excitedly added a sequencer and more to his arsenal, before recording the album in late 1978. When *Goldmine* magazine credited Sylvan with "pav[ing] the way for 80s' [New] Romantic acts," it was *Radio Mercury* that truly signposted the way. Sadly, it, too, has yet to see the light of day.

• • •

Today, there are several Internet projects inviting the era's bedroom pioneers to finally bring their unreleased or painfully rare music out into the open; a growing corpus of CD compilations, too. And even after skimming off the eventual superstars whose earliest strivings are now regarded (at least by them) as formative novelties . . . names like Soft Cell, Thomas Leer, the Human League, Depeche Mode, Blancmange, Orchestral Manoeuvres in the Dark . . . the sheer diversity of what remains is breathtaking.

To sample just the UK side of the equation, from Sheffield to Shepton Mallet; from Bognor Regis to a bedsit in Bangor, D.I.Y. Electro was the sound from *beyond* the suburbs, a nationwide shriek against the hegemony of three guitars and a chord, wordless anarchy in the United Kingdom's decay. Add the United States and Europe to the equation and similar similes pile up like car crashes. Wherever it hailed from, however, at its best, it was the most exhilarating noise on earth.

That is an important caveat—"at its best." As anyone who lived through those times will recall, a lot of pointless farting around was unleashed in the name of electronic music, particularly once the likes of Leer, Robert Rental, and Daniel Miller scored a degree of cultish fandom with their earliest releases, and provoked their own surge of imitators.

But Malcolm Brown's "Sedation Strokes," all thudding footsteps and screaming panic; Inter City Static's "Fractured Smile" ; British Standard Authority's positively demented stab at Rod Stewart's "Do Ya Think I'm Sexy?" . . . so many great performances came busting out of nowhere.

Some acts demanded more than even the most open-minded audience was likely to offer. The likes of Throbbing Gristle and the American Boyd Rice flirted with the furthest extremes of both sonic and cultural propriety. From Akron, Ohio, Devo made mutant disco in lab coats and funny hats. And the intriguingly named 3 Teens Kill 4 delivered dislocated New York post-punk via a series of agitated home recordings scratched out by the simple expedient of turning on the cassette recorder and doing . . . whatever.

Taping things off the radio and inserting them into the soundscape; coaxing mutant, rumbling beats from Casio drum and Korg rhythm machines, 3 Teens Kill 4 concocted a savage collage of urban decay and headline news, wrapped up inside the slinkiest dance sensibilities.

A report on the attempted assassination of Ronald Reagan unfolds around stentorian neo-rap; "Crime Drama" is semispoken word set to sci-fi space junk having a seizure; "Circumscript" is an oasis of pop purity that could have crackled out of any decent new wave jukebox of the age; and "Hut/Bean Song" is seven minutes of robotic S&M set to a foreboding marching beat, before morphing into a childish chant about breast exercises.

Not every experiment along such visceral lines was so successful, but that is always the case. Besides, "success" itself is relative. Some performers were happy simply to get their music down on tape. Others were content with seeing it released, either independently by the wealth of labels that other would-be enthusiasts were launching, or even by a major label.

The fact that they were doing it was enough.

Sparks, on the other hand, were less sanguine about such matters. Their next album to be recorded under Moroder's aegis, *Terminal Jive*, was released less than two months after the final single from *No. 1 in Heaven* had run its course and, initially the portents were good. A review in *Melody Maker* could only delight the album's makers, as writer Harry Doherty declared, "The three tracks that open side two ['Young Girls.' 'Noisy Boys' and 'Stereo'] are persuasive arguments in favor of this being their best-ever album.

"*No. 1 in Heaven* saw Ron and Russell Mael as rock'n'roll people in a disco world, bowing to Moroder's superior experience and technique. *Terminal Jive* reverses the terms of the partnership and has Moroder playing in Sparks' court. It's an even more compelling venture than last year's."

Again, Ron Mael's songwriting was restricted; he penned just two songs solo, and the remainder with Moroder and members of his crew. Sparks' manager Joseph Fleury later revealed that Ron was not even permitted to play keyboards on the record, "and he was never happy about that arrangement. But you have to remember that Giorgio was very powerful at that time, and had done a lot for Sparks, so there was a feeling that he knew the market and what it wanted a lot better than we did.

"So when he said Ron's writing was sometimes a little on the crazy side, and that people needed something else, we thought 'well yeah, and you're the guy who can provide that, because you've had all these hits.' Forgetting that whenever Sparks have been the most successful, it's because Ron is completely off on his own tangent and not paying any attention to the market. We forgot that, but we were reminded of it very quickly, once the record came out."

Neither were Sparks impressed when they discovered that, while Moroder was nominally overseeing the sessions, the bulk of work was to be protégé Harold Faltermeyer, and while the duo had forgiven Moroder for throwing out most of their proffered songs at the outset of their relationship, they were less impressed when Faltermeyer did the same thing.

Twenty new compositions were offered up for consideration; Faltermeyer approved one, although in that instance, his judgment could not be faulted. The ballad "When I'm with You" went on to spend six weeks atop the French chart.

France was, however, the only market that did seem to appreciate *Terminal Jive*, as Ron later admitted. "People suddenly started aligning us with the whole disco thing. We were no longer a real band, we were a synth duo and, at the time, there was no room for synth duos."

"At that time" is a key remark. When Sparks returned with their next album, 1981's *Whomp That Sucker*, they had formed a new band around themselves. Unfortunately, synth duos were now *the* hot ticket.

Ever philosophical, the Maels took it all in their stride, and forty years on from the Moroder adventure, Sparks remains a force in modern rock, with their entire back catalog spread out behind them to the delight of a new generation of fans. And if *Terminal Jive* is still regarded with some suspicion, *No. 1 in Heaven* is widely regarded among the best they ever made.

When Sparks returned to the United Kingdom in 1994 to play a sold-out comeback show at the Shepherds Bush Empire—their first British concert since 1975—"Number One in Heaven" was the song they chose to open with, and it really was one of those moments that you wish you could bottle and keep forever, standing in a shuffling crowd, nobody knowing quite what to expect, and then the familiar synth refrain rising over the crowd noise, the heavenly choirs as the lights went up. . . . It was magical.

They revisited the song again for 1997's *Plagiarism* collection of rerecorded oldies, with Bronski Beat front man Jimmy Somerville now supplying the heavenly vocal; and Sparks even got around to performing all the songs from both *Number 1 . . .* and *Beat the Clock* live for the first time, when they took over Islington Academy in London for twenty nights in May 2008, to run through the entire back catalog, one album per night.

And out in the audience, musicians who might never have even glanced at a synthesizer had they, like the Maels, not first heard "I Feel Love" gathered to pay grateful homage.

15

ARE FRIENDS ECLECTIC?

Gary Numan's emergence was volcanic. One minute, the world had never heard of him. The next, he was everywhere.

Some fifteen years after the fact, Rozz Williams, founder of Los Angeles art rock combo Christian Death, recalled his first exposure to Numan's sound.

"You know what it's like, you're listening to the radio, but not really listening, it's just on, and suddenly they play something that makes you just drop everything.

"That's what happened. . . . 'Are Friends Electric?' . . . came on and I was—'is it Bowie?' And then, 'is it Donna Summer impersonating Bowie?' Because 'I Feel Love' had the same effect and, at that time, they were the only people who had made 'pop' records that sounded like that.

"The relentless synthesizer loop, lots of people in the underground were doing that, Kraftwerk included, but this obviously wasn't them. And it was Tubeway Army, Gary Numan."

Numan is shockingly modest about his accomplishment; and honest, too, regarding the immediate conflict between his image, and his actual intentions. On video and television, and on record as well, Numan came over as distant, dislocated, icicle cold. A robot in a twenty-one-year-old's clothing.

"I never intended it to be like that. I don't know how much of that was due to me having asthma, late teenage anxiety, 'poor little misunderstood me,' there could have been a lot of that. My absolute fear of being in and around people, not knowing what to say, clumsy and awkward."

His own isolation, too, played a role in the image he presented. "I didn't have children or family and [music] was all I wanted to do. Every single part of it was down to my shoulders, and it was made more difficult for me because I didn't have management, and I was with a very little record company at the time. They had no experience either, nobody to guide you or help you with all this huge amount of pressure, the hostility of the press which was pretty extreme at the time, it was a lot to deal with and it was difficult."

He sought refuge in his own thoughts, but there was no respite there. "I did a lot of thinking because some of [what was happening] was great, but some of it was very demoralizing, and I was thinking about that a lot . . . the way I saw it was so slanted, so skewed because it was so massive so sudden.

"[The fame] was pretty much overnight. My whole life was different, even for a mature man that wasn't on the autism spectrum, it was a real challenge not to be affected by that."

Numan effectively recorded just two albums in the vein that established his fame; thereafter, although electronics remained to the fore, his approach to them became more varied with every release—"I remember when I first played *Dance* [1981] to [the record company head], I could see the disappointment on his face. The problem I think I had was, what started out as natural . . . the flow from one thing to another as life gives you new experiences and you keep adapting, it soon became a contrived series of changes and that's may be where I started to lose my way, changing for the sake of change. The person making the music I was making was not who I was, the things that had an impact on me early on stopped having an effect."

Assuming a listener is willing to take the recorded rough with the smooth (his late eighties and early nineties were not a banner period), Numan remains among the most entertaining and intriguing artists to emerge from the post–"I Feel Love" diaspora.

But he was by no means the only one.

Keith Forsey, drummer on so many great Moroder productions and, prior to that, with Amon Düül II and Udo Lindenberg's Panik Orchestra, stepped out in his own right as a producer.

In Munich, his precision chops underpinned a string of Donna Summer albums, Sparks' *No. 1 Song in Heaven*, the Munich Machine's *Whiter Shade of Pale*; elsewhere, Boney M, Lipstique, and Claudja Barry all benefited from his presence.

The Moroder mood, if not exactly its sound, was also in Forsey's mind when he did finally move into production in 1980, helming Generation X's genre-splitting "Dancing with Myself" single.

The band did not disguise the song's inspirations, either musically or in period interviews. Formed in the very first wave of British punk bands, Generation X had mutated considerably in the years since then, and were now drawing their intentions from the sounds and, lyrically, the sights of the discotheque. Recently back from a tour of Japan, bassist Tony James explained, "all the discos have mirrors and the people over there all dance with their own reflections."

Generation X had broken up by the time it was released as a single. But "Dancing with Myself"'s breathtaking collision of punk energy and disco sensibilities posited a private future that few other bands had ever even dreamed of; one that vocalist Billy Idol grasped with both hands. Over the next three years, the Forsey/Idol team continued to triumph, while Forsey was there, too, for Simple Minds' big American breakthrough in the mid-1980s, producing and cowriting "Don't You Forget About Me."

For sheer consistency even over a short period of time, however, only one act truly (if you'll pardon the pun) synthesized the linkage between disco and electronica, between "I Feel Love" and "Are Friends Electric?," between raw sexuality and icy dislocation. Or, as Duran Duran's Nick Rhodes put it, took "the original punk ethic, and [bound] it up with the electronic music of Kraftwerk and Giorgio Moroder and all that disco stuff as well."

In Manchester, in northern England, Joy Division had risen from the post-punk ferment with a sound that was almost revolutionary in its stark monotony, chill and darkness. Yet, though they remain the root cause of the myriad bands that would go on to be described as gothic rockers, Joy Division themselves thought they were actually very danceable.

"It was very unsettling," bassist Peter Hook reflected two decades later. "To go from being nothing, to being lauded as one of the darkest groups known to man, was a trifle confusing." He never understood, he continued, "why people thought we were so miserable, because I thought it was quite exciting."

Musically, it didn't always sound like that, but it is no coincidence that three of the band (following vocalist Ian Curtis's death in 1980) should go on to form the massively successful New Order. And, in among the influences that they carried with them from their debut album, *Unknown Pleasures*, to the sessions for their second, *Closer* . . . Iggy Pop and Kraftwerk, Bowie and the Clash . . . they were also listening to Giorgio Moroder.

They already had the necessary equipment to hand—guitarist Bernard Sumner's ARP Omni-2, producer Martin Hannett's ARP 2600 Modular analogue synth, a Simmons SDS-V drum synthesizer. They just hadn't quite decided what to do with it all. And then, one evening, "we were out in this London burger place and a . . . Moroder track came on."

Talking with *Mojo* magazine forty years on, drummer Stephen Morris could not remember precisely which song it was, but he suspected, "maybe . . . the Patrick Cowley remix" of "I Feel Love." "And one of us said 'wouldn't it be great to do something like this?'"

The album track "Means to an End" was the result. Morris continued, "I remember hearing that played back [in the studio] and thinking, 'fucking hell! People could dance to this!'" In 2012, New Order repaid their earlier selves' debt to "I Feel Love" when they included it on *Back to Mine*, a self-curated compilation of songs that they considered the greatest influence upon their music, past and present.

Closer, Joy Division's second and final album, was released in April 1980, around the same time as Liverpool's Nightmares in Wax debuted with their own, equally personalized interpretation of what electronic dance should sound like.

Fronted by Pete Burns, subsequently of Dead or Alive, Nightmares in Wax's "Black Leather" was an X-rated paean to the joys of "big filthy muscle boys on motorbikes," with a motorik rhythm to match, and a lyric that borrowed from both Iggy Pop and David Bowie's "Sister Midnight" and KC & the Sunshine Band's "That's the Way (I Like It)."

Nor would that influence fade, as Dead or Alive went on to score, in 1984, their first big hit with a (reasonably) straightforward cover of the latter song.

"I Feel Love," too, continued to figure in that band's musical makeup, as guitarist Wayne Hussey, later of the Mission but an integral part of Dead or Alive throughout their formative early eighties, recalled.

"We started going to gay clubs and ['I Feel Love'] was still a big favorite there." He admitted he didn't really pay attention to "I Feel Love" when it was released—"I was a guitar player and there were no guitars on it." But, as Dead or Alive rose up to embrace the Hi-NRG sonics that would characterize their greatest hits, he learned to appreciate it.

"It's classic. I've got the extended twelve-inch of it somewhere . . . yeah, it was a classic. I actually tried to get my guitar to sound like a sequencer; I found a way of doing that, introduced it to Dead or Alive and the result of that was me losing my job. And then Pete [Burns] went off and got some real sequencers of his own."

The other band that melded these same musical sensibilities to a worldview that was poised on the darkest extreme of depravity was Soft Cell. The difference was, whereas Pete Burns would never abandon his outsider status, Soft Cell spent much of

Dead or Alive frontman Pete Burns. (Simon Fowler/Photofest)

their career trying to reclaim it. A worldwide number 1 with the effervescent synthi-pop of "Tainted Love," necessitated that.

A duo formed in the northern city of Leeds by art students Marc Almond and Dave Ball, what became Soft Cell was originally fertilized when Almond and another student, Kris Neate, set themselves up as the brains behind the latest club venture to illuminate the English nightlife.

It was staged ever Monday night at the Warehouse, a self-styled "super-discotheque" launched by one Mike Wyen—according to Almond, the Warehouse already boasted the best sound and lights in the north of England, and played host, too, to the region's most beautiful style-setters, glitterati, who came from far and wide to experience its soon-to-be-legendary hedonism. What Almond and Neate did was open that hedonism even further.

Originally, they saw their venture simply as their hometown's answer to the sudden insurgence of fashionable "new music" niteries elsewhere. Such clubs, after all, were no longer new testing grounds for costumes and outrageousness, alone.

They were a breeding ground for new bands, too: Eric's in Liverpool, from whence Echo & the Bunnymen, the Teardrop Explodes, and Frankie Goes to Hollywood would emerge; Barbarella's in Birmingham, where Duran Duran were fusing disco with the Sex Pistols; and back in London, where a crowded club scene became even more hectic with the arrival of the Cabaret Futura, Hell, and Le Beat Route, the seething funk of Spandau Ballet established them as the entire scene's first true superstars.

Soft Cell played their first ever live show at the Warehouse, very early on into the Monday club's lifetime, interrupting the disc jockey's routine of Bowie, Throbbing Gristle, and Donna Summer with a set that already included future Soft Cell favorites "Facility Girls" and "Metro Mr X," plus the showstopping "Martin," inspired by George Romero's teenaged vampire movie.

Just weeks later, they were a natural homegrown attraction for the Futurama II festival of post-punk music; and had also come to the attention of one of the original Blitz kids, Stevo, as he prepared to launch his own record label, the purposefully misspelled Some Bizzare.

Stevo was already a force to be reckoned with on the scene. Deejaying at the Clarendon Hotel in west London's Hammersmith, his Electro Tunes dance sets ranked among of the most compulsive nights out that London offered. He also compiled the weekly Futurist chart for the weekly music paper *Sounds*, drawn both from the requests he received and his own private tastes.

One chart, from December 1980, captures both the mood and the variety of a typical Stevo set—Bowie's "Ashes to Ashes," Numan's "I Die, You Die," Joy Division and Iggy Pop, the Human League and Ultravox, Cabaret Voltaire and Modern English. By early the following year, the chart had proved so popular that Stevo was now compiling two, one Top 10 for Atmospheric Dance, another titled No Guitars.

Would-be bands paid attention. As Stevo packed up his gear at the end of a night, another pile of home demos would cascade onto his turntables, from bands who'd heard the music Stevo played and hoped he'd find the same qualities in theirs.

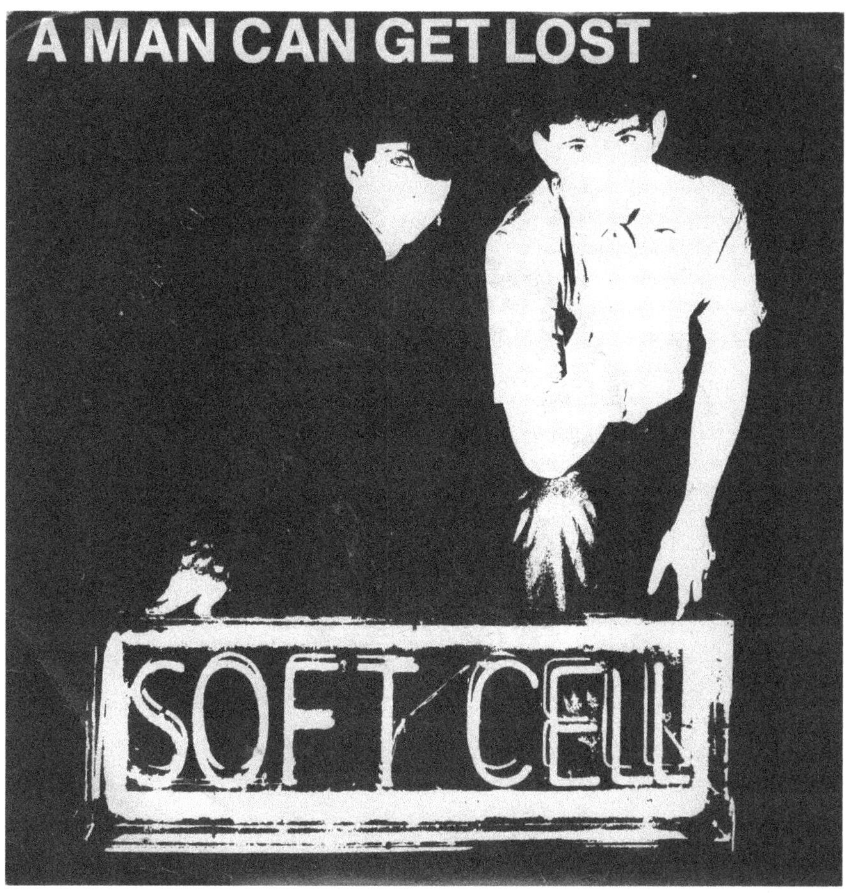

Soft Cell's debut 45 has its B-side top billing on the sleeve. (Author Collection)

A lot of the tapes that he took home (and which also flooded in via the mail) were rubbish, but some showed genuine promise—not enough, maybe, to interest a real record label, but certainly enough to demand a wider hearing. Soon, they too were finding their way into his weekly chart; that same December, a demo by Naked Lunch made the listing. Soon, it would be joined by similar offerings from Soft Cell, Depeche Mode, The The, and Jell. And in January 1981, Stevo released *The Some Bizzare Album*, the definitive anthology of the nascent futurist scene.

Not one of the twelve bands had a deal at the time—within a couple of years, however, four would have scored major hits—Depeche Mode, The The, Blancmange and Soft Cell; while four more—Naked Lunch, B-Movie, the Fast Set, and Blah Blah Blah—at least had their own records out.

Neither had Stevo even scratched the top of the iceberg. The same day as his album was issued, Sheffield's Thompson Twins were self-releasing their first single, "Perfect Game"; within a month, keyboard player Thomas Dolby had revealed his "Urges."

Of all these new arrivals, Depeche Mode were destined to travel the furthest. Thirty miles outside London, in the dormitory town of Basildon, teenagers Vince Clarke and Andy Fletcher formed their first band, No Romance in China, in 1977.

It was a lightweight concern; their live repertoire primarily reflected their love of old pop music, covers of "The Price of Love," "Then She Kissed Me," "I Like It." But Clarke, at least, was constantly wondering how to broaden the project's acoustic duo origins, a question that was answered one night in 1979, when another local band—Norman and the Worms—turned up for a double-header youth club gig with a new addition to their musical arsenal, guitar-playing bank teller Martin Gore's Moog Prodigy synthesizer.

He wasn't the instrument's most adept exponent, later confessing that it took him a month before he realized that the machine could make more than single sound, which he approximated with a loud "waaauuuugh." But Clarke was impressed. He invested in a drum machine, and soon after that, he and Gore were regularly rehearsing—or, at least, studying synth catalogues in readiness for the day when they'd buy another. When Fletcher gravitated to their side, they already had a new band name waiting, Composition of Sound.

By the time vocalist David Gahan joined the band in spring 1980, both Clarke and Fletcher had acquired their synths, and the newcomer suggested they change their name again, to "Dépêche Mode"—"fast fashion." (The accents would swiftly be discarded.)

Clarke, meanwhile, had established himself as the band's premier songwriter, and was now busy turning out a succession of incredibly tuneful pop confections with choruses that clung like ivy, and proved just as hard to get rid of. The world would get its first opportunity to hear one of them, "Photographic," on *The Some Bizzare* album; and another just three months later, as Depeche Mode released their debut single, "Dreaming of Me," on Daniel Miller's Mute label. Two decades on, Depeche Mode celebrated the fortieth anniversary of that first demo tape with the release of an eighteen-CD box set, and a career of unbroken success.

Soft Cell, too, found themselves moving fast. Their debut single, "Memorabilia," barely left the dance floors in terms of sales. But by summer, 1981, Almond and Ball

Dave Ball and Marc Almond of Soft Cell. (Photofest)

were digging back into their shared love for Northern Soul and redesigning Gloria Jones's "Tainted Love" from the ground up. The result took them to number 1 across four continents, gave them a US *Billboard* Top 10, and set up the band for a succession of further hits.

Before that, though; indeed, at the very moment when Soft Cell, Depeche Mode, and the rest of the pack started bedding themselves down as UK chart regulars, a couple of old favorites returned to the fray to show this new generation exactly how things were supposed to be done.

"I Feel Love" first, spinning out of the soundtrack to the cult disco movie *Paul Raymond's Erotica*, to reestablish its dominance of the dance floors; and then, a new album from Kraftwerk.

Three years had elapsed since *The Man Machine*, years during which the group had completely reequipped their Kling Klang studios with computers, and set to work on the appropriately titled *Computer World*. As was always their intention, they scarcely paid attention to anything that was happening in the outside musical world, but when they did reemerge, it was to discover an entire new vista awaiting them.

Britain was in the grip of synthesizer mania, and even as *Computer World* moved up the chart, so the band's UK record company began reactivating Kraftwerk's back catalog.

Trans-Europe Express reappeared in the album chart, and emboldened, EMI decided to release a couple of singles. "Pocket Calculator" first, and then "Computer Love." Both did moderately well, grazing the Top 40, then slipping out of view again. But disc jockeys kept on playing "Computer Love," and, when they got bored with that, they flipped it over and played its B-side, the three-year-old "The Model" instead. And suddenly sales started flickering again.

By early winter, 1981, the single was officially released with "The Model" as the A-side. And now things started to happen.

On January 9, 1982, "The Model" entered the UK chart at number 21. The following week, it breached the Top 10, and on January 23, it hit number 2. It slipped one place the week after that, but it was only a hiccup. On February 6, "The Model" reached number 1, and suddenly Kraftwerk weren't simply the first German band ever to top the British chart, they were the biggest thing in sight. Had they only followed it up, they might have remained so.

Instead they retreated, away from the garish glare of the limelight, away from the record company pressures and the media's demands, away from these strange quirks of timing that could push them to the peak when they least expected it. The future was left, once again, to the futurists, and of course, they kept on coming.

The Human League, sundered by a down-the-middle breakup in early 1981, regrouped and reemerged stronger than ever with the chart-topping "Don't You Want Me." The other half of the group, now doing business as Heaven 17, scored with "We Don't Need This Fascist Groove Thing."

Vince Clarke's Yazoo (abbreviated to Yaz in the United States) formed from a similarly cataclysmic split within the ranks of Depeche Mode. Across the ocean, Chicago-based Ministry emerged with a debut album, *No Sympathy*, which highlights some of front man Al Jourgensen's most humanely listenable confections. A Flock of Seagulls conquered America, and Duran Duran—whose earliest recordings showed a lot more understanding of electronics than their later fame would let on—took on the world.

Not everybody was impressed by the insurgence of synth bands—you might even say the movement's newly coined name of synthipop was itself somehow disparaging, even as it became common coinage.

But the machines had advanced a long way since "I Feel Love"; had, in addition, become so fully incorporated into the sound of myriad acts that many musicians mourned their rise as the death knell to traditional instrumentation.

Why, the aficionados of synth and sampler—an electronic process that had been on the market since the mid-1970s, but was now likewise coming down in price—seemed to be asking, should they spend years learning how to play a guitar, bass, or drums, when the machines could do it for them?

"Because you're putting us out of work," replied the hoary old souls who hitherto had made their living from actually playing their instruments, and both sides had a valid point to make.

Even members of the synth's own traditional constituencies were mortified. Not only did these kids not know how to play conventional instruments, they didn't know how to play electronic ones, either. In a savage reappraisal of the modern concept of "plug and play," a lot of these newcomers appeared to rely simply on "hit and hope."

The day of electronic instruments being regarded as the exclusive preserve of genius-level prodigies was well and truly over, and even that became a badge of pride. In 2020, the Pet Shop Boys' Chris Lowe raised wry, if (by now) distinctly graying, eyebrows when he admitted that the electronic duo's musical arsenal included "a vocoder which we never use because I don't know how to plug it in."

Not everybody appreciated the new approach. Vangelis, the Greek prog rock superstar whose love of synths dated back to the very first time he heard one in the early 1970s, complained in a contemporary interview, "I don't know whether it comes from the business or from the musicians, but to me this sort of music in general sounds like dead animals. You see a beautiful bird or a beautiful whatever—it's fantastic, but it's dead. And it's really sad. It's perfect, the style is absolutely great, but something's missing."

In some cases, too, he is correct. A lot of hideously vacuous music was recorded under the banner of synthipop; a lot of soulless meanderings, too, as electronics became the preserve of the so-called new age community. People who should not have been allowed within spitting distance of a synthesizer suddenly found themselves either cavorting around their newly minted Prophet 5 on MTV, or soundtracking workshops dedicated to unleashing one's inner chi.

Thankfully, most did not survive long and besides, those performers who not only lasted the pace, but also outlived it (the Pet Shop Boys among them), were more than compensation for the sap that dripped in their wake; again, we remember that every new musical movement has its leaders and its followers, and the early eighties 'electro-boom was no exception.

Gary Numan still tours and records today. Depeche Mode remain enormous. Blancmange, now comprising Neil Arthur alone, continue to record some genuinely daring electronic music. And Soft Cell, though they broke up in 1984, are recalled whenever Marc Almond raises himself to perform or record.

He shrugs away the tag of electronic innovator. "Thankfully I had Dave Ball there. I was just the singer." Indeed, talking in 1998, he admitted, "I don't have a computer . . . I don't even have a DAT machine; it took me years to get round to buying a CD player, and even then I can't figure out how to work it. I'm dyslexic, so I just don't know how to . . . you can tell me how to do something, but if it involves programs I forget it five minutes later, I can't retain it."

It was as a songwriter and a singer that Almond excelled, and three albums between 1981 and 1984 so guilelessly walked the line between sexual subversion and pure pop goodness that Soft Cell surely rated among the most divisive acts ever to walk this earth.

On the one hand, after all, was the number 1 "Tainted Love," the schmaltzy "Torch," the drab "Where the Heart Is" . . . on the other, a flickering Polaroid tour of a midwinter red light district, sex dwarves scurrying to get out of the rain, sleazy films reflecting in the oil-slicked puddles, desperate housewives, vengeful lovers . . . a return, in other words, to precisely the same world as "Love to Love You Baby" and "I Feel Love" so bewitched and bewildered, and set to a musical soundtrack that the denizens of any urban nightclub might have recognized from a decade in the past. By the time they broke up, Soft Cell were surely the only band that could make their own a James Bond theme ("You Only Live Twice") and a junkie punk anthem (the Heartbreakers' "Born to Lose"), and still have the time to cover Suicide.

"There was never any animosity over the split," Almond reflected. "We split for a lot of reasons, which were maybe due more to the things that were around us, than us falling out, but we were kind of burned out as people."

Both moved into solo pastures; and sure enough, while Ball's work focused further on electronics, Almond moved . . . more or less everywhere else. "I've played all kinds of parts over the years, I've done the whole seventy piece orchestra thing to death, the Vegas bit . . . [the] intimate, more introspective. . . ."

He has recorded an album-length tribute to Jacques Brel, and transformed the Belgian master's "Jackie" into wild disco cabaret. He even consigned "commercial suicide" to record, in the shape of 1982's *Torment and Torreros*, credited to his Marc and the Mambas side project. "I look back on it as an immensely flawed record, but still a great record for its time. It was like putting a nervous breakdown on a record."

He has resisted, too, the temptation to revisit his early days of electro-themed fame—a couple of remakes here, a solitary Soft Cell reunion there, Almond has generally maintained his own idiosyncratic path across what is now forty years' worth of work.

Once, however, he did delve deep into nostalgic waters, to confirm not only his own role in the development of electronic music, but also his appreciation of the music that inspired him before he ever picked up a microphone.

Bronski Beat were very late arrivals on the synthipop scene, but they easily made up for lost time. According to legend, the group had played just nine gigs before being signed to London Records in early 1984. A trio of vocalist Jimmy Somerville and keyboard/synth players Steve Bronski and Larry Steinbachek, the openly gay and politically outspoken band scored three hits, "Smalltown Boy," "Why," and George Gershwin's "It Ain't Necessarily So" around the release, also in 1984, of their debut album *Age of Consent*.

Their next 45 would be their last before Somerville quit in early 1985, but what a farewell it would prove, as they linked with Almond to record not only a cover of "I Feel Love"—one of Almond's all-time favorite songs—but also, as part of the medley that they built into the performance, "Love to Love You Baby" and, as if to complete the electronic circle that Joe Meek opened with his *I Hear a New World*, "Johnny Remember Me," a Meek production that topped the chart for John Leyton in 1961.

Bronski Beat had already recorded a short version of the medley, "I Feel Love" and "Johnny Remember Me" alone, on *Age of Consent*. It was an oddly lifeless performance, however, feeling more like tired filler than a determined take on either song. But with Almond joining them for an early 1985 remake, they truly hit the heights.

Close to ten minutes in length, it was an astonishing performance, the slinking opening duet across "Love to Love You Baby" gleefully subverting the original's heterosexual assault, but never distracting from its overall sexual*ity.* The combination of Somerville's falsetto and Almond's earthier tones, Somerville told *Quietus*, transformed it completely.

"We wanted to take a song that was gay . . . and make it even gayer." Adding "Johnny Remember Me," he said, was crucial in that respect. "When we got Marc, we basically had two gay men singing this song in which suddenly a man called Johnny appears, and we are both wanting him to remember us.

"It was so radical; when I look back we really did push the boat out with that."

Even Almond's accidental misreading of the third verse of "I Feel Free," singing "What'll it be, what'll it be, you and me" instead of "Falling free, falling free, falling free," could not damage the performance.

Neither was that, despite the split, the end of the original incarnation of Bronski Beat. Onstage at the Brixton Academy in London on April 4, 1987, Somerville reunited with his former bandmates for International AIDS Day (a predecessor to World AIDS Day, introduced the following year), and invited Pete Burns out for the closing number.

Of course, they performed "I Feel Love."

16

HIT THAT PERFECT BEAT, BOY

On the streets of New York City in the late 1970s, and the clubs of Chicago in the mid-1980s, hip-hop and house music both arose around the tireless quest for the perfect beat. Rhythms and riffs were scratched from scratchy vinyl to live again as both foundation and building brick, and it is unlikely that many of these borrowings were ever committed in the knowledge that they were contributing to the afterlife of the records that they were taken from.

British journalists visiting Brooklyn professed themselves astonished to hear the measured tones of Kraftwerk underpinning the boom box symphonies that were the nascent rap scene . . . a far cry indeed from the situation a decade later, when it was more likely to be lawyers listening in, searching for the latest unlicensed sample.

To both, however, it became clear that some records were more likely to be hit upon than others.

It is difficult to confirm even an approximate figure for how many times elements of "I Feel Love" (or any other record) were lifted during the earliest Wild West days of hip-hop.

There was no imperative to request legal clearance . . . nobody would have known what the petitioner was talking about, anyway; and with many examples performed live only, no formal accounting was kept. We have just the fading memories of dancers and disc jockeys to fill the gap, and occasionally a bootleg tape recording in which a certain snatch of sound *might* be it. Or might not.

The house scene is a lot clearer in its intentions—Helen's "I Love You," Hit House's "I Felt Acid House Love," Acid Angels' "Speed Speed Ecstasy," and a clutch of cuts by Divine all knowingly either take, or replay, elements of "I Feel Love," acknowledgment again of its titanic role in the development of dance music through the 1980s.

In amid such activity, it would have been easy for Giorgio Moroder to rest on the laurels of his 1970s success. Yet he had no interest whatsoever in revisiting old pastures. Disco had burned out as a musical force by the very early 1980s; other producers and artists, whether deliberately following in his footsteps or not, had grasped the synthesizer firmly, and Moroder allowed them to follow through.

He would continue his solo career—his own "From Here to Eternity" was a UK hit later in 1977, and in 1979, his *EMC2* album was touted as the world's first-ever direct-to-digital recording.

His production work, too, continued apace, and included several remarkable partnerships, as unexpected in their own way as his years with Sparks.

In 1978, Moroder reinvented Gamble and Huff's Three Degrees, with an album, *New Dimensions*, that opened with an apocalyptic showcase for every electronic effect in the Moroder arsenal, the stunning "Give It Up, Give It In." It was certainly a far cry from the "When Will I See You Again" hit-makers whom Britain's Prince Charles once famously proclaimed his favorite pop group.

Two years later, as he pieced together the *American Gigolo* movie soundtrack, Moroder was in the studio with Blondie. There he fully realized the sound they'd toyed with on "Heart of Glass," and strived for onstage with Robert Fripp, leaving fans to wonder only what might have transpired had they united for a full album. One assumes that Moroder also kept quiet the fact that the song they recorded together, "Call Me," was originally written for Stevie Nicks.

The tantalizing prospect of a fully consummated union between Moroder and Blondie could indeed be ranked among the great missed opportunities of the new decade. Another soundtrack, in 1981, however, saw an even grander combination slip through the participants' fingers, when Moroder combined with David Bowie for "Cat People (Putting Out Fire)."

The pair worked together on just two tracks, the main theme to Paul Schroeder's latest movie, a remake of the 1942 movie *Cat People*, now starring Malcom McDowell and Natassja Kinski, and the instrumental "Paul's Theme." The remainder of the soundtrack was Moroder's province alone. But still the union delivered all that one could have dreamed of.

The lengthy, brooding, and so beautifully monolithic "Cat People (Putting Out Fire)" drew from Bowie a performance which ranks among his most honestly impassioned vocals ever; up there with "'Heroes,'" and probably topping anything he had recorded in a similar vein since the stately balladeering of *Station to Station* in 1976.

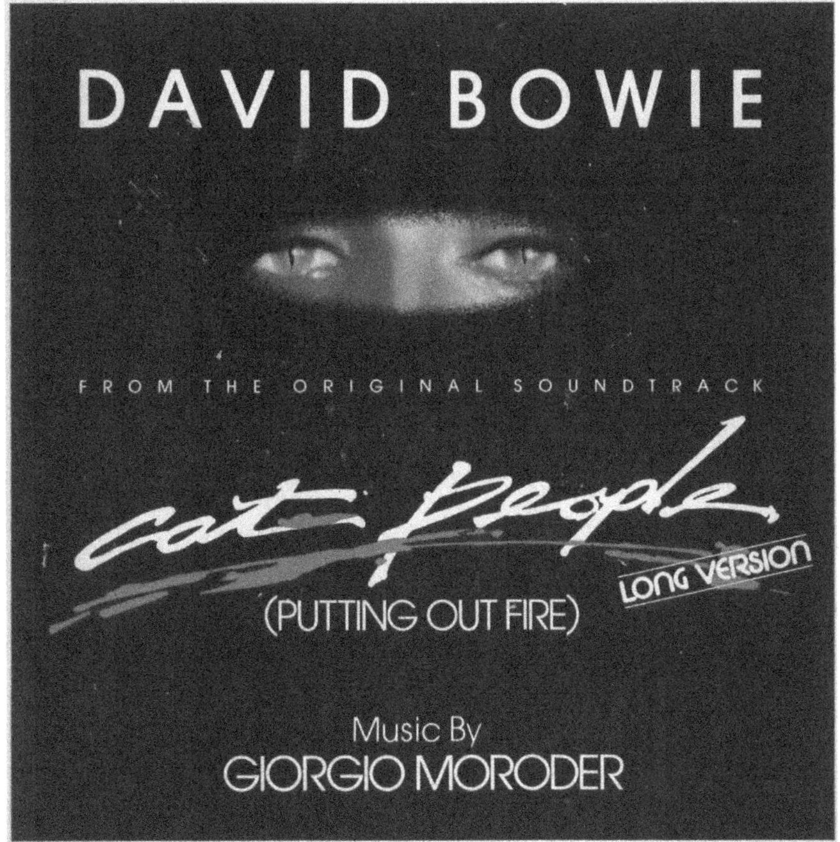

Giorgio Moroder and David Bowie unite for "Cat People (Putting Out Fire)." (Author Collection)

Indeed, though Moroder's own imprimatur was all over the record, the strength of Bowie's vocal was sufficient to render even that an irrelevance. And if it was impressive on record, it worked even better on film, igniting the closing credits with an atmosphere that was both dark and moody, and ecstatically frenetic—at least across the original collaboration. Bowie revisited the song on 1983's *Let's Dance* album, without Moroder's involvement, and he utterly neutered it.

It was during the "Cat People" sessions, incidentally, that Bowie told Moroder the story that the producer has never tired of retelling. He recalled it for insomniac.com in 2017: Bowie was "in Berlin recording the new album with Brian Eno, and the aim there was to find a new sound. Supposedly, Brian Eno came into the studio with a record and said they could forget the new sound: 'Giorgio found it already.'"

Soundtracks would remained Moroder's most visible works through the 1980s, but his love of music had a rival. In 1982, he told PopJustice, he was "on top of the world," only to decide he wanted "to do art, so I moved to New York and did big neon art. If I'd wanted I could have worked so much more [on music], and probably better.

"Even before I retired, I was half-retired already: I had enough money, I had enough hits. But I'm sure I could have continued until now. Musically I know what I can do. When disco went out, I didn't die! [Chic's] Nile Rodgers is still sad that disco went out, because it was his life, but I went on to score movies, I did music for the Olympics, I did the World Cup . . ."

One of those movies was *Electric Dreams* in 1984, for which he drew Human League's Phil Oakey in to voice the title song (and major hit) "Together in Electric Dreams." Another was *Flashdance* (1983); another was *Never Ending Story* (1984). All spun off major hit singles.

He oversaw the soundtrack for *Scarface* (also 1983), and a reimagination of Fritz Lang's silent-era *Metropolis* (1984). But he also produced the solo Freddie Mercury, and brought savage reality to the electro punk dreams of Sigue Sigue Sputnik.

Martin Degville was one of the post-punk drag queen shockers running on the same London nightclub circuit as the then equally unknown Boy George when Tony James, fresh from the ruins of Generation X, and a collaboration with the nascent Lords of the New Church, ran into him in 1982 working the YaYa clothes store in London's Kensington Market.

Having already linked with guitarist Neal X through a *Melody Maker* ad, James's first idea was to recruit Andrew Eldritch from the Sisters of Mercy to his new band; another scheme involved a pre-Eurythmics Annie Lennox. James, however, was immediately fascinated by the be-feathered Degville dancing round the store to old Suicide records, and the search for a vocalist ended.

YaYa became the new band's home base (and wardrobe supplier), and the as yet unnamed group's early demos reflected their fascination with the more sordid aspects of the rock lifestyle—Mick Jagger's "Memo from Turner," the New York Dolls' "Personality Crisis," and a self-composed song about penises, "Wang Wang Wang."

They developed an endless dub version of "Be Bop A Lula," watched a lot of John Waters movies, and toyed with such names as Sperm Festival and Nazi Occult Bureau before playing their first gig, with no name at all, following a Johnny Thunders show

A clean-shaven Moroder in 1984.
(Giorgio Moroder Enterprises/Photofest © Giorgio Moroder Enterprises)

in Paris. Former Generation X drummer Mark Laff (then part of Thunders's band) sat in for the three-song set.

Returning to London, the band recruited Ray Mayhew after he walked innocently into the store one day—he borrowed a drum kit from Topper Headon (ex-Clash); second drummer Chris Kavanagh got his from another Clash alumni, Terry Chimes, while the band's first sound engineer, Mick Jones, had just been sacked as guitarist by the same band. His first "appearance" with the band, manipulating their sound in the same way Brian Eno used to reshape Roxy Music's, was opening for New Model Army in Hastings.

Boomtown Rats manager Fatchner O'Kelly, who had already supplied much of the band's gear, finally named them Sigue Sigue Sputnik from a Russian street gang and, with one of Degville's coworkers, Yana, brought in on keyboards, the band printed up their first T-shirts, and began experimenting with what was, by now, a huge collection of synthesizers, tape machines, and electronics that none of them knew how to operate.

According to James, the crucial moment came when he was bouncing bits of his favorite movies onto a homemade video compilation, over which he'd dubbed Sputnik's "Love Missile F1-11" demo. He hit the wrong button, and the movie's soundtracks—explosions, gunfire, and general destruction—was accidentally layered over the band's master tape. That tape was to shape the entire Sputnik sound.

Their efforts were not unique. Cut-up movie clips, speech, music, and more was already common in hip-hop; had gifted fresh dimensions to 3 Teens Kill 4; and they flavored Mick Jones's next band, Big Audio Dynamite, as well.

But still, a Sputnik interview in the *New Musical Express*, designed simply to catch fans up on Tony James's latest doings, precipitated a frenzy. Eleven record companies turned up to the band's next show at London's Electric Cinema; and Sigue Sigue Sputnik were invited onto television's *The Tube*, a frenzied flurry of color, hair, and psychedelic Mad Max imagery which blew that Friday evening into legend. Close to two years had elapsed since the band took its first steps—now it was to take a massive stride.

Linking with EMI for a reported £4 million (in fact, the figure was vastly inflated, to match the hype already building around the group) Sputnik went into the studio with Moroder in late 1985, with one goal in mind. To do for 1986 what "I Feel Love" did for 1977—that is, rip everything to shreds and insist everything started over again.

They almost accomplished it, too. Released in February 1986, "Love Missile F1-11" was indeed the sound of the future—ear-catching samples flew, the bass line slipped in where your heartbeat's meant to be, the record yelped and pulsed and was quickly selling seventy thousand copies a day.

But where "I Feel Love" united so many disparate tribes, "Love Missile F1-11" divided them. The sheer heft of the hype behind which the dynamically costumed Sigue Sigue Sputnik postured and posed bred distrust; the sonic similarities that hallmarked every track on the album caused disappointment; and, while the single was

Sigue Sigue Sputnik. (Photofest)

certainly *one* of the first major hits to deploy sampling as an instrument in its own right, it was by no means *the* first.

"I Feel Love" was beloved almost everywhere. "Love Missile F1-11" was loved and loathed in equal proportions, and while the group's *Flaunt It* debut album would ride roughshod to glory over a crop of extraordinarily negative reviews, it was clear that this was a one-off adventure, even before the band allowed two years to elapse before following it up.

Moroder's role in crystalizing the Sputnik vision across that LP can never be understated. It would be rash to say that he alone knew how to harness the multitudinous disparate sounds that the band chose to work with, and seamlessly meld them with the ideas that were being thrown at him. But it was the resultant, and so unique combination of his experience and their enthusiasm; his ear for the eclectic and their penchant for drama, that granted *Flaunt It* whatever magic it had.

Yet Sigue Sigue Sputnik's downfall was not limited to approach and marketing alone. Six years later, Moroder himself would encounter similar pitfalls when he masterminded a new album of his own, unpromisingly titled *Forever Dancing*.

The brief should have been a no-brainer—a nonstop dance party digging back through disco's entire history, and redesigning everything in Moroder's own image. From "Shake Your Booty" to "Born to Be Alive," and on, inevitably, to a new take on "I Feel Love," *Forever Dancing* brought modern high-energy technology to what now felt like ancient dance history, only to discover that the new ways aren't always the best.

When it worked, it worked. In 1998, a recent remix of *Forever Dancing*'s reunion with Donna Summer, "Carry On," won the first-ever Grammy for Best Dance Recording. Elsewhere across the album, splitting vocals between Christina Nichols, Joey Diggs, and Melanie Taylor brought just enough variety to the proceedings to keep things interesting.

The problem was, Moroder simply didn't seem to know what to do with the songs he chose to cover: "Boogie Oogie Oogie," bereft of every iota of the original's slinkiness; "That's the Way (I Like It)" as a techno toe-tapper; "Don't Leave Me This Way" in the process of walking out of the door.

Moroder's renewed take on "I Feel Love" is especially disappointing. In 1977, when the machines were limited, he was pushed to the edge of creativity in order to create the record—and it shows. Fifteen years later, with the technology now at everybody's fingertips, and everything he had ever wanted to do on the record suddenly available at the flick of a switch, he seems simply to have just let the machine play itself. Placed close to the very end of the album, it simply sounds like everything else on the record. Which, one suspects, surprised nobody, least of all Moroder.

Music evolves. So does the purpose it is put to, and so do—in the starkest terms—the limits of what one can get away with. In 1969, "Je t'aime . . . moi non plus" was considered among the most shocking and disgusting records ever made, and radio dared not touch it. Today, it's simply a sweet, light orchestral ballad.

We do not single out Serge and Jane alone. No record, once it has been absorbed into music's body politic, can retain the exact same values, be they commercial, creative, or cultural, with which it first arrived on the scene. The most original record in the world will only remain startling for a short while, before the inevitable copycats, covers, rip-offs, and revamps start pouring out. Before everything that made it unique has become a part of the musical landscape.

"I Feel Love" was just weeks, if not days, old before it received its first cover version, courtesy of the UK's *Top of the Pops* series of pocket money–priced albums.

First launched in the late sixties, and averaging one new release every six weeks or so, *Top of the Pops* (not to be confused with the television show of the same name) was targeted at audiences that liked a particular song, but didn't especially care whether they got the hit original, or something that sounded more or less the same.

Recorded at breakneck speed, a dozen songs per album would highlight the biggest hits of the day while they were still hits. It was a scattershot process—some *Top of the Pops* covers are genuinely comparable to the original chart version. Others, to

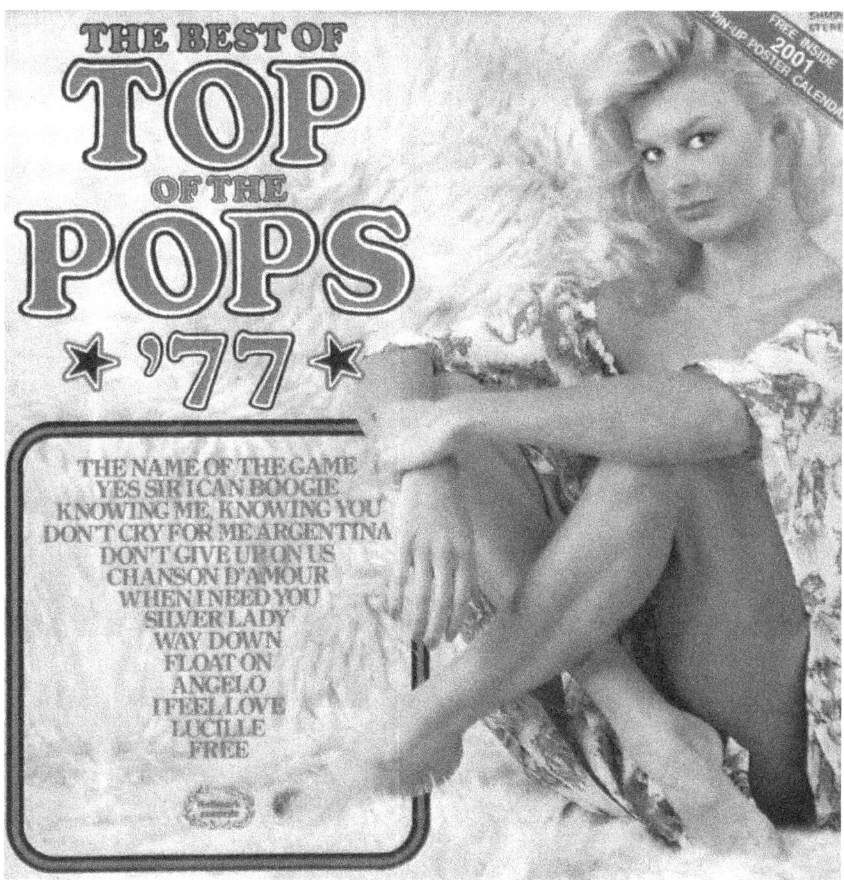

The Top of the Poppers take on "I Feel Love." (Author Collection)

put it bluntly, are grotesque. But the Top of the Poppers' "I Feel Love" falls firmly in the former category, replicating Moroder's original sonic landscape with such aplomb that one wonders why so many other musicians, over the years, have made it sound like such a great accomplishment. After all, if the Top of the Poppers could do it . . . and find the time, too, to add a few little electronic flourishes of their own . . . surely anybody could?

Actually, no. For all the scorn that was poured on these records (and their purchasers) while the series was alive, *Top of the Pops* called upon some of the most adept session musicians around—no household names, no future stars earning a quiet crust while awaiting their big break (famously, both David Bowie and Elton John recorded several sessions for similar albums for rival record companies during the late 1960s). Just good, solid musicians re-creating what they heard to the best of their abilities, and they clearly enjoyed themselves on "I Feel Love" because they kept it going for close to six minutes.

A markedly similar performance was also released in Germany, credited to serial covers band the Hiltonaires; another appeared in Italy, aboard an entire album of Summer covers credited to the Connection Group; yet another in the United Kingdom on a similar project by Dee Dee Smith; and yet *another* by Swedish singer Monica Forsberg, aboard her second solo album, *Sorry, I'm a Lady* (titled for another cover, a recent hit by the Spanish disco duo Baccara).

In every case, the intention was again to perform the song as close to the original as possible. In every case, the song's elusive atmosphere proved to be a breath too far.

Somewhat more inventive, in theory if not actual listenability, was an electro-orchestral extravaganza produced by Le Grand Orchestre de Paul Mauriat in 1977; while another Italian effort, Between the Sheets' 1983 medley of Moroder compositions, productions, and covers crunches a dozen tracks into its ten-minute playing time, but gives "I Feel Love" a full ninety seconds; "Love to Love You Baby" then gets thirty, before the two bleed together for an additional ten.

Elsewhere, on a surprisingly enjoyable album, everything from "Chase" to "Beat the Clock," and on to Queen's Musicland-produced "Another One Bites the Dust" makes an appearance, and while it would be both presumptive and inaccurate to suggest that Between the Sheets at all influenced Bronski Beat's own merging of Donna Summer's first two major hits the following year, they did do it first. There would be further medleys produced over the years, including the Disco Flashback portion of Jive Bunny & the Mixmasters' 1989 *Pop Back in Time to the 70s* album; and, that same year, a "I Feel Love"/"Love to Love You Baby" hybrid by Paul Hardcastle.

In 1981, a truly bizarre version of "I Feel Love" made its way into the soundtrack of the Bollywood movie *Armaan*, as part of a medley with "Rambha Ho Ho Ho," performed by Usha Uthup and Bappi Lahiri. It has little in common with anything else mentioned in this book, but it proves the song's international appeal.

The long-running British comedy/novelty act the Barron Knights were next to handle "I Feel Love," setting it within the context of a Welsh-accented talent contest. Ignoring Donna Summer altogether, "Mr Bronski Meets Mr Evans" does, in fact, pull off a fairly tolerable impersonation of Bronski front man Jimmy Somerville's trademark falsetto, although the humor itself ("that's not singing, you'll do yourself a damage") was probably funnier at the time. Or maybe not. The bit at the end, where the full Welsh choir joins in, however, is remarkably effective.

A decade earlier, Russell Mael wondered what would happen if a disco producer made a record with a rock band. Now, rock bands were wondering what would happen if they made records written by disco producers.

In 1987, the goth metal band Balaam and the Angel took on "I Feel Love" as the B-side to their "I'll Show You Something" single, stripping away the electronics in favor of a scything guitar and dismissing Summer's ecstatic sexuality with a hard rock voice. The resultant smash and grab utterly upends every last feature that had ever drawn dance and electro audiences to the song.

Around the same time, the song made a similarly genre-smashing appearance in the British indie band Crocodile Ride's repertoire, as their contribution to the *Alvin Lives (In Leeds)* compilation of seventies covers. A couple of years later, a folk-rock group from Austin, Texas, Two Nice Girls, created their own acoustic-led blend of "I Feel Love" and Bad Company's "Feel like Making Love," under the title "I Feel (Like Makin') Love."

The floodgates split open. In 1991, the Poster Children produced a fuzz drenched cover for another seventies hits tribute, *20 Explosive Dynamic Super Smash Hit Explosions!*; the following year, shoegazers Curve gave the song their own wide-screen twist for a collection of covers of UK chart toppers *Ruby Trax—The NME's Roaring Forty*.

Space rockers Kingston Wall produced a hybrid, riff-sodden dance version for their 1993 second album, *II*; the end of the 1990s saw dance act Amanda combine

"I Feel Love" with Led Zeppelin's "Whole Lotta Love" for an appallingly clumsy mash-up.

There was still room for more traditional takes, of course. In 1988, Italian actress and singer Ilona Staller included a supremely sexy "I Feel Love" on her Cicciolina alter-ego's *Sonhos Eróticos* album—lining it up, for good measure, alongside versions of both "Je t'aime . . . moi non plus" and "Love to Love You Baby." Into the 2000s, and the Red Hot Chili Peppers took to including the song in their live set, with guitarist John Frusciante taking over lead vocals for the occasion, and pulling off an exquisite falsetto over Flea's bubbling bass line.

But the 1990s house music boom saw Messiah twin with former Eruption singer Precious Wilson for an acid-drenched club floor filler (Vanessa-Mae followed suit, and breached the UK Top 50, in 1997). The punk-rocking Mr T Experience crunched out their own high-energy interpretation; alt-rockers A House covered "I Feel Love" for a 1994 B-side; and the percussion-heavy Blue Man Group linked with Venus Hum to acknowledge their past respect for the song with a deliciously percolating, and wildly guitar-whipped assault.

British singer Tina Charles, who enjoyed her own string of UK disco hits in the mid-1970s, launched a mid-2000s comeback with an album reprising both her own golden oldies and others from the era, a gloriously enthusiastic "I Feel Love" among them. And other versions abound, with the dance and DJ culture of the 2000s spilling out a wealth of interpretations.

Few are much more than dance floor filler; few made a mark beyond whichever clubs aired them. Like R&B bands performing "Johnny B. Goode," or hard rockers dipping their toes into "Smoke on the Water," "I Feel Love" entered the twenty-first century firmly established among those songs that everybody knew, and almost everybody seemed to want to hear . . . no matter how inexpertly it was performed.

Madonna took to covering the song on her 2011 Confessions tour, segueing out of "Future Lovers," but really adding nothing whatsoever to any past interpretation. But the UK's Astralasia worked up a terrific version to play at parties, "for fun," explained Marc Swordfish, "like our [version of] 'Boogie Nights.'"

The Irish acoustic band Ham Sandwich enacted a startling interpretation during their live shows around 2012, fiddle, trumpet, and acoustic guitar utterly inverting the song's traditional propulsion; there was even, remarkably, a prog rock rendition, conjured up by Welsh space rockers Sendelica in 2015, although the opening six minutes of pastoral psych prog and sound effects certainly masked the band's intentions. Even when the rhythm kicked in, it continued a gradual thing.

The Blue Man Group. (Photo by Léo Pinheiro/Picasa Web Albums/Wikimedia Commons)

It took until then, too, for the melody to assert itself, but once it got going, it was unmistakable . . . so long as you could convince yourself that Gong were at the controls the day that Giorgio Moroder first handed the song to Ms. Summer, and Didier Malherbe had sent the synth man out for sandwiches.

"For me ["I Feel Love"] is classic Krautrock," declared Sendelica front man Pete Bingham. "It was great to add twists to this iconic classic and take it somewhere very new." (Neither had the band finished with the song. Unused drum tracks from the recording session were later applied to Sendelica's cover of David Bowie's "Ziggy Stardust.")

In November 2019, "I Feel Love" even found its way into the world of television talent shows, with Kevin McHale's exotically staged performance on *The X Factor: Celebrity*; coincidentally, at precisely the same time as British singer Sam Smith cut a reading for a Target Christmas commercial.

Smith's "I Feel Love" is as lush as such a commission might demand. It is also incredibly faithful to its source, as *Stereogum* critic Tom Breihan noted. "Smith does not attempt to reinvent 'I Feel Love,' which would be pretty much impossible anyway. Instead, [producer Guy] Lawrence simply recreates the original beat as closely as possible, while Smith reaches out for that elusive Donna Summer vocal register. There's also a bit where they chant the lyrics in a spoken monotone, which is pretty funny."

A CD promo of space rockers Sendelica's "I Feel Love" cover. (Author Collection)

There was, however, one significant difference, as residentadvisor.com critic Andrew Ryce noted. "The all-synthesizer song was a world-changing revelation when it came out in 1977. Here, it's karaoke."

Tweeting about the recording, Smith was keen to emphasize the song's relevance to the gay community, echoing Jimmy Somerville's now-thirty-five-year-old remarks about the song's popularity. "I Feel Love" was "an anthem of our community," the four-time Grammy winner declared, "and it was an honor and most importantly so much fun to have a go at it."

"I Feel Love," Smith continued, had "followed me to every dance floor in every queer space from the minute I started clubbing." Smith also described it as the "highest song I've ever fucking sang," so it's ironic that it should result in one of the singer's lowest-charting singles. "I Feel Love" reached number 76 on the British chart.

For a performer with seven chart toppers in the catalog, the most successful Bond theme ever, and a fervently loyal following, it was a strangely subdued showing. Perhaps because Smith never answered one especially cogent question, posed by Andrew Ryce in that same residentadvisor.com review. "What [is] 'queer' about a note-for-note copy made for a corporation?"

Through all of this, Donna Summer, Pete Bellotte, and Giorgio Moroder's original recording continued to sell. In 1982, Patrick Cowley's full-length mix finally made its commercial debut as a British twelve-inch single, and swept the dance floors once more. A seven-inch edit just missed Top 20.

Further remixes followed and, in 1995, two of the best contemporary teams, Masters at Work and Rollo & Sister Bliss, were offered the opportunity to place their own stamp on Summer's original. With Summer herself adding a newly recorded vocal, the single climbed to number 8 in the United Kingdom, in the midst of a pervasive, if somewhat arch, revival of "classic" disco sound and vision from across the musical board.

New acts like Haddaway ("What Is Love") and N-Trance (a cover of the Bee Gees' "Staying Alive") led the way; more established performers like the Pet Shop Boys (the Village People's "Go West") and Erasure (an EP's worth of ABBA tunes), added muscle to the movement.

A seemingly never-ending supply of disco oldies became available for either a fresh remix or a newly recorded makeover. Britpop darlings Pulp shot the video for their "Disco 2000" on a disco-themed set; U2 dressed up as the Village People in the video for a single called "Discotheque," although it was not the best record they'd ever made. "Does disco suck?" asked Gene Loves Jezebel cofounder Michael Aston in 1997. "Only when U2 do it. It was bad enough when Village People did it, but at least they had some class."

Within such a febrile environment, the revived "I Feel Love" could hardly help but hit. Unlike so many other examples, however, the remixes were actually worth hearing, and the song's appeal continued to flourish.

Summer's own rendering of "I Feel Love" returned to the UK chart again at the end of May 2012, when it reached number 45. On this occasion, however, there was less to celebrate. On May 17, the woman who the mainstream media still insisted on calling the "Queen of Disco" passed away.

17

I'M A RAINBOW

Donna Summer and Giorgio Moroder continued working together through the remainder of the 1970s. Musically, the pair were forever pushing the boundaries of what Summer's existing audience might expect, pursuing the kind of following that they believed she deserved. Diana Ross, Elvis Presley, Barbra Streisand—they were the role models that the two were targeting, performers who were adept not simply at following musical trends but influencing them as well; and whose audience exceeded any of the traditional demographic boundaries.

It was a fraught enterprise. While the 1970s certainly embraced musical freedoms that past generations might never have imagined, they were also responsible for firmly locking artists into all-but-escape-proof pigeonholes. If an artist's first hit was a soft rock classic, then a soft rocker was what the artist would remain.

Bands that broke through during Britain's early-decade glam rock fixation were, with the single exception of Bowie, doomed to forever more be termed and regarded as glam, regardless of where their muse might take them—one remembers chuckling wryly to hear Marc Bolan and T. Rex's disco-bound "Dreamy Lady" dismissed as glitter rock by some disgruntled passerby, but *only* after he was told who had recorded it.

Summer had already found herself chained inside the sack marked "disco," and that despite the variety of themes that had populated her albums so far. Nor would Casablanca especially strive to alter that scenario . . . not while disco was still hot and selling, at least.

Yet her reading of "MacArthur Park," no matter how grisly one might find it, was surely hard-core disco by association (and danceable beat) alone, and while there is no doubt that Casablanca was very reluctant for Summer to step too far out of that spotlight when it came to choosing new singles (1979's "Heaven Knows" was both utterly danceable and barely memorable), on record she and Moroder continued pushing forward.

But the plaudits that greeted *Bad Girls*, her final album of the decade, would have meant far more had the reviewers not approached the record as strictly a disco release—in fact, it is one of the most solid soul/R&B LPs of the era, that just happened to be released at a time when any danceable song was being lazily termed "disco."

The health problems that Summer suffered through the latter part of the 1970s, and which culminated in both a reliance on prescription medication and, reportedly, a 1979 nervous breakdown, were at least partially the consequence of that conflict. Summer yearned to break away from her stereotype; the marketing department was equally desperate for her to remain within it, and for now, the salesmen were winning.

In mid-June 1979, Summer had both the number 1 single in America, "Hot Stuff," and the number 1 album, *Bad Girls*. The following week, the album's title track joined "Hot Stuff" in the Top 3, the first time a female artist had ever achieved that particular feat. Incredibly, she would repeat it in November.

In July, Summer was atop the soul chart as well, and she ended the year with further statistical accolades simply raining down. In the eyes of the media, the Disco Queen remained inviolate.

Yet she rounded off the year with a chart-topping duet with Barbra Streisand, and though "No More Tears (Enough Is Enough)" surely ranks among the most lachrymose hits of the age, it also signposted to the world at large where Summer's ambitions lay.

Yet its success also masked another problem. Summer's first self-composed single, "Dim the Lights," was still marching up the chart when Casablanca released the duet. It would reach number 4, but was readily overtaken by "No More Tears," and Summer was livid.

Had the label waited just another few weeks, until it was certain "Dim the Lights" had peaked, not only might she have had another number 1, but more important, she would have achieved it with her own words. For that, too, was her goal, to establish herself as a songwriter in her own right, and not just the voice in front of her producer.

An eponymous television special in the new year added further emphasis to Summer's strivings, while things had changed on a personal level, too, as she rediscovered her Christian religious roots, and suggested that their teachings were more important to her than continuing to dance to Casablanca's tune.

Now it was the label that lived in fear that her next album might be the last for Casablanca—which immediately rushed out the oddly subtitled *On the Radio:*

Greatest Hits Volumes One and Two compilation, to be duly rewarded with double platinum sales.

Summer, however, was resolute. Although she still owed the label one more album (*She Works Hard for the Money* was delivered in 1983), she departed Casablanca early in 1980, to become the first signing for David Geffen's newly launched Geffen Records. She also filed a $10 million lawsuit against her former label. In the event, Casablanca was not long for this world, with or without its legal woes. The label folded (or, more accurately, was absorbed into the Polygram giant) and Summer's case folded with it.

A new Donna Summer album, showcasing her victory, appeared later in the year. Unfortunately, while *The Wanderer* was a purposeful dismissal of the disco sound, the peculiar thing was, it didn't really replace it with anything.

Listened to today, it feels more like a precursor to the generic rock that so scarred the music industry later in the decade; songs that neither said nor did anything much, but which managed to sound impressive—which itself is ironic because Harold Faltermeyer, fresh from the Sparks sessions, later complained that they had not finished with production before Geffen demanded the record be released.

Its sonic deficiencies notwithstanding, *The Wanderer* was a brave release, populated with songs that could, in a less rushed (and, perhaps, uncertain) environment have delivered far more than they ultimately did. But like Sparks before her, Summer was unhappy that much of the work on the album was undertaken by Faltermeyer, rather than her familiar team of Moroder and Bellotte, and the media agreed.

Suggestions that the newcomer offered little more than a watered-down approximation of Musicland's traditional achievements were certainly not dismissed by the album, and though *The Wanderer* was scarcely a failure, its final US chart position of number 13, and the absence of more than one major hit single (the title track) were certainly a far cry from recent glories.

Summer was dismayed, David Geffen was concerned. Knowing that work was already under way on the projected follow-up, an as-yet-untitled double LP, the label head determined to keep a close eye on proceedings, demanding both regular updates and an early preview of the record.

Neither were encouraging, In fact, it would transpire that many of the gestating album's so-called problems were due to the birth of Summer's second child, her daughter Brooklyn, just as the sessions were due to begin, and her understandable preoccupation with that. It was Geffen's impatience that would ultimately damn the project.

Faltermeyer told *Daieda*, "Donna had changed and was going through some things we couldn't help with. Things had changed and scheduled recording sessions were not kept." The studio team were working around her though, and matters were progressing at least somewhat satisfactorily. And then, "when Geffen stopped by the studio to check on progress, he was unhappy with what he had heard. There were only a few songs finished and most were in demo phase."

Despite the team's protests, Geffen pulled the plug on the project. More than that, he demanded Summer break with Moroder and Bellotte.

It was not, Moroder later reflected for *Out*, a soul-destroying rupture. "The last two albums we did, I was not really happy with her. She didn't want to sing this line because there was this word. She wanted to sing a song about Jesus. What can you do? She was my main singer."

Summer, too, had few regrets, although knowing that Quincy Jones had been recruited in Moroder's stead surely sweetened the pill somewhat. She did, however, tell writer Barney Hoskyns, "It was much easier working with Giorgio, for sure, because I kinda grew up with him and Pete [Bellotte], and to make the transition to a new producer is very hard. It's like starting all over again, learning to walk again, learning what to say and what not to say."

The success of the ensuing *Donna Summer* LP proved that Geffen may not have been wrong, after all. Certainly it is intriguing to compare that with the tapes that were ultimately (1996) released as *I'm a Rainbow* and which, even making allowances for its unfinished state, suggests that Summer's partnership with Musicland had indeed reached the end of the road.

Jones, on the other hand, not only offered her a new landscape in which to perform, he and partner Rod Temperton were also more open to (and, perhaps adept at) facilitating Summer's own creative demands.

The contractual obligation album *She Works Hard for the Money* was, perhaps unsurprisingly, something of a backward glance. Yet it was also crucial to Summer's continued success. Produced by Michael Omartian, it was an enjoyable collection of pop dance songs, mostly cowritten by the pair, and after the somewhat off-piste nature of its predecessors, it returned her to the dance floor in an age when "disco" had been placed as far back in the rear view mirror as Summer herself had ever wished it to be.

Donna Summer at the 2009 Nobel Peace Prize concert.
(Photo by Harry Wad/Wikimedia Commons)

Now it was "club" music, energetic and yes, electronic, and with this in mind, Omartian remained at the helm for Donna Summer's next LP, her twelfth, 1984's *Cats Without Claws*. Lightning, however, did not strike twice; indeed, the album quickly established itself as her lowest selling yet, not even receiving a gold disc. At the same time, however, it was becoming clear that Summer's success was not something to be measured in record sales per se, so much as her overall career.

Summer did not, for example, grace the televised Presidential Inaugural Gala in 1985 on the strength of her recent chart performances; she was there because she was indisputably a star, with instant name recognition, a catalog that everybody could sing and dance along with, and no need any longer to try and compete with the hip young guns who were rising up around her in the world of pop.

She had attained that rarified plateau upon which simply *being* is as important as *doing*, and her achievement was only amplified by the knowledge that one would be hard pressed to think of more than a handful of performers from her generation who had reached similar heights.

Geffen, too, appreciated her status, talking of repositioning Summer not as a current artist, but a veteran star. When she suggested her next album should be a solid R&B set, the label quickly agreed and, while sundry critics did murmur uneasily about her moving in on Tina Turner territory, *All Systems Go*—a reunion with Harold Faltermeyer—proved that there was plenty of room for both of them.

Again, sales were (by her 1970s standards) disappointing, and the album would become her last for Geffen, and that despite their having already arranged for her to go next into the studio with the British hit-making team of Stock Aiken Waterman.

It was an odd decision, and the result, *Another Place and Time*, was an odd record, one that sometimes felt as though the singer had been awkwardly shoehorned into her producers' long-established trademark sound, and left to fend for herself. Likewise, its successor, 1991's *Mistaken Identity* was probably her most aptly titled record yet, as Summer tried, but failed, to come to grips with Janet Jackson–esque new jack swing.

It would be churlish to suggest that Summer, already secure in her fame, had more pressing interests in her life than making new records, but there was certainly something very lackluster in her approach these days, a sense that working with a producer whose signature sound had already been established (*Mistaken Identity* was recorded with Keith Diamond) would save her having to develop one of her own. And if that was the case, good luck to her.

Francisca Moroder, Donna Summer, Bruce Sudano, and Giorgio Moroder in 2007. (Photo © Wolfgang Moroder/CC BY-SA 3.0/Wikimedia Commons)

Both *Another Place and Time* and *Mistaken Identity* were thoroughly enjoyable within the context of the time during which they were recorded; both kept her name on the chart. All the while, though, it was in the world outside the studio that Summer's career was focused; on the world tours that never failed to sell out; on the honors and awards that kept her name on far more front pages than a new record ever would. In 1989, she came close to agreeing to a reality-based sitcom revolving around her life with husband, Bruce Sudano, and their three children; in 1992, she was the recipient of a star on the Hollywood Walk of Fame.

But when the opportunity to reengage with Giorgio Moroder presented itself, also in 1992, she had no hesitation. It was for just one song, "Carry On," which in turn would lead off both her next hits collection and Moroder's *Forever Dancing* album, and it would take a 1997 remix to truly show the song in its best light. Nevertheless, it was the best-sounding record Summer had recorded in years, and in 1998, the remix won her the inaugural Grammy for Best Dance Recording.

It would be 2008 before another all-new Donna Summer album, *Crayons*, finally arrived, and 2010 before she mused aloud on her next one, a possible collection of pop standards. Otherwise, she just carried on carrying on, a soundtrack recording here, a gala performance there, the occasional acting role, another awards ceremony. She recorded a Christmas album in 1994, a major VH-1 live special in 1998, and she published her autobiography in 2003.

She did not lose touch with Moroder. There was a brief period, he told *Time Out New York*, when she was living in Nashville and "I . . . lost track of her. . . ." But then she returned to Los Angeles, and "in the last few years, she had the apartment right below me in my high-rise on Wilshire. I . . . invited her for dinner at my place, and she loved it. So she took the apartment below with Bruce [Sudano, her husband].

"We were basically meeting about once a week, for lunch or dinner or whatever. I certainly saw her more during the last few years than I did in the second half of the eighties and the nineties."

But those last few years raced past too quickly. Donna Summer died of lung cancer at her home in Naples, Florida, on May 17, 2012, a nonsmoker whose own conviction was that the disease was born on September 11, 2001, breathing in the poisoned air of that morning's New York terrorist attacks.

So many people paid tribute to her, friends and fellow performers alike. Liza Minnelli, Dolly Parton, Barbra Streisand, Quincy Jones, Gloria Estevan, Mary J Blige. President Obama remembered "A five-time Grammy Award winner . . . [whose] voice was unforgettable . . . the music industry has lost a legend far too soon."

A few of these people . . . actually, a lot of them . . . did squeeze the "Queen of Disco" tag into their tributes. Even the president. And that's okay, because at one point she was. But Beyoncé, in her tribute, acknowledged an even greater truth.

"Donna Summer made music that moved me both emotionally and physically to get up and dance. You could always hear the deep passion in her voice. . . . I've always been a huge fan and was honored to sample one of her songs ["Love to Love You Baby" in the 2003 hit video "Naughty Girl"].

But she reminded us, and everybody, that Summer "was so much more than the queen of disco she became known for, she was an honest and gifted singer with flawless vocal talent."

18

IT ALL COMES ROUND AGAIN

Giorgio Moroder remained active, but barely visible. Having composed the official theme for the 1990 World Cup in his homeland Italy, and released *Forever Dancing*, his 1990s and 2000s were consumed by visual art, interrupted by the occasional remix, and just one new, full-length project, a truly atmospheric soundtrack for a new release of German filmmaker Leni Riefenstahl's *Impressionen unter Wasser* movie.

Signs that he was growing restless in his semiretirement were scant. But in May 2012, just eight days after Donna Summer's death, the French electronic duo Daft Punk announced that Moroder was among the contributors to their forthcoming fourth album, *Random Access Memories*. He had, apparently, recorded a rap.

Moroder was already a fan of their music, and spoke highly of "One More Time," a track from their second album, *Discovery* (2001). But he also saw in the group's eclectic experimentation a vivid reflection of his own early work. When Daft Punk first contacted him regarding a proposed collaboration for the *Tron: Legacy* movie score, he was definitely interested. In the event, that never happened. But they remained in contact.

Daft Punk emerged onto the Anglo-American scene with the 1997 release of their *Homework* debut album. However, its members Thomas Bangalter and Guy-Manuel de Homem-Christo had been working together for almost five years at that point. Indeed, they named this latest project from a particularly uncomplimentary review that one of the English music papers meted out to a band they'd had earlier in the decade.

Bangalter explained, "We had a band when we were sixteen or seventeen, called Darlin', after the Beach Boys song. That was our first record as well, it was released as a split single with Stereolab, and an English reviewer said it was really horrible, just 'daft punk.' And we liked that name better than ours."

Homework was a magnificent record, its insistent dance rhythms and innovative electronics prompting comparisons that ranged from the Chemical Brothers to Chic, with the disco stylings of the latter only amplified when Bangalter revealed that his father, Gérard, had produced and written hits for the Gibson Brothers and Ottawan.

"The success was unexpected," Bangalter admitted. "We did everything very small, for ourselves, and it just took off. We had this electronic equipment set up in my bedroom and a lot of [*Homework*] was us seeing what different things did."

One track in particular, "Rolling and Scratching," summed up Daft Punk's genre-busting ambition, as a standard beat was overlaid with what can only be described as two teenagers pushing buttons to see which noise was the most . . . some critics said it was "annoying"; Bangalter preferred "interesting."

Early Daft Punk releases hit the English-speaking world via the Glasgow underground label Soma; the two teams met up at a EuroDisney rave before unleashing the "New Wave"/"Alive" and "Da Funk"/"Musique" couplings that originally slammed out in horribly limited editions.

"The only people who heard them were the Chemical Brothers," remarked Bangalter. "They asked us to remix 'Life is Sweet' for them, and things started moving."

By the time Daft Punk signed to Virgin, and prepared to reissue the looping psychoses of "Da Funk," the original twelve-inch singles had sold over thirty thousand. For mainstream America, the introduction again came through "Da Funk," courtesy this time of late-night MTV airings for Spike Jonze's brilliant accompanying video.

Moroder was not an altogether visible touchstone on *Homework*, as the track "Teachers" perhaps made clear. A squelchy drum and bass underpins a simple litany of the names of the duo's primal influences: Brian Wilson, George Clinton, Mark Dearborn, Armand Van Helden . . . on and on it goes, with especial attention paid to the giants of the house scene, but no Moroder.

Random Access Memories was Daft Punk's chance to rectify that omission, a tribute to the music of the late 1970s and early 1980s, with the electronic instrumentation played exclusively on period technology: vocoders, drum machines, and a custom-built modular synth.

Moroder would not touch any of the instruments. "They did not let me get involved at all," he said. All he was asked to do was, "tell the story of my life. Then they would know what to do with it."

Electronic dance heroes Daft Punk. (Virgin/Photofest © Virgin)

The result was "Giorgio by Moroder," a nine-minute slice of punishing motorik, over which Moroder narrated his story—including the creation of "I Feel Love": "I knew that it could be a sound of the future but I didn't realize how much impact it would be."

Random Access Memories was released in 2013, by which time the reenergized Moroder had already provided the theme music for *Racer: A Chrome Experiment*, Google's new multiscreen game. He followed that in May 2013 with an appearance at the Red Bull Music Academy in New York, his first ever DJ-ing gig in the United States.

With his assistant Chris Cox alongside him, the seventy-five-minute set marched through Moroder's career, its contents both manipulated and augmented by the gray-haired producer as he stood behind an impressive bank of equipment. "Evolution" (from the score of *Battlestar Galactica*) "From Here to Eternity," "Racer," "Chase," the Three Degrees, Suzi Lane, Sparks, Donna Summer . . . the memories cascaded out.

But there was no mistaking the highlight of the evening, as a solidly packed audience erupted both into applause and delight when the set reached "I Feel Love." At one point, Moroder was all but conducting the crowd as it sang along to the lyrics.

He told *Time Out New York*, "I always wanted to perform. When I was young, I did a few gigs, but I don't have a great singing voice—plus, I always forget lyrics. So at one point, I just said, 'I don't want to do it.' But now, with deejaying—that is almost like performing!

"Plus, I just love dance music. I don't do it because I want to just make money. And I'm not disturbed at all by the volume of the music; even at home, when I listen with headphones, my ears are almost exploding!"

He had the bug. Over the next year, Moroder toured the world, his live remixes growing more confident and bold as he did so. He recorded a Volkswagen commercial and remixed Lady Gaga; he released a new single. "Giorgio's Theme," and in 2015 Moroder uncorked his first new album in almost a quarter of a century, *Déjà Vu*.

It met and, in places, exceeded expectations. One does not, after all, look to a seventy-five-year-old for cutting-edge innovation in any field, let alone one so dependent upon youth as modern dance music. Indeed, as its title made clear, *Déjà Vu* was less a reclamation of his old status than it was a reminder of it.

At the same time, however, Moroder did not rely on the old standards for material; rather, *Déjà Vu* comprised almost all new material, leavened by three covers, and all featuring an array of guest performers that included Britney Spears, Sia, Charli XCX, and Kylie Minogue.

Whether *Déjà Vu* met his live audience's expectations is immaterial—they would have been happy, one imagines, with a simple live recording of the DJ set and, in many ways, that would have been a far more exciting offering.

But still *Déjà Vu* topped the American Dance/Electronic chart, breached the British Top 30 and the Italian Top 20, and if Britain's *Independent* newspaper complained that its impact was "strained and dulled by over-familiarity," *Spin* at least acknowledged "Moroder's humble ability to make our ageist culture forget the fact

Giorgio Moroder on stage in Oslo, during his 2015 European tour. (Tord Litleskare/Alamy Stock Photo)

that he's well past retirement age." A point that Moroder made midway through the disc, with "Seventy Four Is the New Twenty Four."

He continued performing live—a March 2015 Australian tour opening for Minogue, and that September, an appearance at the massive Radio 2 Live in Hyde Park day-long festival in London, now with a repertoire divided equally between selections from the new album and a veritable greatest hits set—"I Feel Love" and "Love to Love You Baby," "Bad Girls," "Flashdance," "Together in Electric Dreams," "Call Me." It was not, on paper, as thrilling a set as his earlier performances, but a packed park did not seem to care. The attendees were seeing a legend, and they seemed to know every word.

He toured the United States in 2018 and the following year, on the road in Europe Moroder took to resurrecting "Looky Looky," from fifty years before, and interspersing the songs with some wry explanations. Introducing "Love to Love You Baby," for example, he told the crowd, "Donna said she wanted to make a sexy record. Then she did a moaning, and then another moaning."

His studio activities, too, took on a new life, recording with Kylie Minogue, producing the Korean band Sistar. He was celebrated by Shooter Jennings (son of country star Willie), whose 2016 album was titled *Countach (For Giorgio)*, to honor the

Giorgio Moroder onstage in Minneapolis, 2018. (Photo by Andy Witchger/Flickr/ Wikimedia Commons)

man whose work "set the foundation for the music of my entire life." And in 2018, the story of his work with Donna Summer became the foundation for a Broadway musical.

First conceived at a workshop directed by Tony Award–winner Des McAnuff in 2016, *Summer: The Donna Summer Musical* was written by Colman Domingo, Robert Cary, and McAnuff; its three acts depicted Summer in her preteens ("Duckling Donna," played by Storm Lever); at the height of her early fame ("Disco Donna," Ariana DeBose), and toward the end of her life ("Diva Donna," LaChanze).

Directed by McAnuff and choreographed by Sergio Trujillo, *Summer* was a rambunctious affair, and not without its faults. Even in its early days at La Jolla Playhouse (where it opened in November 2017), the critical knives were quick to come out.

"In a musical form not known for literary finesse, *Summer* lowers the bar," snarled the *Los Angeles Times*'s Charles McNulty. "The lack of playwriting imagination is startling. If the program didn't state otherwise, I'd be sure the writing was outsourced to Wikipedia," a point that the *Hollywood Reporter*'s David Rooney would reiterate the following year: "[a] tacky little show, a feebly dramatized Wikipedia page with lackluster covers . . .

"The mangling, early on, of two of Summer's most iconic hits sends a clear signal this is going to be painful. 'I Feel Love' and 'Love to Love You Baby' are classics that changed the direction of dance music with their dreamy sensuality and trance-like grooves. Chopping them up with commentary, not to mention anemic arrangements deflates the mood."

But the *New York Stage Review* was perhaps the most withering, noting that "Donna gets sick near the end of the show, but she and her family sing a defiant song, and then she goes on telling her story. If you have only a glancing familiarity with the Queen of Disco's life—and, let's be honest, how many living today have more than that?—you're likely to walk out of the theater thinking, 'Huh, so I guess she's still alive?'"

Nevertheless, *Summer* would appear to have been $12 million well spent. The musical transferred to Broadway's Lunt-Fontanne Theatre for an April 23, 2018, opening and 289 performances took its run through to the end of 2018. The following fall, the musical opened a North American tour with the lead roles now taken by Olivia Elease Hardy, Alex Hairston ("Disco Donna"), and Dan'yelle Williamson.

The bad reviews continued to flow, but so did ticket sales, and it is difficult to resist drawing parallels between the critical lambasting meted out to the musical, and that with which many of its subject's records . . . including most of those featured in *Summer* . . . were greeted upon release. Moods move on, standards shift, music changes.

But it is unlikely ever to change again so abruptly, and decisively, as it did when Donna Summer, Pete Bellotte, and Giorgio Moroder were at the controls. The day they released "I Feel Love."

EPILOGUE

It is unlikely that there will ever be another "I Feel Love"; another song that arrives out of nowhere and hits so many people . . . so many fans of so many different musical styles . . . with equal force and similar consequence.

Other records have forged a change in mainstream direction and taste—few people had even heard of "grunge," for example, before Nirvana's "Smells like Teen Spirit" came along, but a lot went out and formed their own grunge bands afterward. Ditto punk and the Sex Pistols, heavy metal and Black Sabbath, the blues and the Rolling Stones. According to that sequence, "I Feel Love" should have simply sent more would-be musicians scampering to make their own disco records.

Instead, it opened a door through which myriad other disciplines could flood, with each of those then forging its own way forward, and hatching its own brood of yowling offspring. Not, as is so often the case, in thrall to slavish imitation, but in search of the possibilities that "I Feel Love" made so apparent.

From the bands who made an immediate beeline for Giorgio Moroder, to those who merely hired his Musicland Studios; from the artists who were inspired to take their first steps into electronics, to those who completely redesigned their output to accommodate the ideas he presented them with, "I Feel Love" is directly responsible for great swaths of the music we have enjoyed over the past forty years.

As Moroder himself has stated on many occasions, he wanted to visualize the sound of the future. But he had no idea that he would get it so right. Nobody did. . . .

Well, apart from David Bowie and Brian Eno, Robert Fripp and Ron and Russell Mael, Jim Kerr and Charlie Burchill, Pete Burns and Marc Almond, and all the other names who heard "I Feel Love" and decided that was where they wanted to go.

In fact, sometimes it seems as though Moroder was the only person who didn't immediately grasp its unique brilliance, and maybe it's that which makes "I Feel Love" so important.

Nobody . . . not even the man who made the record in the first place . . . saw it coming.

PLAYLISTS

Giorgio Moroder—Selected Discography

Cerca (Di Scordare) (single, 1965)
Bla Bla Diddley (single, 1966)
Stop (single, 1966)
Yummy Yummy Yummy (single, 1968)
Lilly Belle (single, 1968)
Cinnamon (single, 1968)
Looky Looky (single, 1969)
Moody Trudy (single, 1969)
Mah Nà Mah Nà (single, 1969)
Monja (single, 1969)
That's Bubblegum—That's Giorgio (LP, 1969)
Arizona Man (single, 1970)
Mony Mony (single, 1970)
I'm Free Now (single, 1971)
Underdog (single, 1971)
Son of My Father (single, 1971)
London Traffic (single, 1972)
Take It, Shake It, Break My Heart (single, 1972)
Today's a Tomorrow (single, 1972)
The Future Is Past (single, 1972)
Son of My Father (LP, 1972)
Heaven Helps the Man (single, 1973)
Lonely Lovers' Symphony (1973)
Marrakesh (single, 1973)
Giorgio's Music (LP, 1983)
Sinfonia De Los Enamorados Solitarios (Lonely Lovers Symphony—Für Elise) (1973)
Lie Lie Lie (single, 1974)
Bricks and Mortar (single, 1975)
Einzelgänger (LP, 1975)

I Wanna Funk with You Tonight (single, 1976)
Knights in White Satin (LP, 1976)
Let the Music Play (single, 1977)
From Here to Eternity (LP, 1977)
Chase (single, 1978)
Love's in You, Love's in Me (single, 1978)
Midnight Express (Music from the Original Motion Picture) (LP, 1978)
Music from Battlestar Galactica *and Other Original Compositions* (LP, 1979)
E=MC² (LP, 1979)
Baby Blue (single, 1979)
If You Weren't Afraid (single, 1979)
What a Night (single, 1979)
Night Drive (single, 1980)
Hollywood Dreams (single, 1980)
The Seduction (Love Theme) (single, 1980)
American Gigolo (Original Soundtrack Recording) (LP, 1980)
I Wanna Rock You (single, 1980)
Cat People (Original Soundtrack) (LP, 1982)
Solitary Man (with Joe Esposito) (LP, 1983)
The Duel (single, 1984)
Reach Out (single, 1984)
The Never Ending Story (Original Motion Picture Soundtrack) (with Klaus Doldinger) (LP, 1984)
Together in Electric Dreams (with Phil Oakey) (single, 1984)
Philip Oakey & Giorgio Moroder (LP, 1985)
Innovisions (LP, 1985)
Now You're Mine (with Helen Terry) (1984)
American Dream (with Paul Engeman) (1984)
Night Time Is the Right Time (with Edie Marlena) (1985)
Lead Me On (with Teena Marie) (1985)
To Be Number One (single, 1990)
Forever Dancing (LP, 1992)
Déjà Vu (LP, 2015)

Giorgio Moroder—Selected Productions and Compositions

Chicory Tip: Son of My Father (single, 1972)
Chicory Tip: Good Grief Christina (single, 1972)
Roberta Kelly: *Troublemaker* (LP, 1976)
Roberta Kelly: *Zodiac Lady* (LP, 1977)
Munich Machine: Get on the Funk Train (single, 1977)
Munich Machine: *Munich Machine* (LP, 1977)
Three Degrees: *New Dimension* (LP, 1978)
Sparks: *No. 1 in Heaven* (LP, 1979)
Munich Machine: *Body Shine* (LP, 1979)
Japan: Life in Tokyo (12-inch single, 1979)
Suzi Lane: Ooh La La (single, 1979)
Three Degrees: *Three D* (LP, 1979)
The Sylvers: *Disco Fever* (LP, 1979)
Sparks: *Terminal Jive* (LP, 1980)
Blondie: Call Me (single, 1980)
Madleen Kane: *Don't Want to Lose You* (LP, 1981)
David Bowie: Cat People (12-inch single, 1982)
Blondie: War Child (single, 1982)
France Joli: Blue Eyed Technology (single, 1983)
Nina Hagen: *Angstlos* (LP, 1983)
Flashdance (Original Soundtrack from the Motion Picture) (LP, 1983)
Superman III (Original Soundtrack) (LP, 1983)
Freddie Mercury: Love Kills (single, 1984)
Metropolis (Original Motion Picture Soundtrack) (LP, 1984)
Sigue Sigue Sputnik: *Flaunt It* (LP, 1986)
Limahl: *Colour All My Days* (LP, 1986)
Donna Summer: Carry On remix (single, 1997)
Daft Punk: Giorgio by Moroder (LP track, 2013)

DJ Moroder

DJ set, Red Bull Academy, New York, 2013

Evolution / In Love with Love / Lost Angeles / Utopia (Me Giorgio) / From Here to Eternity / Racer / Love to Love You Baby / Bad Girls / Jump the Gun / Beat the Clock / I Wanna Rock You / E=MC² / Hot Stuff / Harmony / Chase / On the Radio / I Feel Love / Giorgio by Moroder

DJ set, Hyde Park, London, 2015
Love to Love You Baby / Tom's Diner / Right Here, Right Now / Flashdance . . . What a Feeling / Hot Stuff / I Feel Love / Together in Electric Dreams / Déjà Vu / Bad Girls / 74 Is the New 24 / Giorgio by Moroder / Call Me

Donna Summer—Early Recordings

Wasserman (as Donna Gaines, with *Hair* ensemble) (single, 1968)
If You Go Walkin' Alone (as Donna Gaines) (single, 1969)
Sally Go Round the Roses (as Donna Gaines) (single, 1971)

Donna Summer/Giorgio Moroder

The Hostage (single, 1974)
Denver Dream (single, 1974)
Lady of the Night (LP, 1974)
Love to Love You Baby (LP, 1975)
A Love Trilogy (LP, 1976)
Four Seasons of Love (LP, 1976)
I Remember Yesterday (LP, 1977)
Once Upon a Time . . . (LP, 1977)
Theme from *The Deep* (single, 1977)
Last Dance (single, 1978)
Je t'aime . . . moi non plus (single, 1978)
MacArthur Park (single, 1978)
Live and More (LP, 1978)
Bad Girls (LP, 1979)
No More Tears (with Barbra Streisand) (single, 1979)
On the Radio (single, 1979)
The Wanderer (LP, 1980)
I'm a Rainbow (LP, recorded 1981, released 1996)

Donna Summer

Donna Summer (LP, 1982)
She Works Hard for the Money (LP, 1983)
Cats Without Claws (LP, 1984)
All Systems Go (LP, 1987)
Another Place and Time (LP, 1989)
Mistaken Identity (LP, 1991)

Carry On (single 1992)
Christmas Spirit (LP, 1994)
I Feel Love (remixes) (single, 1995)
Carry On (remixes) (1997)
Live and More Encore (LP, 1999)
Crayons (2008)
To Paris with Love (single, 2010)
Love Is in Control (Finger on the Trigger) (remixes 2013)
Love to Love You Baby (remixes 2013)
MacArthur Park (remixes 2013)
Enough Is Enough 2017 (remixes, 2017)
Hot Stuff 2018 (remixes 2018)
Encore (box set, 2020)

Sex Sells

Serge Gainsbourg and Jane Birkin; Je t'aime . . . moi non plus (single, 1969)
Los Chakachas: Jungle Fever (single, 1970)
Sylvia: Pillow Talk (single, 1973)
Fancy: Wild Thing (single, 1973)

Electronica: The Experimental Years

Original soundtrack: *Forbidden Planet* (LP, recorded 1956, released 1976)
Daphne Oram: *Oramics* (recorded 1959–1977, released 2007)
Joe Meek and the Blue Men: *I Hear a New World* (LP, 1960, released 1991)
Jean-Jacques Perrey: *Musique Electronique du Cosmos* (LP, 1962)
The Tornados: Telstar (single, 1962)
Delia Derbyshire and Barry Bermange: *Inventions for Radio: The Dreams* (LP recorded 1984, released 2019)
Perrey-Kingsley: *The In Sound from Way Out* (LP, 1966)
Emil Richards: *New Sound Element—Stones* (LP, 1967)
Hal Blaine: *Psychedelic Percussion* (LP, 1967)
The Supremes: Reflections (single, 1967)
BBC Radiophonic Workshop: *BBC Radiophonic Music* (LP, 1968)
United States of America: *United States of America* (LP, 1968)
Walter Carlos: *Switched-On Bach* (LP, 1968)
Dick Hyman and His Electric Eclectics: The Minotaur (single, 1969)

Louise Huebner: *Seduction through Witchcraft* (LP, 1969)
White Noise: *An Electric* Storm (1969)
Perrey-Kingsley: *Kaleidoscopic Vibrations: Spotlight on the Moog* (LP, 1971)
various artists: *Stanley Kubrick's A Clockwork Orange (Music from the Soundtrack)* (LP, 1971)
Delia Derbyshire and Elsa Stansfield: *Circle of Light (Original Electronic Soundtrack)* (LP recorded 1972, released 2016)
Gentle Fire: *4 Systems, Music for Amplified Toy Piano, Music for Carillon, Edges* (LP, 1974)

Electronica: The Pop Years

Chicory Tip: Son of My Father (single, 1972)
Hot Butter: Popcorn (single, 1972)
Roxy Music: *Roxy Music* (LP, 1972)
BBC Radiophonic Workshop: Doctor Who (single, 1973)
Fripp & Eno: *(No Pussyfooting)* (LP, 1973)
Todd Rundgren: *Todd* (LP, 1974)
Tomita: *Clare de Lune* (a.k.a. *Snowflakes Are Dancing*) (LP, 1974)
Ataraxia: *The Unexplained* (LP, 1975)
Brian Eno: *Another Green World* (LP, 1975)
Brian Eno: *Discreet Music* (LP, 1975)
Fripp & Eno: *Evening Star* (LP, 1975)
Fripp & Eno: *Live in Paris 20.08.75* (LP recorded 1975, released 2016)
Philippe Besombes: *Besombes Rizet* (LP, 1975)
Todd Rundgren: *Initiation* (LP, 1975)
Brian Eno: *Music for Films* (LP, 1976)
Jean-Michel Jarre: *Oxygène* (LP, 1976)
Space: *Magic Fly* (LP, 1977)

Krautrock and Kraftwerk

Kraftwerk: *Kraftwerk* (LP, 1970)
Popol Vuh: *Affenstunde* (LP, 1970)
Can: *Tago Mago* (LP, 1971)
Popol Vuh: *In den Gärten Pharaos* (1971)
Tangerine Dream: *Alpha Centauri* (1971)
Can: *Ege Bamyasi* (LP, 1972)

Kraftwerk: *Kraftwerk 2* (LP, 1972)
Tangerine Dream: *Zeit* (LP, 1972)
Kraftwerk: *Ralf and Florian* (LP, 1973)
Tangerine Dream: *Atem* (LP, 1973)
Kraftwerk: *Autobahn* (LP, 1974)
Kraftwerk: Autobahn (single, 1974)
Tangerine Dream: *Phaedra* (LP, 1974)
Kraftwerk: *Radioactivity* (LP, 1975)
Can: I Want More (single, 1976)
Kraftwerk: Les Mannequins (single, 1977)
Kraftwerk: *Trans-Europe Express* (LP, 1977)
Kraftwerk: *The Man Machine* (LP, 1978)

Disco: The Underground Years

Barrabas: Wild Safari (single, 1972)
Billy Paul: Me and Mrs. Jones (single, 1972)
Limmie and the Family Cooking: You Can Do Magic (single, 1972)
The O'Jays: Backstabbers (single, 1972)
The O'Jays: Love Train (single, 1972)
Billy Paul: War of the Gods (full-length version, 1973)
Eddie Kendricks: Keep On Truckin' (single, 1973),
Ike and Tina Turner: Nutbush City Limits (single, 1973)
Patti Jo: Make Me Believe in You (single, 1973)
Zulema: *Ms. Z* (LP, 1973)
Barry White: You're the First, the Last, My Everything (single, 1974)
Disco Tex & the Sex-O-Lettes: I Wanna Dance Wit' Choo (Doo Dat Dance) (single, 1974)
Disco Tex & the Sex-O-Lettes: Get Dancing (single, 1974)
Gloria Gaynor: *Never Can Say Goodbye* (LP, 1974)
Hamilton Bohannon: Foot Stompin' Music (single, 1974)
Minnie Ripperton: Lovin' You (single, 1974)
Rufus featuring Chaka Khan: Once You Get Started (single, 1974)
Spaghetti Head: Big Noise from Winnetka (single, 1974)
Hamilton Bohannon: Disco Stomp (single, 1975)
Harold Melvin and the Blue Notes: Don't Leave Me This Way (full-length version, 1975)

Michael Jackson: Forever Came Today (single, 1975)
Syreeta: Harmour Love (single, 1975)
The Jimmy Castor Bunch: E-Man Boogie (single, 1975)

Disco: The Early Twelve-Inch Years

Andrea True Connection: More More More (12-inch single, 1975)
Banzai: Chinese Kung Fu (Disco Version) (12-inch single, 1975)
Calhoon: Dance Dance Dance (12-inch single, 1975)
Gerri Granger: Can't Take My Eyes Off You (12-inch single, 1975)
Trammps: That's Where the Happy People Go (12-inch single, 1975)
Boney M: Daddy Cool (12-inch single, 1976)
Double Exposure: Ten Percent (12-inch single, 1976)
Jesse Green: Nice and Slow (12-inch single, 1976)

Disco: The Later Years

Candi Staton: Young Hearts Run Free (single, 1976)
Diana Ross: Love Hangover (full-length version, 1976)
La Belle Epoque: Black Is Black (Disco Version) (12-inch, 1976)
Tavares: Heaven Must Be Missing an Angel (single, 1976)
Thelma Houston: Don't Leave Me This Way (12-inch single, 1976)
Tubular Bells: Champ's Boys Orchestra (single, 1976)
Vickie Sue Robinson: Turn the Beat Around (12-inch single, 1976)
Eruption: I Can't Stand the Rain (12-inch 1977)
John Forde: Stardance (12-inch, 1977)
Lipstique: *At the Discotheque* (LP, 1977)
Saint Tropez: *Je t'aime* (LP, 1977)
Alicia Bridges: I Love the Nightlife (12-inch, 1978)
Boney M: Rasputin (12-inch, 1978)
Cerrone: Supernature (12-inch, 1978)
Dan Hartman: Instant Replay (12-inch, 1978)
Karen Young: Hot Shot (12-inch, 1978)
Sarah Brightman and Hot Gossip: I Lost My Heart to a Starship Trooper (12-inch, 1978)
Sylvia: Automatic Lover (12-inch, 1977)
Anita Ward: Ring My Bell (12-inch, 1979)
Lipps Inc: Funkytown (12-inch, 1979)

various artists: *The Dance Decade 1973–1983* (LP box set, 1983)
various artists: *The Disco Years volumes 1–7* (CD, 1990-1995)
various artists: *The Disco Box* (CD box set 1999)

Rock Goes Disco

Todd Rundgren: I Saw the Light (single, 1972)
Hall & Oates: She's Gone (single, 1973)
Robert Palmer: *Sneakin' Sally through the Alley* (LP, 1974)
David Bowie: Fame (single, 1975)
Elton John: Philadelphia Freedom (single, 1975)
Roxy Music: Love Is the Drug (single, 1975)
T. Rex Disco Party: Dreamy Lady (single, 1975)
Rolling Stones: *Black and Blue* (LP, 1976)
Rod Stewart: Do Ya Think I'm Sexy? (12-inch single, 1978)
Rolling Stones: Miss You (12-inch single, 1978)
Mike Oldfield: Guilty (12-inch single, 1979)
Wings: Goodnight Tonight (12-inch single, 1979)

The Northern Soul Crossover

Dee Clark: That's My Girl (single, 1964)
The Tams: Hey Girl Don't Bother Me (single, 1964)
Gloria Jones: Tainted Love (single, 1965)
Tami Lynn: I'm Gonna Run Away from You (single, 1965)
Al Wilson: The Snake (single, 1968)
The Delfonics: La La Means I Love You (single, 1968)
The Peppers: Pepper Box (single, 1973)
various artists: *Disco Demand's Solid Soul Sensations* (LP, 1975)
various artists: *Great Disco Demands* (LP, 1975)
Wigan's Ovation: Skiing in the Snow (single, 1975)
Wigan's Chosen Few: The Footsee (single, 1975)
Gene Farrow: Hey, You Should Be Dancing (12-inch single, 1977)
various artists: *The Odyssey: A Northern Soul Time Capsule* (CD box set, 2015)

Post-Punk Electro: The First Wave

David Bowie: *Low* (LP, 1977)
David Bowie: *"Heroes"* (1977)
Iggy Pop: *The Idiot* (1977)

Ultravox!: *Ultravox!* (LP, 1977)
Ultravox!: *Ha! Ha! Ha!* (LP, 1977)
Boomtown Rats: Like Clockwork (single, 1978)
Cabaret Voltaire: *Extended Play* (EP, 1978)
Human League: Being Boiled (single, 1978)
The Normal: TVOD (single, 1978)
Thomas Leer: Private Plane (single, 1978)
Throbbing Gristle: United (single, 1978)
Ultravox: *Systems of Romance* (LP, 1978)
Cabaret Voltaire: Nag Nag Nag (single, 1979)
Gary Numan & Tubeway Army: Are Friends Electric? (single, 1979)
Gary Numan: Cars (single, 1979)
Human League: Empire State Human (single, 1979)
Human League: *The Dignity of Labour* (EP, 1979)
Thomas Leer & Robert Rental: *The Bridge* (LP, 1979)
Simple Minds: *Life in a Day* (LP, 1979)
Simple Minds: *Real to Real Cacophony* (LP, 1979)
Simple Minds: I Travel (12-inch, 1980)
various artists: *Close to the Noise Floor: Formative UK Electronica* (CD box set, 2016)
various artists: *Noise Reduction System: Formative European Electronica 1974–1984* (CD box set, 2017)
various artists: *Third Noise Principle: Formative North American Electronica 1975–1984* (CD box set, 2019)

Synthipop and Friends

Visage: Tar (single, 1979)
Blancmange: Irene & Mavis (EP, 1980)
John Foxx: *Metamatic* (LP, 1980)
Nightmares in Wax: Black Leather (12-inch, 1980)
Telex: Twist à Saint Tropez (single, 1978)
Ultravox: *Vienna* (LP, 1980)
Visage: Fade to Grey (single, 1980)
Yello: *Solid Pleasure* (LP, 1980)
Yellow Magic Orchestra: *Yellow Magic Orchestra* (LP, 1978)
Depeche Mode: *Speak & Spell* (LP, 1981)
Human League: Don't You Want Me (single, 1981)

Human League: The Sound of the Crowd (single, 1981)
Soft Cell: Memorabilia (12-inch, 1981)
Soft Cell: *Non-Stop Erotic Cabaret* (LP, 1981)
Soft Cell: Tainted Love (12-inch, 1981)
various artists: *Some Bizzare Album* (LP, 1981)
Blancmange: *Happy Families* (LP, 1982)
Soft Cell: *The Art of Falling Apart* (LP, 1982)
Turquoise Swimming Pools: The Winds (LP *To the Shores of Lake Placid*, 1982)
various artists: *The Tears of Technology* (CD 2020)

New York and Elsewhere

Devo: Mongoloid/Jocko Homo (single, 1977)
Devo: Satisfaction (single, 1977)
Suicide: *Suicide* (LP, 1977)
Cristina: Disco Clone (12-inch, 1978)
Devo: Be Stiff (single, 1978)
Devo: Mechanical Man (single, 1978)
Blondie: Heart of Glass (12-inch single, 1979)
Klaus Nomi: *In Concert* (LP recorded 1979, released 1986)
Robert Fripp: *Exposure* (LP, 1979)
Blondie (with Robert Fripp): Heroes (12-inch single, recorded 1980, released 1982)
Polyrock: *Polyrock* (LP, 1980)
Soft Cell: *Mutant Moments* (EP, 1980)
Ministry: I'm Falling (12-inch single, 1981)
Ministry: Cold Life (12-inch single, 1982)
3 Teens Kill 4: *No Motive* (LP, 1983)

Patrick Cowley

Patrick Cowley & Candida Royalle: *Candida Cosmica* (recorded 1973–1975, released 2016)
Michelle: Disco Dance (Mega Mix) (12-inch, 1977)
Donna Summer: I Feel Love (Patrick Cowley Mega Mix) (12-inch, 1978)
Sylvester: *Step II* (LP, 1978)
Sylvester: You Make Me Feel (Mighty Real) (12-inch single, 1978)
Patrick Cowley & Jorge Socarras: *Catholic* (recorded 1975–1979, released 2009)
Sylvester: *Living Proof* (LP, 1979)

Sylvester: *Stars* (LP, 1979)
Patrick Cowley: *Afternooners* (LP recorded 1979, released 2017)
Tantra: Hills of Katmandu (Mega Mix) (12-inch, recorded 1979, released 1984)
Patrick Cowley: *Muscle Up* (recorded 1973–1980, released 2015)
Patrick Cowley: *Mechanical Fantasy Box* (recorded 1973–1980, released 2019)
Patrick Cowley: *Menergy* (LP, 1981)
Patrick Cowley: *Megatron Man* (LP, 1981)
Patrick Cowley: *School Daze* (LP recorded 1973–1981, released 2013)
Two Tons o'Fun: I Got the Feeling (Patrick Cowley Mega Mix) (12-inch, 1981)
Patrick Cowley: *Mind Warp* (LP, 1982)
Paul Parker: Right On Target (12-inch single, 1982)
Sylvester: Do You Wanna Funk (12-inch single, 1982)
Patrick Cowley: *Patrick Cowley's Greatest Dance Party* (recorded 1981–1982, released 1983)
Patrick Cowley: *12 by 12—The Patrick Cowley Collection* (recorded 1981–1982, released 1988)

I Feel Love Covers

Top of the Poppers (1977)
The Hiltonaires (1977)
Le Grand Orchestra de Paul Mariat (1977)
Monica Forsberg (1977)
The Connection Group (1978)
Dee Dee Smith (1979)
Klaus Nomi (live version) (recorded 1979, released 1986)
Blondie with Robert Fripp (live version) (recorded 1979, released 1995)
Usha Uthup (medley with "Rambha Ho Ho Ho") (1981)
Between the Sheets (medley) (1983)
Bronski Beat (1985)
Bronski Beat/Marc Almond (1985)
Barron Nights ("Mr Bronski Meets Mr Evans") (1986)
Balaam and the Angel (1987)
Bronski Beat/Pete Burns (live performance) (1987)
Acid Angels: Speed Speed Ecstasy (sample) (1988)
Cicciolina (1988)
Helen: I Love You (sample) (1989)

Hit House: I Felt Acid House Love (sample) (1989)
Jive Bunny (medley) (1989)
Paul Hardcastle (medley) (1989)
Crocodile Ride (1990)
Two Nice Girls (1990)
Poster Children (1991)
Curve (1992)
Messiah featuring Precious Wilson (1992)
Kingston Wall (1993)
Mr T Experience (1993)
A House (1994)
Vanessa Mae (1997)
Drew's Famous (1997)
Amanda (1998)
Montefiori Cocktail—Count Indigo (2000)
Paul Gilbert (2002)
Blue Man Group featuring Venus Hum (2003)
Red Hot Chili Peppers (live version, 2004)
Jorane (2004)
Cobra Verde (2005)
DJ Space (2006)
Tina Charles (2007)
Kas featuring Fat Brothers (2008)
Moondust featuring Misal (2009)
Niki Evans (2009)
Jimmy Jørgensen featuring Liv Lykke (2010)
Electra (2011)
Madonna (live version) (2011)
Marston Smith (2011)
Ham Sandwich (live version) (2012)
Annaleigh Ashford (within Donna Summer medley) (2015)
Sendelica (2015)
LaChanze (Diva Donna & Ensemble) (*Summer* musical, 2017)
DJ Pierre feat. Chic Loren (1979 Club Disco Mix) (2017)
Samantha Jade (2018)

LaChanze (2018)
Giorgia (2018)
Sam Smith (2019)
Kevin McHale (television performance) (2019)
Dan'yelle Williamson (Diva Donna & Ensemble) (*Summer* musical, 2019)

BIBLIOGRAPHY

Unless otherwise noted, all quoted material is drawn from my own interviews and conversations with those listed in the acknowledgments or from the sources below.

Books

Almond, Marc. *The End of New York.* Ellipsis London Ltd, 2001.

Almond, Marc. *Tainted Life*. London: Pan Macmillan, 2001.

Blot, David, and Mathias Cousin. *The Song of the Machine: From Disco to DJs to Techno, a Graphic Novel of Electronic Music.* New York: Black Dog & Leventhal Publishers, 2019.

Brewster, Bill, and Frank Broughton. *Last Night a DJ Saved My Life: The History of the Disc Jockey*. New York: Grove Press, 2014.

Cowley, Patrick. *The Mechanical Fantasy Box: The Homoerotic Journal of Patrick Cowley*. Dark Entries Editions, 2019.

Disco Patrick and Patrick Vogt, eds. *Disco: An Encyclopedic Guide to the Cover Art of Disco Records*. Soul Jazz Books, 2014.

Edison, Mike. *Sympathy for the Drummer: Why Charlie Watts Matters*. Lanham, MD: Backbeat Books, 2019.

Flür, Wolfgang. *Kraftwerk: I Was a Robot*. London: Omnibus Press, 2017.

Gamson, Joshua. *The Fabulous Sylvester*. New York: Picador, 2006.

Hamsley, David. *To Disco, with Love: The Records That Defined an Era.* New York: Flatiron Books, 2015.

Hollern, Andrew. *Dancer Before the Dance*. New York: Harper Perennial, 2001.

Lawrence, Tim. *Love Saves the Day: A History of American Dance Music Culture, 1970–1979*. Durham, NC: Duke University Press, 2004.

McLeod, Kembrew. *Downtown Pop Underground: New York City and the Literary Punks, Renegade Artists, DIY Filmmakers, Mad Playwrights, and Rock 'n' Roll Glitter Queens Who Revolutionized Culture.* New York: Harry N. Abrams, 2019.

Nowell, David. *The Story of Northern Soul: A Definitive History of the Dance Scene That Refuses to Die*. London: Portico Books, 2012.

Pawul, Jan Yahu: *Silent Records: Disco History.* Self-published, 2015.

Stubbs, David. *Future Days: Krautrock and the Birth of a Revolutionary New Music*. London: Melville House, 2015.

Summer, Donna. *Ordinary Girl: The Journey*. New York: Villard Books, 2003.

Ure, Midge. *Midge Ure: If I Was—An Enhanced Updated Autobiography*. Amazon Services LLC, 2015.

Magazines

Abbey, John. Donna Summer interview. *Blues & Soul,* February 1976.

Aletti, Vince. "Discotheque Rock '73. Paaaaarty!" *Rolling Stone*, September 13, 1973.

Aletti, Vince. *Record World*, various columns 1973–1978.

Azzopardi, Chris. "The Big Daddy of Dance." *Between the Lines*, August 6, 2015.

Bohn, Chris. "Kraftwerk: A Computer Date with a Showroom Dummy." *New Musical Express*, June 13, 1981.

Brewster, Bill. "The Master: Patrick Cowley Created the Definitive 'I Feel Love' Remix." *Mixmag*, June 23, 2017.

Brewster, Bill. Giorgio Moroder interview. *Mix Mag*, June 22, 2017.

Burke, Tom. "Struttin' His Stuff." *Rolling Stone*, June 15, 1978.

Cromelin, Richard. "Donna Summer: Love on the Road." *Rolling Stone*, March 25, 1976.

Dery, Mark. Ralf Hütter interview, *Keyboard*, October 1991.

Esposito, Jim. "The Great Rocking Orgasmic Renaissance of AM Radio." *Oui*, September 1976.

Fong-Torres, Ben. "A Disco Queen Is Born Again." *Austin American-Statesman*, November 1, 1981.

Freeman, John. "Homage Not Fromage: Jimmy Somerville Interview." *Quietus*, March 25, 2015.

"Giorgio Moroder: I Hated the Moustache." PopJustice, January 26, 2015, www.popjustice.com/articles/giorgio-moroder-interview-i-hated-the-moustache.

"Giorgio Moroder: I Was Always Interested in the Hits." *Purple Fashion*, December 17, 2014, www.stage.the-talks.com/interviews/giorgio-moroder.

Greene, Jo-Ann. "Your Mission, Barbarella: Find Duran Duran." *Goldmine*, January 16, 1998.

Hancock, David. "They're Gonna Put Me in the Movies." *National RockStar*, January 15, 1977.

Hanson, Amy. "More, More, More! A Brief History of Disco." *Goldmine*, October 24, 1997.

Harriman, Andi. "Music from Hell: An Interview with Nervous Gender." PostPunk.com, December 1, 2014.

Holleran, Andrew. "Dark Disco: A Lament." *Christopher Street* magazine, December 1978.

Hoskyns, Barney. "From Sex Goddess to Superwoman." *New Musical Express*, December 18, 1982.

Iqba, Nosheen. "*Giorgio Moroder:* I Don't Even Like Dancing." *Guardian*, February 9, 2019.

Jones, Allan. "It Wasn't Until July 1977 That Fripp Was Able to Be Fripp." *Melody Maker*, April 28, 1979.

Juzwiak, Rich. "The AIDS Masterpiece of a Lost Disco Pioneer." gawker.com, October 31, 2013.

Katz, Robin. "Donna und Blitzen!" *Record Mirror*, October 15, 1977.

Katz, Robin. "Hot Stuff." *Smash Hits*, June 14, 1979.

Lamphier, Jason. "The Comeback of the Summer: Disco King Giorgio Moroder." *Out*, May 5, 2015.

Mahler, Jonathan. "Summer of 1977." *New York Times*, June 30, 2002.

Male, Andrew. "Regiurm: Joy Division." *Mojo*, March 2020.

Matos, Michaelangelo. "Donna Summer 'I Feel Love.'" insomniac.com, February 9, 2017.

Mintz, Elliot. Donna Summer interview. *Penthouse*, July 1979.

Moby. Giorgio Moroder interview. *Interview*, April 23, 2015.

Moulton, Tom. *Billboard*. Various columns 1974–1978.

Nechamkin, Sarah. Vince Aletti interview. *Interview,* December 7, 2018.

Nika, Coleen. "Meet Giorgio Moroder, the Godfather of Modern Dance Music." Time.com, February 12, 2015.

Petridis, Alexis. "Pet Shop Boys: The Acoustic Guitar Should be Banned." *Guardian*, January 24, 2020.

Schmidt, Torsten. Giorgio Moroder interview. *Red Bull Academy*, May 2013.

Smith, Rupert. "Klaus Nomi." *Attitude*, July 1994.

St Mark, David. "Harold Faltermeyer/Flood of Memory: the Summer Reign on Sunset Blvd." *Daeida*, October 2012.

Tantum, Bruce. "The Iconic Giorgio Moroder: Producer, Songwriter, Composer . . . and Disc Jockey." *Time Out New York*, May 13, 2013.

Tobler, John. David Bowie interview. *ZigZag,* January 1978.

Waldern, Celia. Jane Birkin interview. *Telegraph*, October 13, 2009.

Witter, Simon. "Kraftwerk: *Autobahn*." *New Musical Express*, July 6, 1985.

ACKNOWLEDGMENTS

Thanks to everybody who made time to speak with me during the writing of this book, and in the years before then:

Marc Almond (1996), Neil Arthur (2019), Michael Aston (1995), Philippe Besombes (2015), Kevin Bond (2014), Tim Bowness (2019), Gavin Bryars (2016), Pete Burns (1985), Lawrence Casserley (2016), Tim Cross (1981), Holger Czukay (1999), Keith Emerson (1995), Wolfgang Flür (1996), John Foxx (2019), Florian Fricke (1995), Frankie Gaye (1993), Don Gordon (1995), Bob Gruen (2020), Eddie Holland (2018), Peter Hook (1997), Mike Hurst (1997), Wayne Hussey (2019), Jim Kerr (2019), Stanley Lunetta (2016), Athan Maroulis (1997), Hilly Michaels (2019), Roger Nelson (2019), Nico (1982), Gary Numan (2019), Andy Prince (2020), Phil Rambow (2020), Todd Rundgren (2019), Alan Lee Shaw (2019), Marc Swordfish (2017), Thomas Thorn (2020), Midge Ure (2019), Alan Vega (1986), Mel Wesson (2019), Keren Woodward (2019).

Also, as always, thanks to Amy Hanson, who has now heard almost as many different versions of "I Feel Love" as I have; Jo-Ann Greene, for advice and suggestions that I may or may not have acted upon; Mike Edison; Steve Malins; Matt Ingham; Fiona Bloom; Erika Tooker; Pat Prince; my agent Lee Sobel; and everyone at Backbeat Books for shepherding us through the entire process—John Cerullo, Carol Flannery, and Barbara Claire.

And to Oliver and Trevor, for not walking across the keyboard as I wrote; George, for doing the complete opposite; the gremlins that live in the heat pump; Karen and Todd; Kate Poole; and to all the old friends who lived some of these pages with me, but steadfastly avoided some others.

INDEX